Deleuze and Time

Deleuze Connections

'It is not the elements or the sets which define the multiplicity. What defines it is the AND, as something which has its place between the elements or between the sets. AND, AND, AND – stammering.'

Gilles Deleuze and Claire Parnet, *Dialogues*

General Editor
Ian Buchanan

Editorial Advisory Board

Keith Ansell-Pearson
Rosi Braidotti
Claire Colebrook
Tom Conley

Gregg Lambert
Adrian Parr
Paul Patton
Patricia Pisters

Visit the Deleuze Connections website at:
www.edinburghuniversitypress.com/series/delco

Deleuze and Time

Edited by Robert W. Luzecky and
Daniel W. Smith

EDINBURGH
University Press

Edinburgh University Press is one of the leading university presses in the UK. We publish academic books and journals in our selected subject areas across the humanities and social sciences, combining cutting-edge scholarship with high editorial and production values to produce academic works of lasting importance. For more information visit our website: edinburghuniversitypress.com

Edinburgh University Press Ltd
The Tun – Holyrood Road
12(2f) Jackson's Entry
Edinburgh EH8 8PJ

Typeset in 10.5/13 Adobe Sabon by
Cheshire Typesetting Ltd, Cuddington, Cheshire
and printed and bound in Great Britain

A CIP record for this book is available from the British Library

ISBN 978 1 4744 8920 1 (hardback)
ISBN 978 1 4744 8922 5 (webready PDF)
ISBN 978 1 4744 8923 2 (epub)

Contents

Part III: Expressions of Time

Introduction:
The Many Aspects of Duration

Robert W. Luzecky

In a text on the relation between the music of Pierre Boulez and the literature of Marcel Proust, Deleuze observes that the nameless narrator of Proust's expansive masterpiece was a person haunted by time (2007: 297). Indeed, the same might be said of Deleuze himself. Temporality is a near constant theme from Deleuze's earliest publications (on Hume, as well as a scintillatingly brief review of Simondon) to his final publication ('Immanence: A Life'). Much like Bergson did with his unique concept of duration, Deleuze continually added further nuances to his philosophy of time. Temporality is a theme to which Deleuze continually returned throughout the twenty-five monographs that were published during his lifetime, in countless seminars and interviews, as well as in the texts co-authored with Félix Guattari – the two *Capitalism and Schizophrenia* volumes, the book on Kafka and *What is Philosophy?*

The ambit of Deleuze's philosophy could scarcely be more expansive. In the Foreword to Éric Alliez's *Capital Times: Tales from the Conquest of Time*, Deleuze explicitly affirms Plotinus' claim that time is involved in the movements of the universe's soul (1996: xii). A few lines later – through oblique reference to Fitzgerald, Iberall, the Stoics, Nietzsche, Kant and Shakespeare – Deleuze further characterises these movements as aberrant, in the sense that they are akin to the decoupling of a door flying off its hinges; time is a cosmic dice throw that affirms the actualisation of possibilities. In his two *Cinema* texts, as well as his other works on Bergson's philosophy, Deleuze suggests that temporal movements involve the ongoing creation of virtual and actual modes of being. (Here, one might also observe a subtle modification of Étienne Souriau's aesthetics.) The sheer number of texts that Deleuze published also hints at a further aspect of his philosophy of time: it is non-reducible to the thought of one key figure – to encounter Deleuze's concept of time is to participate with a plurality of thinkers. Though there are certainly some philosophical figures to which Deleuze often returns (as though a morsel of time might be regained by the arduous reworking of near forgotten claims from the history of western philosophy), it must be observed that a robust sense of Deleuze's concept of temporality involves bringing philosophical thought into conversation with the thought of a dizzying array of filmmakers, physicists, painters, poets, anthropologists and literary artists. In concrete terms, elaborating Deleuze's philosophy of time requires a multiplicity.

In addition to this introduction, the present volume has eleven chapters, arranged into three sections – Concepts of Time, History of Time and Expressions of Time.

In the first section, Dorothea E. Olkowski, Thomas Nail and Daniel W. Smith elaborate on Deleuze's concept of time. Developing claims from contemporary physicists, Bergson and Pierce alike, Olkowski observes that Deleuze conceives of time as a real, complex, continuum that participates in the creation of new existents. Beginning from Boltzmann's observation that the physical universe tends to present as macroscopic disorder, in which entities – i.e., particles, atoms – enjoy movement along non-identical trajectories, Olkowski suggests that temporality is the continuum which expresses the modification of the universe. Elaborating on themes from Bergson and Peirce, Olkowski observes that Deleuze tends to conceive of time as a complex self-sustaining continuum that involves the ongoing actualisation of potentials – time produces the conditions for modifications of the universal soul.

Perhaps one of the most radical suggestions of Deleuze's philosophy of time is that the temporal continuum – the duration which comprehends all of the memorial past and the lived present, and which gives rise to the indeterminate future – is autonomous from the movement of physical entities. In concrete terms, time is something other than the measurement of the spatial displacement or qualitative modification of existent entities. Is this aspect of Deleuze's concept of time correct? Here, one might to turn Lucretius for the beginning of an answer. In his nuanced chapter – which involves a detailed reading of Lucretius brought into conversation with Carlo Rovelli's reflections of the nature of time – Thomas Nail suggests that the entirety of time (including its analytically discrete domains of past, present and future) is a development of the indeterminate kinetic processes (i.e., movements) of material entities. In this sense, spacetime is ontologically dependent on the swerve of atoms.

The suggestion that Deleuze's philosophy of time is non-monolithic does not diminish the fact that the concept enjoys privileged elaboration in key texts. Daniel W. Smith observes that Deleuze developed his theory of time primarily in two moments of his career: first, in the books published in 1968 and 1969, *Difference and Repetition* and *The Logic of Sense*, and then, sixteen years later, in his 1985 book *The Time-Image*, the second volume of his work on cinema. There is, of course, a development in Deleuze's thinking about time from one period to the other, and his later work makes a claim that was only hinted at in *Difference and Repetition*, namely, that a revolution in our philosophical conception of time took place with Kant. This is the point where Smith's analysis begins. In antiquity, the concept of time was subordinated to the concept of movement. In Kant, time is liberated from movement and assumes an autonomy and independence of its own. Smith traces out the history of this revolution and shows how in Kant time becomes *a pure and empty form*, which is marked by the three syntheses of habit, memory and the new. Smith's chapter presents a perspicacious overview of Deleuze's entire theory of time.

If the swerve of elementary particles is an aspect of the emergence of time, then perhaps it should also be observed that Deleuze seemed to never tire of suggesting that aspects of the creation of time enjoy expression through reference to Nietzsche's concepts of the eternal return and the will to power. In some of the most beautiful passages of *Nietzsche and Philosophy* and *Difference and Repetition*, Deleuze suggests that the eternal return and implicated will to power may be characterised as a dice throw that yields the creation of the new. In his fascinating chapter on Deleuze's reading of Nietzsche, James Mollison observes that Deleuze tends to identify the will to power as a metaphysical selection. Perhaps no phrase in all of Nietzsche's philosophy has endured so much – sometimes deliberate – misinterpretation as 'the will to power'. Erroneous early interpretations suggested that the will to power may admit of psychological interpretations – as though it were merely an aspect of the personality of a psycho-social entity. Though Deleuze tends to characterise the creation of the new as an affirmation of an emergent circumstance, Mollison elegantly observes that, for both Nietzsche and Deleuze, this characterisation is not an expression of a dubious anthropomorphisation of philosophical concepts. (In this sense, the will to power is more akin to Spinoza's concept of *conatus* than it is to any psychological drive.) Mollison further specifies that the eternal return is an actualisation of a singularity – i.e., a point of inflection – which involves aspects of evaluation and selection. He concludes by suggesting that Deleuze conceived of temporality as the eternal actualisation of difference.

Perhaps one of the greatest philosophical friendships in the history of philosophy was that between Gilles Deleuze and Michel Foucault. In his chapter, Strand Sheldahl-Thomason elaborates how Deleuze's and Foucault's concepts of time are profoundly intertwined. Though Deleuze tends to be more inclined to metaphysics than Foucault – whose texts tend to be more aptly characterised as metaphysically informed histories – Sheldahl-Thomason carefully observes that both thinkers tended to eschew appeals to the transcendent, static or continuous, in favour of characterising time as a multiplicity of discontinuous, complicated, disjunctive relations. In *Individuation in Light of Notions of Form and Information*, Gilbert Simondon observes that the apparent tension between discontinuous and continuous may be resolved if both are implicated as aspects of a complex process of production of phenomena (2020: 92). Sheldahl-Thomason suggests that, for Deleuze and Foucault (who were both influenced by Simondon), this constitutive relation of becoming is an expression of temporality.

The claim that temporality involves an immanent expression of the actualisation of difference subtly diminishes the explanatory value of the relation of temporal succession – the series t_1, $t_{2 \ldots}$, t_n, where each moment t is identified as a 'now' which is similar to that which preceded it in the series. Henry Somers-Hall begins with a detailed analysis of Deleuze's and Merleau-Ponty's modification of Kant's account of the constitution of temporal experience. Kantian metaphysics tends to conceive space and time as the forms of intuition by which perception is organised. One of the negative implications of the Kantian approach is that time seems to be stripped of all positivity – time is characterised as an empty form. Somers-Hall deftly observes that both Deleuze and Merleau-Ponty were critical of this Kantian time. The claim is that a more adequate account of time might be afforded by conceiving of it as an immanent constitution of a process of ongoing modification. Citing an often overlooked passage from *Difference and Repetition*, Somers-Hall notes that Deleuze explicitly observes that temporal succession is inadequate to account for the complex ways in which time constitutes human experience. Further, in what is surely one of the most astute observations in this text, Somers-Hall specifies that this thesis is echoed in Merleau-Ponty's phenomenology. These complex analyses yield the claim that temporal constitution tends to be far more complex than that gestured to by Kant.

Peter Trnka's chapter is perhaps the most explicitly political contribution to this volume. Beginning with the observation that the lived experience of political subjects tends to suggest that time is a complex assemblage of both physical and non-physical processes, Trnka argues that the complex mutual implication of these processes yields the creation of utterly new circumstances. Here, Trnka observes that a properly Deleuzian concept of temporality involves weaving together aspects from the thought of Nietzsche, Bergson, Marx and – perhaps most of all – Spinoza and Negri. Trnka elegantly develops Negri's elaboration of Marx's observation (in the second volume of *Capital*) that temporality is intertwined with the economic modes of production. Indeed, for Marx, economic production influences all rates of temporal progression, the material expression of time, as well as the values associated with duration. Trnka further observes that (in the *Ethics*) Spinoza suggests that time is ongoing production – the *conatus* is expressed as the immanent constitution of time. Spinoza is explicit: the *conatus* is bereft of internal limitation. In terms of its essence, the *conatus* may be characterised as pure affirmation. Taken together, these claims suggest that time enjoys an immanent creation that is expressed as ceaseless variation.

One of the key claims that emerges from a synthesis of the first chapters of this volume is that Deleuze conceived of time as a complex dynamic multiplicity composed of a manifold of irreducible, mutually implicated, ontological and axiological processes. It might further be observed that this multiplicity is explicitly transformative, in the sense that it involves modifications of each of its elements as well as a transformation of the whole. Charlene Elsby observes that these spatiotemporal modifications are entirely non-metaphorical – they are literal, metaphysical, actual variations. In her chapter on Deleuze's and Guattari's reading of Kafka, Elsby presents a nuanced account of how a literary text expresses these transformations. Though Deleuze and Guattari frequently use philosophical terms which might be read as metaphorical in nature – e.g., rhizome, desert, black hole, body without organs – it should be observed that throughout his philosophical career Deleuze repeatedly expressed hostility toward metaphorical thought. In *Cinema 2* he observes that it would be dubious to assume that images of deserts (in Antonioni's *Red Desert* and *Zabriskie Point*) are metaphoric representations of a generalised alienation or malaise. In the second volume of *Capitalism and Schizophrenia*, Deleuze and Guattari are perhaps even more stark when they observe that analyses of metaphor and metonymy are 'disastrous' attempts to discern meaning in a text (1987: 76–7). The claim here is that metaphor is a linguistic device that tends to obscure the precise determinations of philosophical concepts. Elsby resolves this implied tension between philosophical statement and practice with the suggestion that Deleuze tends to conceive metaphorical representation as stymieing the deterritorialisation of language. In concrete terms, metaphor attempts to establish a signifying relation between the linguistic terms of a text and putatively signified concepts which obtain as externalities to the text. Echoing Ingarden's critique of Husserl, Elsby observes that reading a text metaphorically is an act of philosophical arrogance, in the sense that it tends to diminish the immanent becomings of the text in favour of some ready-made concept. Taken together, these analyses yield the complex claim that the meaning of time is expressed through a non-metaphorical – and thus non-representational – dynamic union of reader and text. To read a text literally is to participate in its immanent transformations. The implication here is staggering: in the act of reading a text, one involves oneself with the modification of spacetime.

I continue these elaborations of the aesthetics of time in my chapter on cinema and time. When the Lumière Brothers unveiled their Cinématographe to the viewing public in 1895, this heralded a radical change in our understanding of the nature of time. No longer did time have to languish under the inadequate concepts that consigned its dynamism to the mere measurement of the relation of the movement of discrete entities; cinema revealed entities to be dynamic elements of a non-decomposable duration. I suggest Deleuze's thought on the nature of temporal expression in film may be characterised as a Bergsonian philosophy of film that Bergson never found the time to write. One might suggest that the film affords an adequate representation of reality, in the sense that it presents entities in a manner that approximates how various represented objectivities appear to us in reality; in film things appear to move. This appearance of motion – the dove flying toward the sky at the end of Ridley Scott's *Blade Runner*; the nearly sublime spectacle of the crowd of workers threshing in Terrence Malick's *Days of Heaven* – is what Bergson identified as falling victim to the cinematographic illusion. The Bergsonian cinematographic illusion involves the presentation of a series of still images at rapid succession to yield the appearance that each of elements of the series are in uninterrupted motion. Deleuze observes that filmic sequences of shots are unified blocks of duration of duration – i.e., they are identified as complex metastable networks of mutually implicated virtual and actual aspects undergoing variation. The negative claim is that the relation of mutual implication is non-identical to succession. The progression of a series is discrete from the modifications associated with duration. This suggests that the relation of temporal succession is inadequate to elucidate the beguiling temporality expressed by cinema. Taken together, these claims imply that the relation between memorial past and lived present is more complex than mere temporal succession. In concrete terms, Deleuze's elaborations of the nature of temporality expressed in film reveals time to be a duration in which the tension of virtual and actual yields the simultaneous constitution of the memorial past and lived present. The beguiling magic of cinema is that it presents the creation of time.

Vernon W. Cisney's chapter elaborates on the role of the powers of the false in admitting variation (i.e., the new) into temporal progression. Carefully weaving together claims from Nietzsche's 'Vision and the Riddle' (from *Thus Spoke Zarathustra*) and Proust's observation that time involves virtual aspects which are 'real without being actual, ideal without being abstract', Cisney observes that the temporal is a singularity, i.e., a time crystal, which (due to its internal interplay of mutually implicated forces) actualises both the past and the future. In this sense, the singularity is a rigorous determined ontogenetic field from which time, truth and history, as well as the vast menagerie of existent entities, are born. Perhaps it is worth observing that the minimal ontological condition which must be met for an entity to exist is that it obtains as something of which truth might be predicated; i.e., existing, individuated entities enjoy the truth of being. Cisney observes that this minimal truth subsists from the ontogenetic field. Stated again: the singularity is the expression of non-individuated, mutually implicated forces, which create truth. In perhaps one of the most heartening passages of this text, Cisney observes that art is particularly adept at expressing the creative powers of the false. This suggests that artists have the capacity to create (and populate) a new world.

In his wonderful chapter – which is informed by the ongoing project of translating Deleuze's seminars into English – Charles J. Stivale elaborates on the temporal aspects of Deleuze's lived experience. He offers a delightful demonstration of the concord between philosophical thought and philosophical practice when he observes that the conceptual, ontological and epistemological disjunctions associated with Deleuze's philosophy of time gain expression in the real obstacles that Deleuze encountered in his lectures on Spinoza, Leibniz and cinema. After a visitation from the ghost of his dead father, Shakespeare's Hamlet observes that the linear flow of time seems to have fallen out of joint. This is the first of the four 'poetic' formulas that Deleuze invokes to summarise Kantian philosophy (2003: vii). Stivale suggests that Deleuze's seminars involved a plurality of factors which seemed to interrupt the regular progress of temporal succession. It is as though time was forced out of joint by the frustratingly cramped and overcrowded lecture theatres, and various unwelcome events that all too often stymied the timely delivery of course materials. Stivale observes that in one seminar Deleuze reflects on how Nietzsche's example of a thinker who shoots arrows without foreknowledge of their intended target might apply to his own teaching. The suggestion here is that to participate in one of Deleuze's seminars was perhaps to catch of glimpse of one of those rare, beautiful moments in which Deleuze became something of singularity – a point of inflection that marshals key moments of the memorial past only to propel them into an undisclosed future.

The complex analyses contained in this volume promise to change the way future generations of scholars will conceive of Deleuze's philosophy of time. Indeed, they indicate that elaborating on Deleuze's concept of temporality requires specifying the nature and function of mutually implicated aspects of a complex phenomenon. Deleuze's thought on the nature of temporality demonstrates that it is a protean entity which – because of the ongoing modification of its aspects – expresses fragile indeterminacy. If it is to be suggested that the concept of time must – by ontological necessity – still enjoy unity, then perhaps we might now observe that this unity should be identified as the unity of a multiplicity. In this sense, it may be better to use the nominal term 'time' in a plural sense: when elaborating on the nature of temporality with reference to the thought of Gilles Deleuze, perhaps the philosophers of the future will identify the object of their study as 'the times of Deleuze'.

References

Deleuze, G. (1996), 'Foreword', in Éric Alliez, *Capital Times: Tales from the Conquest of Time*, trans. Georges Van Den Abeele, Minneapolis: University of Minnesota Press.

Deleuze, G. (2003), *Kant's Critical Philosophy: The Doctrine of the Faculties*, trans. Hugh Tomlinson and Barbara Habberjam, Minneapolis: University of Minnesota Press.

Deleuze, G. (2007), 'Occupy without Counting: Boulez, Proust, and Time', in *Two Regimes of Madness: Texts and interviews 1975–1995*, ed. David Lapoujade, trans. Ames Hodges and Mike Taormina, South Pasadena: Semiotext[e].

Deleuze, G. and F. Guattari (1987), *A Thousand Plateaus: Capitalism and Schizophrenia*, trans. Brian Massumi, Minneapolis: University of Minnesota Press.

Simondon, G. (2020), *Individuation in Light of Notions of Form and Information*, trans. Taylor Adkins, Minneapolis: University of Minnesota Press.

CONCEPTS OF TIME

Chapter 1

Time is Real: Deleuze and Guattari, from Chaos to Complexity

Dorothea E. Olkowski

Creation?

Philosophy, as defined by Gilles Deleuze and Félix Guattari, is 'the art of forming, inventing, and fabricating concepts' (1994: 4).[1] More specifically, it is 'the discipline that involves *creating* concepts', because concepts are not ready-made, and even though they are incorporeal, what we usually refer to as intellectual or mental, there is no heaven of concepts; they must be created (1994: 5, 21). There are creators; creators are not persons but personae, a force of ideas that provide a signature, a name like Descartes or Kant that is a cluster or assemblage of concepts, and every concept is a multiplicity as there is no concept with only one component. Every concept has some sort of history as well as a becoming; it undergoes evolution, and so is both absolute with respect to the problem it addresses but also relative to its components, as well as infinite in its *survol*, its reach, but finite with respect to its Leibnizian indiscernibility (Deleuze and Guattari 1994: 15–21). Although many things can be said about this designation, what I wish to draw attention to here is the problem of the creation of concepts. What does it mean to say that the creation of concepts is possible? How can we justify even the possibility of creation, not merely as a linguistic phenomenon but as a reality, even if an incorporeal one?

The reason creation rises to the level of a problem has to do both with Deleuze and Guattari's own philosophy and with the mathematical and scientific framework, which their philosophy must confront in utilising the tools offered by the mathematics and cosmology upon which they are reliant. Beginning with a schematic history of philo-scientific accounts of the universe, and not simply of nature, western philosophy of science was formalised by Plato's (fourth century BC) and Ptolemy's (100 AD) models of the universe, both grounded in the idea of heavenly bodies moving in perfect circular motion guided by either Plato's 'pilot' (in *The Statesman*) or Ptolemy's Aristotelean god's realm of heavenly perfection in which nothing that is true undergoes change. Much later (1687) there is Newton's similarly eternal and cyclical universe (inherited by Albert Einstein) in which any event, no matter how improbable, must occur an infinite number of times (Smolin 1999: 143–4). As the physicist Lee Smolin sums this up: '[i]n a world of atoms governed by deterministic laws, chance alone plays the role of the pilot who returns the universe from time to time to an ordered state that makes life possible' (144), but only as an improbable fluctuation in an otherwise dying universe.

The point of this selective account is to take note that from Plato to Einstein, physics posits a world governed by deterministic laws and improbable events, and fails to describe a world in which things – corporeal and incorporeal – arise and evolve; that is, the creation of something new does not seem possible. This problem is further exacerbated by the nineteenth-century theory of thermodynamics which postulates the law of entropy, which states that the disorder of systems in the direction of equilibrium must always increase (Smolin 1999: 147). The law of increasing entropy predicts the eventual heat death of the universe because collections of atoms are more likely to arrive at a disordered state of equilibrium than an organised, creative configuration. Together, the Newtonian worldview along with thermodynamics give us a sad picture of reality as both deterministic and dead.

Deleuze famously critiques the Platonic view of the universe, directly addressing the argument of *The Statesman*. The Statesman, the shepherd of men, is well founded, but below him lie the auxiliaries and slaves, and the evil power of simulacra and counterfeits (Deleuze 1990: 255–6). The motivation for such divisions is, as Deleuze argues, 'to distinguish essence from appearance, intelligible from sensible, Idea from image, original from copy and model from simulacrum' (256). Plato's goal, according to Deleuze, is to distinguish good from bad copies: to distinguish well-founded copies, internally and spiritually balanced and endowed with resemblance to the Idea, from simulacra engulfed in dissimilarity, underhandedly failing to pass through the Idea and internally unbalanced. It is of consequence in this model that at the top of the hierarchy there is a knower who possesses knowledge of the unchanging and eternal Idea. Below this is the possibility of right opinion, not knowledge of the eternal but a good copy. Lowest is the imitator who has access only to simulation due to their inability to master the eternal and unchanging Idea or even right opinion. The imitator advocates for a distortion that evades the equal, the Same and the Ideal, sinking into an unlimited becoming that challenges the authority of the knower and the known (Deleuze 1990: 258).

In the Platonic eternality, Justice is just and so the Same; the copy is at least the Similar. Although Plato introduces this model, it is Aristotle who codifies it through the division into genus and species, which delimited and specified the role of representation and made it easier for Christianity to celebrate the infinitely great of the genus of Being and the infinitely small of species – all in God's domain – to the exclusion of the eccentric and the divergent (Deleuze 1990: 259).

Nietzsche's attack on Platonism was supposed to have reversed it, abolishing the eternal world of essences as well as its impoverished bastard – the world of appearances. But Deleuze is not entirely satisfied with Nietzsche's effort, which remains all too abstract, failing to uncover Plato's motivation. Thus the true overturning of this eternalist model requires affirming the rights of simulacra to deny the claims to truth of the original eternal Idea and its copy and assert the 'triumph of the false pretender' (Deleuze 1990: 262). The resemblance of the similar to the Same is abandoned for the sake of internalised difference, and the identity of the Same is differentiated into the 'identity' that is the Being of the Different, so that what is, is only as difference. As even Nietzsche noted, under every formerly eternal foundation, there exists a more profound subsoil, another cave, another subterranean world (Deleuze 1990: 263; Nietzsche, *Beyond Good and Evil*, sect. 289).

It might now seem to be the case that Deleuze has profoundly freed his thought from the eternal and the inevitable or deterministic, but we have yet to deal with the Newtonian version of the universe. The question is what to make of Newtonian laws and absolute space and time if simulation is now understood as the process of disguising, where behind any mask is another and another, because, as Deleuze notes, '[s]imulation understood in this way is inseparable from eternal return' (1990: 263). Wise to the implications of this, Deleuze quickly revises the meaning of eternal return. It is not, he claims, the eternal return of the Same, but the power of affirming chaos, an affirmation whose meaning it is not a simple matter to discern. For Plato, chaos was defined in relation to order or laws; it is the 'rebellious matter' to be subjugated by the Demiurge (Deleuze 1994: 68). Chaos can be currently defined in physics as 'a deterministic mechanism that generates the *appearance* of randomness' and is sensitive to initial conditions (Casti 1994: 103). For Deleuze, chaos is defined as 'virtual chaos', where virtuality is the 'potential' through which states of affairs take effect (Deleuze and Guattari 1994: 153). The task ahead is to connect this view of chaos from both early and late Deleuze texts to a new cosmology, one that is not situated in relation to a timeless deterministic universe.

Time is Real

'Time is real.' When I spoke these words to an astrophysicist at a seminar on cosmic and human time, he – along with several members of the audience, which included a number of physicists – may have thought, 'no it's not, time is only a psychological phenomenon'. This is because, for the astrophysicist, time is an illusion, and temporal flow and its somewhat recently revealed consequence – complexity – indicate the existence of nothing more than a temporary fluctuation arising from some special initial conditions in our region of an otherwise deterministic universe governed by the time-reversible laws of classical mechanics. This is what is called the Newtonian paradigm. Its conditions are that the space under consideration – configuration space – is timeless, and solving a specific set of equations gives the entire future of the system, a system that exists in the present because the laws governing the system are also timeless (Smolin 2014: 139). The effect of this paradigm is that 'time is inessential and can be removed from the description of the world', and the initial conditions of the universe determine the future down to the smallest detail (167–8). And crucially, the laws of Newtonian physics can be reversed. The initial conditions follow the laws to a final configuration. Starting from that configuration, the laws can be run in the opposite direction back to the initial conditions, so that if it were possible to make '[f]ilmed motions of the whole solar system', then run them backward, the result would be an orbit allowed by Newton's laws that is indistinguishable from its forward motions (111).[2]

This leaves us with the dispiriting notion that our sense of time as real is nothing more than an illusion, that the real universe is timeless, and that the so-called history of the universe is merely a system of causal events in a block universe (Smolin 2014: 150–1). The concept of the block universe allows for the treatment of time as a dimension of space, a fourth dimension since '[a]n event taking place at a moment of time is represented as a point in spacetime, and the history of a particle is traced by a curve in spacetime called its worldline' (151). In this geometricised version of the universe, photons are represented as moving at 45 degree angles, and other particles – because they move more slowly than the speed of light – are represented at steeper angles. Hermann Minkowski devised this representation, the light cone, sometime between 1907 and

1909. It is the translation of motion in time into a visual representation of a timeless geometry (Smolin 2014: 154–5).[3]

This widely accepted view of a timeless and deterministic universe was disrupted by the second law of thermodynamics, which states that no process is possible whose sole result is that energy is transferred from a cooler to a hotter body (Schneider and Sagan 2005: 45).[4] When Ludwig Boltzmann, who is credited with unifying classical thermodynamics with Newtonian mechanics, modified thermodynamics allowing for the 'perception of linear time', this was met with scepticism from Friedrich Nietzsche and Jules-Henri Poincaré, who maintained, along with many others (including Albert Einstein and Bertrand Russell), that even though randomised conditions tend toward equilibrium and thus, increasing entropy, eternal return is still possible and there is no global direction for time (Schneider and Sagan 2005: 47, 57). Why? Because, they argued, future states are fixed by the initial condition and its rules of motion, but over an infinite amount of time nothing prohibits the return of an earlier state (Casti 1994: 87).

Like Newtonian mechanics, classical thermodynamics operates in accordance with a specific set of restrictions. Its systems are isolated, allow for no variables, and they are driven toward equilibrium at a constant temperature (Schneider and Sagan 2005: 25–6; Cortês and Smolin 2018). Of course this is not the full account of thermodynamics. In addition to isolated systems, there are systems, such as chemical reactions, that are merely closed. They allow energy but not matter to be exchanged across their boundaries and they allow for some variables.[5] Ecosystems exchange both matter and energy across borders, making them the clearest example of open systems, but 'stars, burning nuclear fuel and producing high-quality light', along with exploding supernovas, as well as cities and bodies, all exchange matter and energy across boundaries (Schneider and Sagan 2005: 26). Moreover, the further from equilibrium any system is, the more difficult it is to predict its behaviour due to the uncertain relations between changes in variables.[6]

Far from equilibrium systems are instances of the threshold where fluctuations lead to unstable behaviour. Lucretius referred to this as the clinamen, a spontaneous, unpredictable deviation that describes turbulence, irregular on the macroscopic scale, but *highly organised* microscopically (Prigogine and Stengers 1984: 141; Serres 2000). This transition from the macroscopic to the microscopic, from chaotic to highly organised, coherent behaviour, from stable flows to turbulence, is now viewed as *self-organisation* (Prigogine and Stengers 1984: 141). When a system interacts with the outside world, exchanging energy and matter, these nonequilibrium conditions may be the setting for so-called dissipative structures that do not exhibit the characteristics of energy loss but become the sources of order – that is – order out of chaos.

Boltzmann recognised that irreversible increases of entropy reflect disorder on the molecular scale, a broad approximate description with few variables, but that there is also a movement in the direction of *increasing probability* on the microscopic scale, where there is a precise description of the positions and motions of all the atoms in a system (Smolin 2014: 501–2). A macroscopic state of disorder and symmetry corresponds to maximally probable *microscopic states* where as many particles will be moving in one direction as in the other Prigogine and Stengers 1984: 124–5). The number and type of microstates that add up to a macrostate indicate the amount of entropy in a system. The greater the number of microstates, the less the entropy. We can visualise this as the difference between a square building made of nearly identical macrostate bricks, each of which can replace any other, and architect Daniel Libeskind's Denver Museum of Contemporary Art, a model of microstates (Smolin 2014: 502–3). For the latter, there is only one possible way to assemble the titanium and granite siding – each element has a specific and necessary placement – but for the former, any brick will do.

The classical model does not take into account sensitivity to initial conditions, the reality that even two very proximate initial conditions will follow very different trajectories, but insofar as there is only one universe we have no way to test this on a cosmological scale (Casti 1994: 90). And yet, 'we see no evidence for our region of the universe being a low-entropy fluctuation in a static world in equilibrium. We see instead a universe evolving in time, with structure on every scale developing as the universe expands' (Smolin 2014: 516).

Deleuze, Bergson and Intuition

How to decide between these apparently contradictory views of the universe, between an entropic deterministic bloc universe and our encounter with self-organisation moving from chaos to complexity on multiple scales? This is a considerable problem, and one that Deleuze's philosophy takes up along several trajectories, including Henri Bergson's conceptualisation of intuition and duration, which proves useful in confronting the problem. Essential to Deleuze is Bergson's revolt against Platonic ideas, something for which Bertrand Russell criticised him intensely on the basis of what Russell took to be Bergson's failure to understand mathematics and physics (Petrov 2013: 892). As Russell sees it, mathematics conceives change, even continuous change, as constituted by a series of states; Bergson, on the contrary, contends that no series of states can represent what is temporally continuous, and that 'in change a thing is never in any state at all', a claim supported by Bergson's account of intuition and duration (Petrov 2013: 895; Russell 1914: 17).

It is possible that what we commonly refer to as intuitions are not really intuitions at all but merely a poor use of our reflective capacity – a reflection on static logical formulae grounded in a perspective that assumes the existence of unchanging laws of nature and traces them to their apparently inevitable end, which is a deterministic and timeless universe punctuated by fluctuations that give rise to otherwise inexplicable novelty and complexity. This was the source of the conflict between Bergson and Einstein that was fuelled by Russell. Bergson's commitment to what he called the philosopher's time – duration and its tendency intuition – led him to resist Einstein's claim that there is only one time, the eternal time of the physicists and mathematicians, and resulted in numerous accusations that Bergson did not understand relativity and so did not understand the true nature of reality (Canales 2015: 5).[7]

Possibly we have forgotten the history of intuition beginning at least with René Descartes, who in spite of rejecting sensory perception and memory – even intellectual and mathematical memory – still argued that pure intuitions are the most potent source of ideas. After all, how did Descartes come to discover the cogito? Rejecting even this, we have turned to science and the scientific method – physics and mathematics in particular – in order to make sense of the world around us. For us and for Deleuze, Bergson revives our interest in and our affection for temporal intuition.

According to Bergson, it was his reflection on duration that led him to what he calls the philosophical 'method of intuition', in which intuition does not stand in opposition to intelligence (Bergson 1946: 33). For Bergson, what undermines the classical binary approach to intuition and intelligence is that space is intellectualised time; it is the externalisation of internal temporal duration, which he defines as the 'uninterrupted prolongation of the past into a present which is already blending into a future' (35). We may refer to this as continuity, although not the classical mathematical continuity of infinitesimal points on a line, but the continuity of an immediate consciousness hardly able to be distinguished from its object. Duration does not end with consciousness because intuition reflects not only consciousness but also what is vital; it enfolds an intuition of life as evolution and duration such that both are reality (36). This occurs insofar as intuition is never static. It always begins with movement, with the perception of movement as reality and the perception of change as essential (37). 'Intuition, bound up to a duration, which is growth, perceives in it an uninterrupted continuity of unforeseeable novelty; it sees, it knows that the mind draws from itself more than it has, that spirituality consists in just that, and that reality, impregnated with spirit, is creation' (39). It is in this manner that intuition is also reflection; it is the mind drawing from itself (103).

Deleuze has a great deal to say about this. Initially, he characterises Bergson's intuition in two ways. First, it is not inferred from something else but arrives in person. This is why, for Deleuze, there is still philosophy and not only science, as science 'separates us from things and from their interiority', whereas, presumably, it is only philosophy that seeks out the interior (Deleuze 2004: 23). Secondly and necessarily, intuition arrives as a return; it is a return from space, intelligence and science, and so it puts us in things, which for Deleuze is what restores us to a philosophical relationship with the world. Intuition is one movement but it involves two directions – the intelligible and the sensible – one ending in the object and the other turning back, retracing the movement from which it emerged. The return is intuition's power of negation. Like Socrates' demon, it forbids. It turns away from and so forbids the infusion of accepted ideas, evident theses, and affirmations passing for science. It says no, 'impossible' (Bergson 1946: 129).

How does intuition carry out the return in two directions? It does so as image; the image is what reaches the soul of a doctrine, as the image is both nearly matter and nearly mind (Bergson 1946: 139). When a philosophical doctrine takes shape, images arise 'following the philosopher through the evolutions of his thought' (140). Such images may be or perhaps are always unclear – they are the chaos, or as Deleuze comes to define this, virtual chaos. But the philosopher takes them up because she has two means to express herself – the concept and the image. 'It is in concepts that the system develops; it is into an image that it contracts when it is driven back into the intuition from which it comes' (141). If the philosopher supersedes or overrides the image, the intuition likely loses its vitality, becoming insipid, uninteresting and banal, and the philosopher falls back into vague, general concepts.

Bergson introduces the chaos of images at the beginning of *Matter and Memory* when he situates himself in the presence of the vaguest of images (1988: 17). He is there in the midst of what can initially be described as a thermodynamic system that is also a system accommodating chaos, when chaos is properly defined as 'a deterministic mechanism that generates the *appearance* of randomness' and is sensitive to initial conditions (Casti 1994: 103). He begins his account with chaos, with the appearance of randomness, which is to say, a less well-organised sensibility knowing nothing about theories of matter or spirit, or reality or ideality, and from this he articulates how such images may lose their vitality.

> All these images act and react upon one another in all their elementary parts according to constant laws which I call laws of nature, and,; as a perfect knowledge of these laws would probably allow us to calculate and to foresee what will happen in each of these images, the future of the images must be contained in their present and will add to them nothing new. (Bergson 1988: 17)

If these images exist in a block universe and are the effect of reciprocal actions and passions following deterministic laws of nature, then even if they are initially apparently chaotic they should become highly ordered – even homogeneous – and this system would operate deterministically.

But evolution and creation call for intuition, and intuition falls within duration, that which differs from matter but more profoundly differs first from itself. Thus intuition's third and possibly most significant characteristic, Deleuze notes, is that it is the method that seeks difference, differences in nature or kind and articulations of the real (2004: 26). 'Space breaks down into undifferentiated matter and differentiated duration, and duration is differentiated into contraction and expansion' (26–7); thus quality and quantity, instinct and intelligence, vital and geometric order, metaphysics and science, are dualities that are tendencies not opposites or contradictories. Duration is the change in nature, quality, heterogeneity, and crucially, difference from itself, and intuition takes advantage of this to return, to seek difference between two tendencies, and so to reflect on its own images.

There is a fourth characteristic. Given that space is differentiated into matter and duration, and duration is differentiated into contraction and expansion, the method of intuition rediscovers the simple; that is, what persists as a convergence of probabilities (Deleuze 2004: 27). Deleuze points to the *élan vital*, the virtual chaos and its actualisation, the prolongation of the past into the present, but Bergson does not merely remain within biology, he also points to the universe that *endures* because duration is not merely cognitive or psychological (28). 'The more we study the nature of time, the more we shall comprehend that duration means invention, the creation of forms, the continual elaboration of the absolutely new. The systems marked off by science *endure* only because they are bound up inseparably with the rest of the universe'

(Bergson 1983: 11), and only insofar as those systems are reintegrated back into the 'Whole' – like our sun, which radiates heat and light into the universe, and along this 'very tenuous' thread transmits, even to the smallest particle of our world, the duration immanent to the *whole of the universe* (10–11).

Deleuze affirms this Bergsonian method with the confirmation that the reality of time is the affirmation of actualisation, the invention of the virtual on any scale insofar as the virtual is the whole (2004: 30). This is what makes it possible, in Bergson's thought, for matter to be the most relaxed degree of duration even as it returns and contracts as differentiation into the past that is present and the past-present that creates the temporally new and so creatively endures bound up with the universe (31).

Deleuze, Peirce and the Continuum

Charles Sanders Peirce (1839–1914) would appear to have no visible connection to either Bergson or to the concepts of duration and intuition or chaos and complexity, but that view might be short-sighted. Bergson's solution to the problem of insipid generalisation in a deterministic universe is that the general idea will have been felt and passively experienced in intuition and that it will be virtual prior to being thought, and this can be found as well in Peirce's unique conception of the continuum as Thirdness and its manifestations Firstness and Secondness. Let us turn to his refutation of mechanical generalisation: for Peirce, 'every general concept is, in reference to its individuals, strictly a *continuum*', but 'no collection of individuals could ever be adequate to a concept in general' (CP 4.642, 5.526; cited in Zalamea 2012: 7).[8] Although Peirce goes on to define continuity similarly to Bergson, as fluidity, he also admits that continuity has been defined mathematically as a line consisting of infinitesimal parts.

This does not suffice for Peirce, for whom infinity in the strictest sense appears to exceed the possibility of direct experience. And yet, there is one 'real world', one 'positive direct evidence of continuity', that he can cite with some confidence, an instance surprisingly similar to that given by Bergson:

> We are immediately aware of only our present feelings – not of the future, nor of the past. The past is known to us by present memory, the future by present suggestion. But before we can interpret the present feeling which means memory, or the present feeling that means suggestion, since that interpretation takes time, that feeling has ceased to be present and is now

past ... I am trying the hypothesis that it [continuity] is real ... If this is real, the past is really known to the present ... Then we must have an immediate consciousness of the past ... by four units, by eight units, by sixteen units, etc. ... Now, this is only true if the series be continuous. Here, then, it seems to me, we have positive and tremendously strong reason[s] for believing that time really is continuous. (CP 1.167, 1.168, 1.169)

For Peirce's conception, just as for Bergson's duration, continuity arises from feeling, a present feeling immediately present in consciousness as well as present memory and present suggestion, continuous with one another. Peirce claims that according to this reasoning, space, quality and other things, even all things, might be continuous, since, after all, Peirce's continuum is merely a discontinuous series with 'additional possibilities', and the best hypothesis is the one that 'leaves open the greatest field of possibilities' (CP 1.170). And just as relevant is the argument that when a portion of the mind acts on any other, it must be immediately present to it, for all things 'swim in continua' (CP 1.171).

Real continuity arises from feeling or quality but it is a generality, a general, because it is an absence of distinction of individuals and leaves room for possible variables that cannot be exhausted by any multitude of existents (CP 5.103, 5.431; Zalamea 2010: 10). This structure is formalised in Peirce's semiotics and his argument for the character of continuity, wherein parts and wholes are regularised. But also, and perhaps unexpectedly, it has to do with evolution, that is, diversification, the passage from the unorganised to the organised, from what we have called chaos to complexity, which Peirce refers to as an increase in variety (CP 1.174).[9] Can we say that this is crucial for an open system? As Peirce argues, 'were things simpler, was variety less in the original nebula from which the solar system is supposed to have grown than it is now when the land and sea swarms with animal and vegetable forms ...?' (CP 1.174).

This view of nature and the universe, this theory, this idea of continuity and evolution on all scales was and continues to be strongly opposed by the scientific 'algebraical apparatus of mechanical law', which has been asserted to be the one and only, the 'very idea of law', because laws are absolute and cannot grow (CP 1.174, 1.175). The problem with this view is that it makes the laws of nature blind and inexplicable; how can we possibly explain the universe, the formation of its galaxies, planets, stars and life itself on the basis of a single chance, a single role of the dice? Whereas if continuity and the evolution of laws are real, there is no reason not to think that the universe has undergone 'a continuous growth from non-existence to existence' (CP 1.175). In chaos, there is no regularity and so no existence, there is quality or feeling. In the embrace of the principle of real continuity, the only explanation of the universe and of things in the universe is that they have evolved.

Continuity is understood by Peirce to be the generality that makes prediction possible, which he calls Thirdness. The immediate present of which one is conscious, the quality that is immediate consciousness, is the feeling of Firstness, as is the whole of consciousness (CP 1.318, 1.342). Thus, it is '[f]eeling implied in Firstness', because feeling is 'not referring to anything, not lying behind anything'; it is 'fresh, original, spontaneous, and free', potentiality without existence, to the point that to describe it is already to falsify it (CP 1.327, 1.355, 1.356, 1.357). As with any image, it is still utter indeterminacy (CP 1.1405). In the midst of Firstness, there arises a feeling of struggle between our feeling and some sort of stimulus. The feeling of struggle is the realisation of Secondness, which is brute actuality, hard fact, the resistance of the door that refuses to open, the not-self, reality (CP 1.322). There can be no brute reality, limitation, conflict or constraint, no Secondness, 'the external dead thing', without quality, the feeling of Firstness, of freedom and freshness as quality (CP 1.358, 1.361).

The relation between Firstness and Secondness is mediated by Thirdness; that is, Secondness is the Firstness of Thirdness, but only when a singular and blind reactive compulsion in a moment of struggle is replaced by a meaning, something embodied in an event of thought. This is why Peirce calls Thirdness a sign that stands for the idea it produces or modifies. A sign conveys meaning and the idea to which it gives rise is its interpretant. The meaning of a representation is another representation.

In fact, it is nothing but the representation itself conceived as stripped of irrelevant clothing. But this clothing can never be completely stripped off; it is only changed for something more diaphanous. So there is an infinite regression here. Finally, the interpretant is nothing but another representation to which the torch of truth is handed along; and as representation, it has its interpretant again. Lo, another infinite series (CP 1.339).

Given this, it is no wonder that we have a strong tendency toward scepticism with respect to finding any real meaning in laws. But only 'skepticism of the innocent and wholesome kind that tries to bring truth to light' is worthwhile (CP 1.344).

In *Difference and Repetition*, Deleuze argues that the Idea is 'an n-dimensional, continuous, defined multiplicity', where dimensions refer to variables upon which a phenomenon depends, and continuity is 'a set of relations between changes in these variables' (1994: 182). This statement resonates deeply with Peirce's conception of the continuum. We noted that for Peirce continuity is generality: 'the possible is general, and continuity and generality are two names for the same absence of distinction of individuals' (Zalamea 2012: 10; CP 4.172). In fact, continuity is generality that is understood as conformity to one Idea; that is, the continuum is 'all that is possible' in a field so crowded that units loose identity and so become continuous (cited in Zalamea 2012: 15; CP 7.535, n. 6; Peirce 1989: 160). As a result, the continuum is *supermultitudinous*, a collection so great that its constituents have no hypothetical existence except in their relations to one another expressive of the continuum and so are not distinct (Zalamea 2012: 12, 20, 21; CP 3.86–7, 3.95).

This seems to be what Deleuze is aiming at when he refers to the *ideal continuity*, especially because the continuum is reflexive and so cannot be composed of points; it is *mise-en-abyme*, that is, the whole can be reflected in any of its parts (Deleuze 1994: 179). This implies that the continuum is synthetic, unable to be analytically reconstructed, and also inextensible, unable to be divided, thus unable to be composed of points (Zalamea 2012: 14). A continuum, where it is continuous and unbroken, contains no definite parts; its parts are created in the act of defining them and the precise definition of them breaks the continuity. In other words, given that the continuum consists in real and general possibilities that far exceed anything that exists, 'existence is a rupture', a discontinuity, which is a second, Secondness. Peirce's account thus fills in the structure of Deleuze's claim that solutions are like discontinuities, as discontinuity implies an existence that is the fulfilment of a possibility.

Like Peirce, Deleuze insists that the continuum, that multiplicity that consists of virtual events, that virtuality is the 'potential' through which states of affairs take effect (Deleuze and Guattari 1994: 153). For Peirce, the richness and possibilities of the continuum far exceed the realm of existents (Zalamea 2012: 15). Moreover, the continuum has multiple dimensions and a plasticity that never ruptures (CP 4.512).[10] Points of time or space are 'ideal limit[s]', the mathematical notion of limit being what is approached infinitely closely without ever actually being reached in dividing time or space (Zalamea 2012: 23; Peirce 1982–2000: 3.106). Or, as Deleuze and Guattari understand this: 'states of affairs leave the virtual chaos on conditions constituted by the limit (reference): they are actualities, even though they may not yet be bodies or even things, units, or sets' (1994: 153).

In the broader context, Deleuze has argued that '[i]deal connections constitutive of the problematic (dialectical) Idea are *incarnated in real relations* which are constituted by mathematical theories and carried over into problems in the form of solutions', where the solutions are like *discontinuities* (1994: 179). Deleuze locates the concept of the problematic in relation to differential calculus, stating that 'solutions are like the discontinuities compatible with differential equations, engendered on the basis of an ideal continuity', where the latter is situated as the trajectory that traces the calculated speed and direction of an entity (179).

This calls for a structure that allows something to be grasped as a sign, and this is the structure of the Idea that differentiates; it is the generality that actualises quality. When Deleuze argues that problems are always dialectical, this appears to be what he means. By contrast, solutions are mathematical, physical, biological or sociological. Still, the continuity in the development of mathematics has made 'differences in kind between differential calculus and other instruments merely secondary' (Deleuze 1994: 181). This is because, as Deleuze argues, the dialectical Idea, the problematic, is a system of differential relations, and dialectical Ideas are the differentials of thought (Thirdness) engendered or incarnated in various domains (Secondness), each of which is characterised by its own differential calculus as determined by the problematic Idea.

In addressing the problem of how to characterise the relationship between things and thought without resorting to dualism or certain versions of idealism and without the bloc universe and determinism, Deleuze has made ample use of both Bergson and Peirce. For Bergson, it is the continuity duration-intuition that moves an image from banal generality by returning it to intuition, each time creating a new image. For Peirce, the richness and possibilities of the continuum far exceed the realm of existents (Zalamea 2012: 15). The continuum cannot be constructed starting from existents or particulars and so neither can the virtual chaos. But the state of affairs is inseparable from the potential through which it takes effect and which sustains its activity and development. The continuum, the virtual chaos, the continuity of images which may be what we refer to as complexity, continues to act as a catalyst in the face of new or unanticipated problems (Deleuze and Guattari 1994: 153).

Notes

1. Some of the material in this essay appeared initially in my book *Deleuze, Bergson, Merleau-Ponty: The Logic and Pragmatics of Creation, Affective Life, and Perception* (Bloomington: Indiana University Press, 2021).
2. Newtonian mechanics, quantum mechanics and Einstein's Special and General Relativity are all time-reversible (see Smolin 2014: 112).
3. Smolin shows that the block universe depends on the *relativity of simultaneity*.
4. The statement is that of Rudolf Clausius and is cited in Atkins 1984: 25.
5. See Schneider and Sagan 2005: 26. 'An example of a closed system is a chemical reaction in a closed flask where excess heat from the reaction is permitted to move outside the flask into the surroundings.'
6. See Schneider and Sagan 2005: 28. 'A change in one variable may lead near-linearly to a change in another variable; or it may trigger unpredictable changes that cannot be modeled with relatively simple mathematical equations.'
7. These accusations continue to the present day.
8. References for Peirce are to *The Collected Papers of Charles Sanders Peirce*, abbreviated to CP followed by volume and page number.
9. Peirce attributes this idea to the advocate of evolutionary theory, Herbert Spencer.
10. Deleuze does not appear to follow Peirce into the 'logic of vagueness', bypassing excluding the law of the excluded middle in favour of the concept of virtuality.

References

Atkins, P. W. (1984), *The Second Law: Energy, Chaos, and Form*, San Francisco: W. H. Freeman and Co.

Bergson, H. (1946), *The Creative Mind*, trans. Mabelle L. Andison, New York: Citadel Press.

Bergson, H. (1983), *Creative Evolution*, trans. Arthur Mitchell, Lanham, MD: University Press of America.

Bergson, H. (1988), *Matter and Memory*, trans. Nancy Margaret Paul and W. Scott Palmer, New York: Zone Books.

Canales, J. (2015), *The Physicist and the Philosopher: Einstein, Bergson, and the Debate that Changed Our Understanding of Time*, Princeton: Princeton University Press.

Casti, J. (1994), *Complexification: Explaining a Paradoxical World through the Science of Surprise*, New York: Harper Collins.

Cortês, M. and L. Smolin (2018), 'Reversing the Irreversible: From Limit Cycles to Emergent Time Symmetry', *Phys. Rev. D* 97, 026004.

Deleuze, G. (1994), *Difference and Repetition*, trans. Paul Patton, New York: Columbia University Press.

Deleuze, G. (2004), *Desert Islands and Other Texts, 1953–1974*, ed. David Lapoujade, trans. Michael Taormina, Los Angeles, Semiotext(e).

Deleuze, G. and F. Guattari (1994), *What Is Philosophy?*, trans. Hugh Tomlinson and Graham Burchell, New York: Columbia University Press.

Peirce, C. S. (1931–35, 1958), *The Collected Papers of Charles Sanders Peirce*, ed. Charles Hartshorne, Paul Weiss and Arthur Burks, Cambridge, MA: Harvard University Press.

Peirce, C. S. (1976), *New Elements of Mathematics*, The Hague: Mouton.

Peirce, C. S. (1982–2000), *Writings*, ed. Nathan Houser, Bloomington: Indiana University Press.

Peirce, C. S. (1989), *Reasoning and the Logic of Things*, Cambridge, MA: Harvard University Press.

Petrov, V. (2013), 'Bertrand Russell's Criticism of Bergson's Views about Continuity and Discreteness', *FILOZOFIA* 68 (10): 890–904.

Prigogine, I. and I. Stengers (1984), *Order Out of Chaos: Man's New Dialogue with Nature*, New York: Bantam Books.

Russell, B. (1914), *The Philosophy of Bergson. With a Reply by Mr. H. Wildon Carr*. Cambridge and London: Macmillan.

Schneider, E. D. and D. Sagan (2005), *Into the Cool: Energy Flow, Thermodynamics, and Life*, Chicago: University of Chicago Press.

Serres, M. (2000), *The Birth of Physics*, trans. Jack Hawkes, Manchester: Clinamen Press.

Smolin, L. (1999), *The Life of the Cosmos*, Oxford: Oxford University Press.

Smolin, L. (2014), *Time Reborn: From the Crisis in Physics to the Future of the Universe*, Boston: Mariner.

Zalamea, F. (2012), *Peirce's Continuum: A Methodological and Mathematical Approach*, Boston: Docent, at <https://uberty.org/wp-content/uploads/2015/07/Zalamea-Peirces-Continuum.pdf>.

Chapter 2

The *Movement* of Time

Thomas Nail

We talk about the movement of time but does time *move*, or does movement occur *in time*? This is a fundamental question in the philosophy of time that philosophers and physicists are still trying to answer. Interestingly, one of the most original and shockingly contemporary answers to this question was given by the first-century Roman poet Lucretius almost two millennia ago. Lucretius believed that nature was composed of continually moving matter whose spontaneous swerving occurs in 'no determinate time and space' (*incerto tempore, incertisque loci*). Some ancient philosophers and scientists believed that time was linear, others that it was cyclical. Virtually no one thought it was 'indeterminate'. So, unfortunately, Lucretius' theory of time sounded so strange that it was either ignored or misinterpreted as a reference to the soul's freedom.

It was not until the French philosopher Gilles Deleuze returned to this idea in his 1969 book, *Logique du sens*, that Lucretius' theory of time's 'swerve' was taken seriously. In the appendix of his book, Deleuze was the first to argue that Lucretius had put forward an indeterminate (non-linear and non-chronological) theory of time. Deleuze argued that the swerve of falling atoms in Lucretius' philosophy was not the result of a determinate collision with other atoms but was caused by a vital force or *conatus* immanent to them. This was a brilliant and vital insight but also a strange one. Lucretius was a materialist, not a vitalist, and never used the word *conatus* to describe the swerve of matter. Therefore, it is hard to reconcile Deleuze's *conatus* theory of the temporality of the swerve with Lucretius' text. It is even harder to reconcile Deleuze's 'static' view of time in *Difference and Repetition* with Lucretius' kinetic materialism. Deleuze explicitly subordinates movement to time: 'The [third] synthesis is necessarily static, since time is no longer subordinated to movement; time is the most radical form of change, but the form of change does not change' (1994: 89). Similarly, in *The Logic of Sense*, Deleuze subordinates movement and matter to time in his theory of 'an empty form of time, independent of all matter' (1990: 62).

This chapter is an intervention into the strange history of the 'indeterminist' theory of time first put forward by Lucretius and partially recovered by Deleuze. I argue that Deleuze left out the *material* and *kinetic* aspects of Lucretius' theory of time and that this has caused problems for Deleuze's theory of time. Alternately, I propose to recover these aspects with a kinetic theory of time drawing on Lucretius.

Deleuze, Lucretius and the Temporality of the Swerve

Deleuze's work played an essential and pivotal role in shaping the current revival of interest in Lucretius and the philosophy of time. Since Karl Marx, he was the first to return to Epicurus and Lucretius and try to revive a philosophy of immanence. Unlike Marx's dissertation, however, people read Deleuze's *The Logic of Sense* and were directly influenced by it. Let's take a closer look at three critical innovations in Deleuze's reading of Lucretius and the unique temporality of the swerve discussed there.

1. The essence of the atom is to course and flow

Deleuze was the first philosopher since Marx to interpret the essence of atoms as *flows*. 'The ancient atom is entirely misunderstood if it is overlooked that its essence is to course and flow' (Deleuze and Guattari 1987: 489). This is no small gesture since the prevailing and almost universal interpretation of atoms is that they are discrete, self-identical units. Deleuze explicitly credits Marx's dissertation for this wild idea.

In his dissertation, Marx used Hegel's idea of dialectics from *The Philosophy of Nature* to reinterpret Epicurean atomism's key concepts as only dimensions or moments of a single continuous unfolding process. This meant taking some significant liberties with Epicurus' minimal extant corpus of three letters. Needless to say, a dialectical reading of Epicurus had very few followers in classical philology or Marxism.

I will not go into the technical details of Marx's incredible reading of Epicurus here, but here is one memorable quote:

> The consequence of this for the monads as well as for the atoms would therefore be – since they are in constant motion – that neither monads nor atoms exist, but rather disappear in the straight line: for *the solidity of the*

atom does not even enter into the picture, insofar as it is only considered as something falling in a straight line. (Marx 2006: 111; emphasis added)

Marx uses dialectics to completely sublate the atom's discreteness into its fall, swerve and movement. Deleuze was likely the first to pick up on this idea's wild originality and run with it. In *The Logic of Sense* he does not credit Marx explicitly, but in *Nietzsche and Philosophy* he does provide a short note saying that this was where he got the idea (Deleuze 1983: 6–7).

2. The swerve is non-spatiotemporal and not epistemologically indeterminate

Deleuze also emphasised the *ontologically unassignable* nature of the atom's swerve in Lucretius. Many commentators have treated the swerve as merely an *epistemological* uncertainty and treated atomism as an otherwise standard determinism (Spencer 2014). Deleuze, by contrast, writes:

'*incertus*' does not mean indeterminate, but rather unassignable; '*paulum*', '*incerto tempore*', '*intervallo minimo*' mean 'in a time smaller than the minimum of continuous, thinkable time'.

This is why the *clinamen* manifests neither contingency nor indetermination . . . [but] the irreducible plurality of causes or of causal series. (Deleuze 1990: 270)

Deleuze thus emphasised the non-mechanistic nature of the swerve, against the early modern interpretation of atoms as agreeing with deterministic and assignable laws of nature. In Deleuze's reading, the swerve is neither random nor deterministic but rather irreducibly plural and relational. There is no single law that could predict its motion, not because the movement of matter is random but because it is so entangled and relational that there is no objective view that can capture the ontological plurality of relations. This is not merely a limit of human knowledge but a feature of an immanent ontology where the universe is, as Spinoza says, 'cause of itself' (*Ethics*, Book 1, Def. 1). This move also eschews any philosophy of time where time is made of fundamentally discrete and assignable spatiotemporal now points. The temporality of the swerve, according to Deleuze, occurs below the minimum of any thinkable or assignable temporal point (1990: 270). This is an extraordinary and radical notion.

3. The swerve is immanent to the atom and not caused by something else

The final key idea of Deleuze's reading of Lucretius is the idea that the swerve is irreducible to external causality. Lucretius is explicit that external collisions do not cause the swerve but that the swerve is imma-nent to the movement of matter. This may sound like a straightforward reading of Lucretius, but Cicero, Plutarch and many other commen-tators and critics thought this was a completely ridiculous and even embarrassing idea. It was the reason why so many modern philosophers rejected the concept of the swerve and replaced it with mechanistic materialism. They also inserted God, the soul and human freedom back into Lucretius' philosophy. In short, they were unwilling to affirm the consequences of an immanent swerve. Here, Deleuze tries to affirm the consequences of an immanent causality. Matter swerves without any external causality. Deleuze writes:

> The *clinamen* or swerve has nothing to do with an oblique movement which would come accidentally to modify a vertical fall. It has always been present: it is not a secondary movement, nor a secondary determination of the movement, which would be produced at any time, at any place. The *clinamen* is the original determination of the direction of the movement of the atom. (Deleuze 1990: 270)

The idea of an immanent swerve in matter is of crucial importance to the philosophy of time. The swerve's temporality does not occur in any assignable time or space, and one cannot reduce it to a linear causal sequence. It is a kinetic indeterminacy. Time without causality is a very different notion of time. In a strict sense there is no succession of anything at all. There is a differential process of iteration more or less similar in each moment but never any underlying identity. All attempts to define an external causality of matter's motion are claims to tran-scendence or something outside nature.

These are the three excellent ideas that I think we should take from Deleuze's short but profound intervention in the reception of Lucretius and his theory of time. There are, however, some less desirable and even inaccurate aspects of Deleuze's interpretation that I think we should leave behind if we want to think about the temporality of the swerve.

The Problems with Deleuze's Interpretation of Lucretius

Even when there is a core of good ideas in their interpretations, it is also important to acknowledge where Marx or Deleuze have gone entirely outside the text to make their points. Epicurus did not have, and certainly did not mention, any theory of a materialist dialectic in his letters. We have zero evidence that he said or believed anything like what Marx said about him in the passage quoted above. Nonetheless, the idea of atomism without discrete, isolated atoms is not entirely lacking in the case of Lucretius, who never used the word 'atom'.

In any case, let's take a closer look at three key places where Deleuze's reading goes astray from the text in a way we may not want to connect to the temporality of the swerve.

1. Lucretius does not use the word 'atom' and never says it is discrete

Deleuze, like virtually every other commentator, talks about 'atoms' in Lucretius. Still, Lucretius never used the Greek word *atomos*, nor did he use the Latin word *atomus*, which Cicero created later to talk about atoms. Instead, Lucretius multiplied his terms for matter, complicating any unified concept of matter in his work.

Furthermore, in all his terms for matter, Lucretius never says that matter is discrete or that it is particle-like. This makes the following claim by Deleuze not quite textually accurate:

> The sensible object is endowed with sensible parts, but there is a minimum sensible which represents the smallest part of the object; similarly, the atom is endowed with parts that are thought, but there is a minimum thought which represents the smallest part of the atom . . . the indivisible atom is formed of thought minima. (Deleuze 1990: 268)

There is absolutely zero textual evidence in *De Rerum Natura* (*The Nature of Things*) to suggest that Lucretius thought that atoms have 'parts'. Firstly, this is because Lucretius does not use the word atom or an equivalent. Second, even if this were the definition of an atom for Epicurus, it would not necessarily be true for Lucretius. Deleuze does not offer any source citation or translation to support this claim either.

2. *Lucretius does not say that atoms are made of thought*

I suspect that Deleuze may have been trying to reconcile Spinoza's philosophy with Epicurus in suggesting the existence of thought-atoms. It's only a hunch based on what he says in the following passage:

> The atom is that which must be thought, and that which can only be thought . . . The atom is to thought what the sensible object is to the senses: it is the object which is essentially addressed to thought, the object which gives food to thought, just as the sensible object is that which is given to the senses. (Deleuze 1990: 268)

Lucretius indeed believes that one cannot see *corpora* or bodily matters with the eye because they are *processes, not objects*. However, this does not mean that matter *is* thought. Deleuze offers no textual support from *De Rerum Natura* for this claim because there is none. Instead, he cites Epicurus as saying that 'the atom moves "as swiftly as thought"' (1990: 269). He then extrapolates this to mean that the atom's reality is in thought. If Marx mixed ancient materialism with Hegel, Deleuze mixed it with Spinoza. Deleuze had some creative insights but also made some wildly non-textual claims. 'In agreement with the nature of the atom, this minimum of continuous time refers to the apprehension of thought' (269). Deleuze tries to make matter simultaneously thought. Although this position is consistent with Spinoza, Deleuze does not directly credit him here. We may want to adopt this Spinozist interpretation for other reasons, but it is not something Lucretius said. It is inconsistent with Lucretius' philosophy because there are no atoms, no parts, and certainly no thought-atoms. My worry about this claim is that it heads in an idealist direction and threatens to transform Lucretius' radical materialism into an idealism or panpsychism (see Nail 2018b, 2018c, 2020; Nail et al. 2019).

3. *Lucretius does not say that the swerve is* conatus *(vital striving) or that nature is power*

Deleuze does not explicitly use Spinoza's name, but the term *conatus* and the philosophy of nature as power are sufficient to recall Deleuze's massive dissertation on Spinoza. Deleuze says that 'The *clinamen* is the original determination of the direction of the movement of the atom. It is a kind of *conatus*' (1990: 269). This is a key point for thinking about the temporality of the swerve. We might surmise that time is not assignable, causal or linear because it is the pure vital striving of being.

Deleuze does not attempt to find a textual equivalent of *conatus* in Lucretius. We have no direct textual evidence of what Epicurus thought of the swerve, only *testimonia* (the most important being Lucretius). In Lucretius' poem, the swerve of matter is nowhere described as a vital power or striving. Lucretius writes about the movement, fold or curvature of matter without attributing any external transcendent vital cause or any immanent vital power of any kind. Matter moves, and swerves.

As much as Deleuze rejects the early modern attempts to explain the movement of matter by something else (god, soul, freedom, force, etc.), he can't keep from assigning an immanent motive power to movement in the form of a vital striving or *conatus*. This is not the same as a transcendent explanation of the swerve, but it is nonetheless completely unnecessary and not textually supported in Lucretius or Epicurus. Deleuze imports a vitalist temporality unknown to Lucretius.

Deleuze also claims that 'Nature, to be precise, is power. In the name of this power things exist *one by one*' (1990: 267); and that 'There is the power of the diverse and its production, but there is also the power of the reproduction of the diverse' (271). These lines might as well be straight from his book on Spinoza. Yet, Lucretius nowhere says that nature is power. He says that nature moves and that it is material, but terms like power, force and energy do not have any special status that is not, in the end, reducible to matter in motion. If power were something other than matter or motion then it would have no place in Lucretius' materialist philosophy. However, if one used the term 'power' merely to describe matter's movement, then it would be completely redundant and unnecessary.

Deleuze knew what he was doing with this interpretation. The paper trail is explicit in a parenthesis in his earlier book, *Nietzsche and Philosophy* (1962). There, Deleuze subordinates matter and motion to *force*, contrasting himself and Nietzsche (and implicitly Spinoza) against Lucretius' and Marx's kinetic materialism:

> Only force can be related to another force. (As Marx says when he interprets atomism, 'Atoms are their own unique objects and can relate only to themselves' – Marx, *The Difference Between the Democritean and Epicurean Philosophy of Nature*. But the question is; can the basic notion of atom accommodate the essential relation which is attempted to it? The concept only becomes coherent if one thinks of force instead of atom. For the notion of atom cannot in itself contain the difference necessary for the affirmation of such a relation, difference in and according to the essence. Thus atomism would be a mask for an incipient dynamism. (Deleuze 1983: 6–7)

Deleuze finds the idea of materialism insufficient because he cannot imagine how matter could be internally differentiated without the existence of a vital power. He cannot imagine movement without a cause or something else to explain it. In *Difference and Repetition* Deleuze is explicit that 'the *clinamen* is by no means a change of direction in the movement of an atom, much less an indetermination testifying to the existence of a physical freedom' (1994: 184). Matter does not have agency and freedom on its own without some kind of dynamic power or force.

However, I have argued elsewhere on several grounds that motion can be differentiated without assuming any force or vital striving power (Nail 2018a, 2020). For instance, Lucretius defines the swerve as an indeterminate movement of matter. As a materialist, he does not attribute the swerve to any vital force or power. For him, matter is capable of novelty on its own. I see no reason why *conatus* is needed to make matter swerve, and I have tried to show this textually in my books on Lucretius.

Therefore, I suggest that we leave this aspect of Deleuze's interpretation where it belongs: with Spinoza. This is the case for textual reasons but also for philosophical reasons. I think the concepts of *conatus* and power are unnecessary and add nothing to our understanding of Lucretius and the indeterminate temporality of the swerve. At the worst, they are likely to lead readers to conflate it with Margaret Cavendish's early modern vitalist interpretation of Lucretius.[1]

In the next section, I would like to focus on what Lucretius says about the temporality of the swerve and show how we can use it to develop a material and indeterministic theory of time.

Lucretius and the Movement of Time

One of the things that is so interesting to me about Lucretius is that he is one of the few in the western tradition who says that matter moves indeterminately without any other explanation. There is no trace of transcendence or vital forces whatsoever in his work. For Lucretius, the indeterminate movement of matter does not occur in space and time (which would precede motion) but produces space and time. Movement is thus not a movement from point A to point B (points in space traversed over time) – it is the process that produces the line and points AB in the first place. If this sounds Bergsonian, it is because Lucretius was Bergson's first intellectual love. Bergson's first book was a line-by-line commentary on Lucretius' great poem *De Rerum Natura*.

In Bergson's final lectures, *La Pensée et le mouvant* (*Thought and Mobility*, 1934), he returns to the primacy of movement, claiming that 'time is mobility' (2007: 8). Becoming is the continual mobility of reality itself. 'Reality is mobility itself' (46). In this final work, Bergson could hardly be any more clear or unequivocal when he writes that '[i]f movement is not everything, it is nothing' (155). Whatever apparent primacy Bergson had given to so-called vital force/impetus or time/duration should now be understood to be *nothing other than the primacy of motion itself*.

In my view, the philosophy of time, like force, is another historical instance of philosophers and scientists trying to explain why matter moves.[2] Force was popular in the early modern period, and time was popular in the nineteenth and twentieth centuries. Most ontologies and theories of time treat it as the ultimate *a priori* of nature (or of human existence). Historically, this was supported by Einstein's theory of general relativity, even though there were still exceptional 'singularities' (in black holes, for example) left unexplained by that theory. Matter, in general relativity, moves across a pre-existing curved spacetime. If quantum theory is correct, however, there should be a quantum theory of gravity, including space and time, in which spacetime emerges from the laws of quantum physics. In particular, energetic vibrations below the level of space and time should produce space and time like ripples on a pond's surface.

Contemporary theoretical physics points in this direction – even if the formalisms of 'quantum gravity theory' have yet to be experimentally verified. The race is on to prove them. Lucretius was already the precursor to this idea 2,000 years ago, and at least one quantum gravity theorist has acknowledged this (Rovelli 1998). Matter, for Lucretius, produces space and time through its indeterminate motion. In other words, I think we have finally come back to Lucretius. Perhaps this indicates that it is time to shift focus from ontologies of time to ontologies of motion. Maybe it's time to consider a new perspective. This is what I think Lucretius can offer us: a kinetic theory of time.

Time, for Lucretius, is the kinetic dissipation of matter. Matter tends to move from denser to less dense regions, and this provides the arrow of time that we experience as regional beings. This is entropy: the spreading out of matter. This does not mean that time is chronological. Where would the past go when it passes? The past is still with us in the immanent material that we are. The future, too, is here in the matter that we are. As Bergson said in his final lectures, time is nothing but movement: the transformation or redistribution of an open whole. At every moment, the entire universe kinetically transforms its entire distribution of space and time. There is no static nature to which the present can refer as past nature. The whole thing is continually different from itself – but tending regionally toward energetic dissipation (Bergson 1988: 47, 197; 2007: 46, 155).

In my reading, Lucretius was right about the primacy of movement over time. Deleuze got very close but ended up inserting the ideas of *conatus*, vitality, power and force. He even claims that this dynamic time is 'necessarily static, since time is no longer subordinated to movement' (1994: 89). The form of change does not change, and so Deleuze calls it a 'static genesis' in *The Logic of Sense*. Deleuze's idea that time is *formal* and *static* sounds much more like the strobe-like 'occasions' or 'Cambridge changes' of Alfred North Whitehead than like Bergson or Lucretius.[3] According to Whitehead, change is only 'the difference between actual occasions comprised in some determined event', and thus it is 'impossible to attribute "change" to any actual entity' (1978: 73, 59). 'Thus an actual entity never moves: It is where it is and what it is' (Whitehead 2014: 73). For Whitehead, change and motion relate to a succession of actual entities and are constituted only by the *differences* among them. Every entity is 'what it is', and it 'becomes' as the whole of reality enters a succession of different states, but technically nothing ever changes or moves.

The Temporality of the *Clinamen*

In what follows, I would like to take Deleuze's study of the temporality of the swerve in a more materialist direction, leaving vital forces and Spinoza's *conatus* behind. In my view, Deleuze's critical insight about Lucretius' theory of time is that it does not occur in an assignable time or space. However, in my reading, this leads us to an indeterminate and materialist philosophy of time.[4] This also significantly changes our understanding of matter as a substance or an attribute of a substance. Lucretius has a unique process definition of matter. I want to show that this is a better way to think about the swerve's temporality in Book II of *De Rerum Natura*.

In his well-known description of the swerve, Lucretius highlights two key features. It 'occurs in an indeterminate time and space', and it is a 'change in motion' (2003: 2.216–20).

Illud in his quoque te rebus cognoscere avemus, corpora cum deorsum rectum per inane feruntur ponderibus propriis, incerto tempore ferme incertisque locis spatio depellere paulum, tantum quod momen mutatum dicere possis.

In this matter, there is this, too, that I want you to understand, that when the first bodies are moving straight downward through the void by their own weight, at times completely undetermined and in undetermined places they swerve a little from their course, but only so much as you could call a change of motion.

Corpora (flows of bodily matters) move downwards, carried by their energy and momentum through and by making space (*deorsum rectum per inane feruntur ponderibus propriis*) (Lucretius 2003: 2.217–18). Without any measurable discrete time or space (*incerto tempore ferme incertisque locis spatio*) (2.218–19), the *corpora* change, modulate or deviate (*depellere*) (2.219) their motion (*momen mutatum*) (2.220) to the smallest possible degree (*paulum*) (2.219). This is not the result of any other external or oblique motion but is internal to the corporeal flow's motion. Like the turbulent currents of air that drive dust motes, the corpora's movement is also fundamentally turbulent because it changes its motion on its own (*momen mutatum*).

These turbulent twists do not happen in spacetime but create spacetime through their collisions. Time, for Lucretius, is nothing apart from the relative motion, rest and sensation of things (*tempus sentire fatendumst / semotum ab rerum motu placidaque quiete*) (2003: 1.462–3). Movement is always material, and matter is always in continual motion. There is no stasis in nature and nothing ontologically discrete.[5] 'Discontinuous movement' is just the difference between divisible points of spacetime and has nothing to do with movement at all. Therefore, if we want to say that being actually moves, such movement cannot emerge from ontological discontinuity but must emerge from the twin conditions of an unbroken process (*solida*) and motion (*flux*).

Lucretius is clear that the movement and modulation of the *corpora* or matters do not occur in time and space (*nec tempore / loci certo*) (2003: 2.259–60). *Corpora* are not spatial or temporal; they are the material conditions of space and time itself. Therefore, we cannot say that there is a point of spacetime that the *corpora* have not yet reached and then measure how long it takes for them to get there. Their movement produces space and time as it goes. We thus reach the radical and paradoxical-sounding conclusion that the speed of matter is simultaneous, only on the condition that we understand matter to be productive of space itself.

Showing how matter in motion produces spacetime through swerving and folding is the holy grail of contemporary physics. There are numerous theoretical models of how general relativity might be unified with quantum physics to explain the emergence of space and time. These are called 'quantum gravity theories'. None have been experimentally demonstrated, but physicists are presently trying to gather experimental data that might do so.

A consequence of Lucretius' materialist philosophy of time is that matter can instantaneously move since space and time are material. This was an absurd-sounding scientific idea for hundreds of years, but not any more. Quantum entanglement experiments show that particles can make coordinated changes simultaneously without any action at a distance. Two electrons can be entangled and then physically separated. At a distance, the two electron spins change simultaneously in correlation with one another. This is possible because, when one spin is changed, it does not 'cause' the other to change by communicating information to the other.

The electrons are two topological regions of the same quantum field. There is no transfer of information across the quantum field. The field, which spreads out over vast distances, changes what it is as a whole. Quantum movement is an intensive transformation of the whole. We can locate a particle in spacetime, but spacetime itself is an emergent and metastable feature of swerving quantum matter.

These experimental findings are consistent with Lucretius' idea that *corpora* are not reducible to space and time. Furthermore, if the swerve happens on a pre-given immaterial background of space and time, then space and time would have emerged ex nihilo. This is the limit of general relativity. It can describe spacetime dynamism, but it cannot explain how spacetime itself emerged. For Lucretius, we should also not assume that something immaterial like static formal spacetime can give birth to something mobile and material like the swerve.

Simulacral Time: *Brevi spatio, temporis in puncto*

The other place where Lucretius writes about his materialist theory of time is in Book IV of *De Rerum Natura*, where he discusses the simulacra. Deleuze also references this section in his reading of Lucretius. For Lucretius, matter makes spacetime by moving. This is a radical thesis. As matter flows, it weaves figures or patterns that Lucretius calls simulacra. Simulacra are metastable and entangled 'things' (*simulacra rerum*). Deleuze was correct to read them as very different than copies of copies or resemblances of something else.[6] In contrast to the primary flows of matter that Lucretius calls *corpora* or *primordia*, simulacra are relatively discrete and spatiotemporal.

In the final lines of Lucretius' description of simulacra, he puts forward perhaps the most revolutionary physical thesis of Book IV, and perhaps in all of *De Rerum Natura*. He argues that the origin of the emergence of simulacra occurs in *'brevi spatio, temporis in puncto'*. This echoes the indeterminate spacetime of the swerving of the first-threads in Book II, *'incerto tempore, incertisque loci'*:

> *ergo multa brevi spatio simulacra genuntur, ut merito celer his rebus dicatur origo.*

Therefore many images are produced in a brief space,
so that deservedly the birth of these things is said to be quick.

> *necessest*
> *temporis in puncto rerum simulacra ferantur*

it is necessary that images
be carried off from things in a point of time (Lucretius 2003: 4.159–60, 4.163–4)

Simulacra are things (*simulacra rerum*), and things are by definition spatiotemporal and relatively discrete – as Lucretius described in great detail in Books I and II. Simulacra are produced (*genuntur*) or thrown off from larger composite things in the fastest possible spacetime. If they were not, then there would be some thing between them, which would lead to an infinite regress. This is the explicit point of these lines.

However, the implicit question Lucretius is posing is: 'What is between spatiotemporal simulacra?' Or even more dramatically stated: 'What is the origin of spacetime itself?' In effect, Lucretius has already given us the answer to this question. The *primordia* or first-threads of matter are the origins of spacetime. Just as the flows of matter weave things through folding, so spacetime itself emerges from the indeterminate movement of matter. In the lines above, Lucretius temporalises space – *'brief* space' – and spatialises time – *'point* of time'.

How fast do simulacra fly off of things? They fly off at an indeterminate speed that is not assignable to a fixed space or time. Discrete spacetimes are, like simulacra, folds in the threads of matter. Since we know from Book II that matter flows by indeterminately swerving *'incerto tempore, incertisque loci'*, we conclude that determinate spacetimes, like simulacra, emerge from indeterminate fluctuations of matter. This sounds incredible, but like most theses in Lucretius, strikingly contemporary. Today, most theoretical physicists agree that spacetime is not an *a priori* or metaphysical given but rather an emergent property of our quantum universe. More specifically, the emergence of spacetime is a quantum effect of the

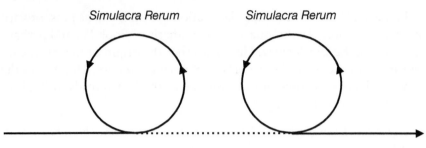

Simulacra Rerum   *Simulacra Rerum*

Indeterminate

flux of indeterminately high energies at work below the level of measurably discrete spacetime fluctuations called the 'Planck limit'. Energy does not vanish below the Planck length but instead becomes so radically indeterminate that the known laws of physics break down. For instance, if you put a particle in a box the size of the Planck length or smaller, the indeterminacy of its position would be greater than the size of the box, and its mass would produce a black hole whose radius would be double the Planck length. The time it would take to cross this radius would be four times the Planck time (Siegel 2019). At these ultra-intense energies, the fluctuation and curvature of space become so indeterminate that we cannot calculate anything meaningful about it, even with quantum gravity theories.[7] Indeterminacy becomes more considerable than any prediction we can make. Statistical mechanics and probability theory run aground on the shores of this radical indeterminacy at the heart of things.

Spatiotemporal discreteness is something that emerges from a more fundamentally indeterminate flux or inclination of energy/matter. Lucretius was thus perhaps the first to pose a version of quantum gravity theory *avant la lettre*. Even more surprising is that his answer is not inconsistent with what we currently know about the nature of the indeterminately high vacuum fluctuations that lurk beneath the fabric of spacetime itself.

How then does something like our experience of the chronological passing of time emerge from an indeterminate material process? In brief, matter swerves into metastable patterns or loops that seem relatively discrete and stable. The present is a metastable state which forms like an eddy as matter moves from hotter to colder states. What we call the passage of present moments is the dissipation of relatively stable metastases and the formation of new ones. Time flows because of the swerving matter that supports it and dissolves it. Time is nothing other than the flowing, folding and unfolding of material processes. It is not a static genesis but a kinetic genesis.

Conclusion

At the turn of the eighteenth century, the philosophy of 'forces' faced a brutal empiricist critique from Hume and others. Empiricists deemed forces metaphysical entities with no reality. However, it was not until nearly the end of the eighteenth century that Immanuel Kant began to replace the metaphysics of force with a new ontologically primary descriptor: time.

At least since Aristotle, time had been considered ontologically subordinate to motion and other terms. It was not until Kant that one of the most historically derivative ontological categories, time, became the most primary. After Kant, almost every nineteenth- and twentieth-century ontologist took up the ontological primacy of time.

Modern ontology became increasingly critical of the idea that space, eternity and force were ontologically foundational categories. Time, however, remained mostly immune to the same critiques. Time became the new name for being – ushering in an age of generalised chronophilia. With only a few exceptions, almost all modern ontologies of the eighteenth through twentieth centuries, in one way or another, accept the reality and foundational nature of time. Everything occurs in time, but time itself was not created by or derived from anything else.

This chapter's thesis is that time, like space, eternity and force, is a fundamentally kinetic process. Time is derived from motion in at least three ways.

First, by definition, time is a division between three tenses: past, present and future; before, during, after. Without such a division, it does not make sense to use the word time without confusion. Time, as a divided and differential phenomenon, presupposes that which it divides, namely the flow and swerve of motion. If temporal division were fundamental, being would already be divided, and movement would be reduced to a mere juxtaposition of vacuum-sealed fragments, as Whitehead and the occasionalists describe. Nothing would secure or allow for transition between divided points. It would be a 'static genesis'. Time, in my view, is therefore derivative of movement. I have tried to show the origins of this idea in Lucretius' theory of the swerve and the simulacra. Motion is how metastable moments emerge and pass.

Second, contemporary accelerationist cosmology confirms the derivative nature of time. Before the existence of the known universe, most physicists postulate a rapid unfolding of matter (as quantum fields) moving (exploding) outward – in a stochastic process of differentiation and combination. All forms of current division and discreteness come from the primary movement of indeterminate quantum fluctuations below the Planck limit. Without matter in motion (the explosion) there would be no spatial division or distinction, no rotational images of eternity in the heavenly bodies, no forces or relations between bodies, and no temporal division among a before, during and after. Temporal division (linear or circular) is only possible based on a more primary explosion of motion or entropic materialisation. Therefore, time is possible only because the universe moves in a certain way and because we *happen to exist in a low-entropy universe*. In high-entropy universes, or at the Planck scale, things move differently. Therefore, it seems that time is not ontologically foundational but derived from the kinetic process of cosmic acceleration and materialisation (Rovelli 2018: 83–4). What we call time is a series of metastable states in an indeterminate flow of matter.

Third, and relatedly, thermodynamics also confirms this thesis. According to thermodynamics, time appears to us as irreversible because it is *derived* from matter in entropic motion. Since heat is fundamentally kinetic (bodies in motion), and since motion is fundamentally pedetic, some motion is always lost or escapes any given circulation (entropy). However, according to the law of entropy that defines this thermodynamic foundation of time, entropy itself is *not absolute*. It is only a macroscopic *tendency*, not a fundamentality. In other words, it is the pedetic movement of matter that is the condition for both the emergence and the destruction of time.

If time existed independently from matter in motion, then it would be logically reversible. However, the postulation of such a reversal, independence and fundamentality of time is the result of a metaphysical presupposition in the mathematical disciplines that can demonstrate the so-called reversibility of time *in equations*. Mathematicians first run an equation (including stochastic equations) forward, laying out the formula and inputting the physical variables. Then, having concluded, they see if they can derive the variables from the conclusion. Invariably, they do. What this shows, however, is not the reversibility *of time* but the reversibility *of equations*. Starting with the solution and working backward confirms what they discovered in the initial formula and observations.

What the difference between thermodynamics and mathematics shows on this point is that if time existed independently from matter and motion, as it does in mathematics, then it would be macroscopically reversible. However, according to thermodynamics, real matter and motion do not actually behave this way in this macroscopic region of our universe. The metaphysical and mathematical-idealist description of time existing independently from material motion has no absolute reality. The movement of time forward and backward has a strictly physical definition because it is tied to kinetic energy. This does not mean, however, that our *description* of time has no reality. What thermodynamics shows us is precisely this fact: time is a description given by bodies in motion *of* bodies in motion and nothing else outside of this. What we are describing when we describe time can certainly be called sequence and seriality. Being really does move and change continuously, and it can be divided into various dimensions we can call past, present and future. The question then is, 'What is the kinetic status of such dimensions and seriality?'

In this chapter, the answer I have proposed, using Deleuze and Lucretius, is that past, present and future are emergent features of indeterminate material fluctuations.

Notes

1. This can be seen in several essays in Ellenzweig and Zammito 2017.
2. For a wonderful chapter arguing that time is only matter in motion see Righini Bonelli 1973.
3. For a more detailed account of the difference between my process philosophy and Bergson's, Whitehead's and Deleuze's, see Nail 2018b, chapter three.
4. My reading of the swerve differs from Althusser's since it is relational and not random or 'aleatory', as Althusser calls it (2006: 163).
5. Plotinus has an interesting theory of the soul as more like a movement than a thing, but for him, the soul is not material and certainly doesn't swerve.
6. Dan Smith elaborates on the characteristics of simulacra excellently in Smith 2012: 12–16. See also Deleuze's account in *The Logic of Sense* (1990: 257–67) and *Difference and Repetition* (1994: 69).
7. This is what Susskind calls 'black hole complementarity' (2008: 237).

References

Althusser, L. (2006), *Philosophy of the Encounter: Later Writings, 1978–1987*, London: Verso.
Bergson, H. (1988), *Matter and Memory*, trans. Nancy Margaret Paul and W. Scott Palmer, New York: Zone Books.
Bergson, H. (2007), *The Creative Mind: An Introduction to Metaphysics*, New York: Dover Publications.
Deleuze, G. (1983), *Nietzsche and Philosophy*, trans. Hugh Tomlinson, New York: Columbia University Press.
Deleuze, G. (1990), *The Logic of Sense*, trans. Mark Lester with Charles Stivale, New York: Columbia University Press.
Deleuze, G. (1994), *Difference and Repetition*, trans. Paul Patton, New York: Columbia University Press.
Ellenzweig, S. and J. H. Zammito, eds. (2017), *The New Politics of Materialism: History, Philosophy, Science*, London: Routledge.

Lucretius (2003), *On the Nature of Things (De Rerum Natura)*, trans. Walter Englert, Newburyport, MA: Focus.

Marx, K. (2006), *The First Writings of Karl Marx*, ed. Paul M. Schafer, New York: Ig Publishing.

Nail, T. (2018a), *Lucretius I: An Ontology of Motion*, Edinburgh: Edinburgh University Press.

Nail, T. (2018b), *Being and Motion*, Oxford: Oxford University Press.

Nail, T. (2018c), 'The Ontology of Motion', *Qui Parle: Critical Humanities and Social Sciences* 27 (1): 47–76.

Nail, T. (2020), *Lucretius II: An Ethics of Motion*, Edinburgh: Edinburgh University Press.

Nail, T., C. N. Gamble and J. S. Hanan, 'What is New Materialism?', *Angelaki: Journal of the Theoretical Humanities*, 24 (6): 111–34.

Righini Bonelli, Maria Luisa (1973), 'Time and Motion: Reflections on the Non-existence of Time', trans. Thomas B. Settle, in Joseph Needham, Mikuláš Teich and Robert M. Young, eds., *Changing Perspectives in the History of Science: Essays in Honour of Joseph Needham*, London: Heinemann Educational.

Rovelli, C. (1998), '"Incerto Tempore, Incertisque Loci": Can We Compute the Exact Time at Which a Quantum Measurement Happens?', *Foundations of Physics*, 28 (1031–43).

Rovelli, C. (2018), *The Order of Time*, London: Penguin.

Siegel, E. (2019), 'What Is The Smallest Possible Distance In The Universe?', *Forbes Magazine*, 26 June.

Smith, D. W. (2012), *Essays on Deleuze*, Edinburgh: Edinburgh University Press.

Spencer, J. M. (2014), 'Left Atomism: Marx, Badiou, and Althusser on the Greek Atomists', *Theory & Event* 17 (3).

Susskind, L. (2008), *The Black Hole War: My Battle with Stephen Hawking to Make the World Safe for Quantum Mechanics*, New York: Back Bay Books.

Whitehead, A. N. (1978), *Concept of Nature*, Cambridge: Cambridge University Press.

Whitehead, A. N. (2014), *Process and Reality*, New York: Free Press.

Chapter 3

The Pure and Empty Form of Time: Deleuze's Theory of Temporality

Daniel W. Smith

Deleuze argues that a fundamental mutation in the concept of time occurred in Kant. In antiquity, the concept of time was subordinated to the concept of movement: time was a 'measure' of movement. In Kant, this relation is inverted: time is no longer subordinated to movement but assumes an autonomy of its own, becoming the *pure and empty form* of everything that moves and changes. In what follows, we will examine how the inversion of the relation between time and movement came about, and how Deleuze's own theory of time builds on Kant's revolution and extends it further.

Originary, Aberrant and Ordinary Time

1. Originary time: the ancient coordination of extensive and intensive movement

For the ancients, the concept of time was subordinated to the concept of movement. Aristotle, in the *Physics*, writes that time is the measure or 'number of movement'.[1] A day is a unit that measures a single revolution of the earth on its axis (the movement from sunset to sunset); a month measures a single revolution of the moon around the earth (a cycle of the moon's phases); a year measures a single revolution of the earth around the sun (a cycle of the seasons). But since there is a plurality of movements, there is necessarily a plurality of times. When a lion chases a gazelle, the different movements of each animal cannot be said to unfold in a homogeneous time. Each movement has its own duration, its own articulations, its own divisions and subdivisions; in subduing the gazelle, the lion incorporates the gazelle into its own movements, its own time. This heterogeneity of movements is equally true of celestial bodies, and the complex history of the calendar is a history of attempts to coordinate and impose order on these heterogeneous movements (see Aveni 1989). Given the heterogeneity of movement, the ancients were led to ask the question: Is there something immobile or invariant, outside of movement – or at least a most perfect movement – through which all other movements could be measured? Is there a movement of movements in relation to which all other movements could be coordinated – a great celestial schema, or what Leibniz might have called a kind of 'metaschematism'?[2] This question wound up being answered in two different ways because there existed two fundamental types of movement: the *extensive* movements of the cosmos and the *intensive* movements of the soul. In antiquity, Plato and Plotinus provided the paradigmatic conceptions of time for these two kinds of movement.

In the *Timaeus*, for instance, Plato sought to incorporate the extensive movements of the cosmos into a vision of a 'planetarium' comprised of eight globes, with the immobile earth at the centre, surrounded by a sphere of 'the fixed' (the stars) turning on its axis, following a circuit that, by some calculations, was thought to last 10,000 years. It was precisely this movement of movements that provided a reference point by which all other extensive movements were to be measured: an invariant, a permanence. Time, in this manner, was subordinated to eternity, to the non-temporal. In Plato's famous formula, time was 'the moving image of eternity' (*Timaeus*, 37d).

But Aristotle observed that time not only measures the extensive movements of cosmic bodies, but also the intensive movements of the soul, that is, *the passage from one internal state to another*. 'If any movement takes place in the mind', he wrote in the *Physics*, 'we at once suppose that some time also has elapsed' (IV.11.219a5). Husserl's celebrated study of *The Phenomenology of Internal Time-Consciousness* would later become the classic analysis of the structure of these internal movements, such as protention and retention (Husserl 1964).

But the shift from the cosmos to the soul entails a profound change in the nature of movement, since intensive quantities are very different from extensive quantities.[3] Suppose I have twenty bottles each filled with a litre of water whose temperature is 50 degrees. I can pour the water of all these bottles into a separate container: though the volume of water will now be 20 litres, its temperature will remain 50 degrees. This is because volume is an extensive quantity, whereas temperature is an intensive quantity. Extensive quantities are additive, but intensive quantities are not. If they were, as Diderot quipped, you could simply add snowballs together to produce heat.[4] Extensive quantity is a *parts–whole* relation: the parts are external to each other (the exteriority of relations), and one part does not contain another part; what contains parts is always a whole, even if this whole is itself a part in relation to another whole. Intensive quantity, by contrast, is a *zero–unit* relation. What distinguishes two intensive quantities is the variable *distance* through which one comprehends their distance from zero intensity, although these distances are non-decomposable. The distance of 40 degrees from zero is 'greater' than the distance of 30 degrees from zero, but neither of these distances is divisible into parts (though the function of thermometers is to convert intensive qualities into extensive units) (see Knowles Middleton 1966). If time is the measure of movement, then time becomes something different when it measures intensive movements rather than extensive movements.

Plotinus' analysis of the soul, Deleuze argues, was modelled on the concept of intensive quantity, and his greatness was to have incorporated the intensive movements of the soul into his vision of the movement of the 'One', with its emanative processes of procession and conversion. Plotinus' dialectic proceeds in terms of a series of *powers*, beginning with the One, and proceeding through thought, the soul, nature, phenomena and so on (Plotinus 1991: 213–32). Intensive movement is an ordination of non-decomposable distances, that is, an ideal *fall* (French: *chute*, 'decrease' or 'drop') that marks the relation of a series of powers to zero.[5] Time emerges as the measure of intensive movement in two ways. Eternity (*aeon*) designates the fact that all 'powers' are each internal to the other insofar as they are 'One'. The 'now' (*nun*) is a privileged point in the internal movement of the soul that is intrinsically distinguishable from other points thorough their differing degrees of power, dividing into a pure past and a pure future, while nonetheless remaining united in the One. This act of distinction is thus at the same time a synthesis, and Deleuze argues that the Neo-Platonists were the first to see that time is inseparable from an act of synthesis.[6]

What one sees in both Plato and Plotinus, then, is the formation of an *originary* time that serves as a measure for movement, whether it is derived from the extensive movements of the cosmos (Plato) or the intensive movements of the soul (Plotinus). In both cases, the result was a hierarchisation of movements depending on their proximity to or distance from the eternal, an originary time marked by privileged positions in the cosmos or privileged moments in the soul. The discovery of this invariant was itself the discovery of the true, since truth required a universally commensurable time and space over which it could govern.

One should note that the common distinction between 'objective' and 'subjective' time does not mark a break with the ancient subordination of time to movement. Objective 'clock time' (or physical time) and the subjective experience of 'time consciousness' *both* measure movement, the sole difference being the type of movement. Objective movement measures the extensive movement of objects in the cosmos, whereas subjective movement measures the intensive passage from one state to another, even though the extensive *object* and the intensive *state* are only artificial 'snapshots' or 'cuts' extracted from the transition or passage of time.[7] Moreover, it is clear that modernity no less than antiquity still subordinates time to movement: the International System of Units (SI) defines a second in terms of the motion of a caesium atom (Crease 2011: 252, 264). In physics, special relativity had its roots in the problem of the synchronisation of clocks, and if 'time moves more slowly' for an object moving faster than another object, it is because the clocks on each object are measuring different movements.[8] In this sense, special relativity remained tied to the ancient conception of time and might even be said to have completed it.[9] Despite these practical exigencies, the fundamental issue in the theory of time is not the distinction between objective and subjective time but rather the relation between time and movement.

2. Derived time: aberrations of movement

The Kantian revolution was prepared for by the fact that both these domains – the extensive movements of the cosmos and the intensive movements of the soul – were haunted by fundamental aberrations of movement, where a *derived* time increasingly tended to free itself from the posited originary time. The closer one came to the earth – what the Greeks called the 'sublunar' domain – the more the extensive movements of the cosmos tended to become anomalous: the unpredictability of meteorological movements, for instance, or the movement of what comes-to-be and passes-away (becoming). Scientists can precisely predict the time of a solar eclipse, for instance, but they cannot predict whether or not they will be able to see it, that is, they cannot predict with precision the 'sublunar' weather. The entire corpus of Aristotle shows how anomalies of movement, with their accidental causes, were already marking a new form of time that could no longer simply be defined as a measure of movement.[10]

In short, the invariant provided by the 'movement of movements' was threatened by *crises* when cosmic movements became increasingly aberrant. Similarly, the intensive movement of the soul became marked by a *fear* that its restless movements in derived time – a *real* fall – would take on an independence of their own and would cease to be submitted to the originary time of the One, and the 'now' of the soul would fall into its double, the non-being of 'instant', a pure disappearing. In the doctrine of the Fall developed later in Christian theology – notably by Augustine – this Neo-Platonist notion of a real fall, and its correspond-ing fear, would take on enormous proportions.[11]

Aberrant movements provoked *crises* in the extensive movements of the cosmos and *fear* in the intensive movement of the soul. It is not by chance that, in French and many Latin languages, the same word is used for time and weather – *le temps* (from the Latin, *tempus*) – and the term has various cognates that are used to describe the aberrant motions of the cosmos (*tempest, temperature, temperate*) as well as aberrant motions of the soul (*temper, temperament, tempestuousness*) (see Serres 2000: 67; 1994: 100). The question then became: Does the sublunary world, with its *tempests* and *tempestuousness*, obey the metaschema-tism, with its proportional rules? Or does it enjoy an independence from it, with its own anomalous movements and disharmonies? The Pythagorean discovery of irrational numbers had already pointed to a fundamental incommensurability between the speed and position of the various cosmic spheres, and the search for 'universals' in philosophy is, in a sense, a remnant of the fear provoked in the intensive time of the soul: the very term is derived from the Latin word *universus*, meaning 'turned toward the One' (*uni-* 'one' + *versus* 'turned', the past participle of *vertere*).

In Deleuze's interpretation, these aberrant or derived movements – marked by meteorological, terrestrial and spiritual contingencies – remained a downward tendency that still depended on the adventures of movement. They too posed a problem, a choice: either one could try to 'save' the primacy of movement ('saving the appearances', in the Greek phrase), or one could not only accept but *will* the liberation of time with regard to movement. In effect, there were two ways in which movement could be saved. The extensive harmony of the world could be saved by an appeal to the rhythms of work in the *rural time* of the countryside, with the seasons and harvests as privileged points of reference in the originary time of Nature ('works and days', in Hesiod's phrase; or the rhythm of 'autumn' and 'spring' in China).[12] The intensive harmony of the soul could be saved by an appeal to *monastic time*, with its privileged moments of prayers and vespers (the clock was initially invented to mark the hours of prayer of the monasteries); or more generally, by an appeal to a spiritual life of interiority (Luther, Kierkegaard). By contrast, the liberation of time would take place in the city, an 'enemy' that was nonetheless engendered by both the rural communities and monasteries themselves. The time of the city is neither a rural life nor a spiritual life, but the time of everyday life. There is no longer either an originary time or a derived time, but what might be called an *ordinary* time or an *everyday* time: an abstract, uniform and homogeneous time.[13] Although Newton may have provided its initial scientific expression in his theory of absolute space and time, ordinary or everyday time has above all become the conventional time of our quotidian banality: the time of clocks, watches, calendars, time zones and daylight savings.[14]

3. Ordinary time: toward the liberation of time

The sources of this liberation of time from movement were multiple, having socio-cultural roots in the Reformation as well as the development of capitalism. Max Weber, for instance, showed that the Reformation became conscious of this liberation of time by joining together the two ideas of a 'profession' – one's profession of faith and one's professional activity – so that mundane professions like that of a cobbler were deemed to be as dignified as any sacred calling. Unlike the monk, whose duty was to be otherworldly, denying the self and the world, the fulfilment of one's duty in worldly affairs became the highest form that the moral activity of individuals could take. There was only one time – everyday time – and it is in this time that we would now find our salvation.[15]

Likewise, Marx showed that this vision of *temporal activity* ('What do you do with your time?'), which is no longer grounded in a cosmic rhythm or a spiritual harmony, would eventually find a new model in the 'abstract' time of capitalism, which replaced the privileged moments of agricultural work with the any-instant-whatever (*l'instant quelconque*) of mechanised work. Time became money, the form under which money produces money (usury or credit); and money itself became 'the course of time': the abstract time of capitalism became the concrete time of the city.[16] It was Heidegger who would ultimately produce a prodigious philosophical concept of the everyday and its relation to time, though to some degree he still maintained the old distinction between a derived (inauthentic) time and an originary (authentic) time (Heidegger 1962a).[17]

This liberation of time resulted in a fundamental change in the relationship of philosophy to the thought of everyday life (opinion). Up until the seventeenth century, one could say that, philosophically, everyday life was suspended in order to accede to something that was not everyday, namely, *a meditation on the eternal*. By contrast, the ordinary time of urban everydayness would no longer related to the eternal, but to something very different, namely, *the production of the new*. In other words, given the flow of average everydayness, I can either raise myself vertically toward the transcendent or the eternal, at least on Sundays (or Saturdays, or Fridays), through understanding or faith; or I can remain at the horizontal flow of everydayness, in which temporality moves toward the new rather than the eternal. The *production of the new* will be the correlate of ordinary time in exactly the same way that the *discovery of the true* was the correlate of originary time with the ancients. The aim of philosophy would no longer be to *discover* pre-existent truths outside of time but to *create* non-preexisting concepts within time.[18]

The Kantian Revolution

1. The pure form of time: 'the time is out of joint'

Deleuze argues that Kant was the first philosopher to give expression to this new conception of time.[19] In the anomalies of motion, time had begun to free itself from its subordination to movement. What Kant did in the *Critique of Pure Reason* was to derive the necessary consequences from these anomalies, whether cosmological (the movements of the universe) or psychological (the movements of the soul), in order to reverse the movement–time relation definitively and to render time independent and autonomous. Deleuze finds a poetic expression of this first aspect of Kant's revolution in Hamlet's phrase, 'the time is out of joint'.[20] The 'joints' are the privileged positions of the cosmos or the privileged moments of the soul that characterised originary time. Ordinary time, however, brings about a rectification of time: time 'out of joint' becomes a *straight line* that imposes its determination on every possible movement (Deleuze 1997: 28). On the surface, this is a surprising claim, since the common and simple image of time as a succession of instants on a line (the 'timeline') is an image that most philosophers of time have attempted to break with. (The word 'succession' is derived from an old French term meaning 'inheritance', and the presumption that time is successive was initially derived from the practice of measuring time though the succession of kings or dynasties, where time would begin again with each new reign.[21] Paul J. Kosmin has shown that the Seleucid Empire was the first to introduce a uniform and linear calendar that did not restart with each successive dynasty, which became the condition for the appearance of the first apocalyptic eschatologies of the 'end times'.[22]) But for Deleuze, the straight line indicates, paradoxically, that time has become a 'simple, terrible, inexorable' labyrinth that can only be comprised of the abstract and ordinary positions and instants irreducible to both bodies and souls (Deleuze 1997: 28).

The consequence of Kant's revolution was that time was freed entirely from cosmology and psychology, as well as the eternal. Such is the conclusion Kant draws in the Transcendental Dialectic, where the Self (the soul), the World (the cosmos) and God (the eternal) are all shown to be transcendent illusions of reason that are derived from our new position in time. Time is no longer dependent on *either* extensive movements (the cosmos) or intensive movements (the soul), and it thereby ceases to be a measure of movement. Instead, all movements – whether originary or derived, anomalous or aberrant – are now seen to take place within the labyrinth of time.[23]

Deleuze summarises these analyses by saying that Kant reconceived time as the *pure and empty form* of everything that changes and moves. Deleuze is here giving the concept of 'form' a new sense, since the form of time is not an eternal form, in a Platonic sense, but rather the pure form of what is *not* eternal (Deleuze 1997: 29). When time is liberated from movement, it ceases to be a cosmological or psychological time in order to become a formal time: a pure deployed form. The pure form of time is necessarily *static*, since time is no longer subordinate to movement. Time is the most radical form of change, but *the form of change does not itself change*: 'the *a priori* determinations of time are fixed or held, as though in a photo or a freeze-frame' (Deleuze 1994: 89, 294). If the form of time itself was changing or successive, it would have to succeed in another time, to infinity (Deleuze 1997: 28).[24]

2. The pure form of time: 'I is another'

But there is a second aspect to Kant's revolution, which can be seen clearly in the 'Analogies of Experience' section in the *Critique of Pure Reason*. Before Kant, time had largely been defined by succession, space by coexistence and eternity by permanence.[25] In Kant, succession, simultaneity and permanence are all shown to be *modes* or *relations* of time itself. Succession, as extensive movement, presupposes a plurality of times: empirical time (within the pure form of time) is composed of different times, and succession is the mode of relation between the different *parts* of time. Simultaneity, as intensive quantity, is what exists at the same time, it is the determination of the *content* of time (every sensation that fills time has an intensive quantity) (Deleuze 1994: 38). Permanence, finally, is the rule of what endures for all times (substance), which constitutes the ground of both successions and simultaneities. Put summarily, succession is the rule of what is in *different* times; simultaneity is the rule of what is at the *same* time; and permanence is the rule of what is for *all* times. As an individual, for instance, I exist *in time* as something permanent that has simultaneous states and that successively passes from one state to another.

Yet succession, simultaneity and permanence are all modes or relations of time; they are not time itself. When Kant defines time as the immutable form of what changes, he tells us repeatedly that 'time cannot by itself be perceived'.[26] Because I exist in time, I am eaten away and worn down by a time that I cannot perceive. Time is 'no less capable of dissolving and destroying individuals than of constituting them temporarily' (Deleuze 1994: 38). In a sense, the form of time dis-integrates: it devours succession, it devours simultaneity, and it devours permanence. From the viewpoint of succession, time is a straight line which the parts of time are unmade at the moment they are made (*elles se défont à mesure qu'elles se font*). From the viewpoint of simultaneity, time is an instant that, in terms of content, is emptied out at moment it is being filled (*un instant qui se vide à mesure qu'il se remplit*). From the viewpoint of permanence, time decomposes an enduring substance into something that is ceaselessly undoing and emptying itself (*ne cesse pas de se défaire et de se vider*).[27] Proust would later write, 'Time, which is usually not visible, in order to become so seeks out bodies and, wherever it finds them, seizes upon them in order to project its magic lantern on them', quartering the features of an aging face according to its 'distorting perspective' (Proust 1993: 342, 344; translation modified; cited in Deleuze 2000: 18, 160).

The only way to extract ourselves from the disintegrating power of time is through the power of *synthesis*. As Kant shows in the first Transcendental Deduction, synthesis is a triple operation – apprehension, reproduction and recognition – that is carried out by the activity of the 'I think' or consciousness (1929: 129–38, A98–110). Since every sensation that appears in time is a manifold and has a multiplicity of parts, consciousness must synthesise these parts in an act of *apprehension*; it must also *reproduce* or remember preceding parts when the following ones appear if a synthesis is to take place; and this sensible complex of parts can only be *recognised* if it is related to the form of the object (the 'object = x', which is the objective correlate of the 'I think'). Synthesis is an activity – or in Kant's language, a spontaneity – that is exercised by the mind on both the parts and the content of time.

But what Kant's analysis makes clear is that the new status of time introduces into the individual a profound 'fracture' (*fêlure*) – a scission between the disintegrative and synthetic aspects of time that Deleuze summarises in a second poetic formula taken from Rimbaud: 'I is another' (Rimbaud 1975: 101, 103).[28] On the one hand, my existence is that of 'a passive, receptive, phenomenal subject *appearing within time*', a time that is being undone at the moment it is constituted (Deleuze 1994: 86). On the other hand, the *unity* of my experience in time depends on the active and spontaneous temporal syntheses carried out by the *a priori* categories of the transcendental 'I think'. For Deleuze, this fracture between the passive self (intuitions in time) and the active self (the categories of the understanding) marks 'a precise moment in Kantianism, a furtive and explosive moment that is not even continued by Kant, much less by the post-Kantians' (58). Whereas Kant himself, as well as post-Kantians such as Fichte and Hegel, would tend to focus primarily on the 'I think' and the 'transcendental unity of apperception', Deleuze's analyses will attempt to penetrate the passive self and the pure form of time.[29] In other words, Deleuze will ultimately carry the Kantian revolution in a different direction than Kant himself.

3. From Kant to Heidegger to Deleuze

In moving beyond Kant, Deleuze was no doubt influenced by the 'ecstatic' conception of temporality developed by Heidegger in *Being and Time* (1927), and Heidegger would himself highlight the importance of the Kantian revolution in *Kant and the Problem of Metaphysics* (1929). Heidegger, however, had focused his analysis on the role of the transcendental imagination, that is, on the activities of synthesis and schematisation.[30] Yet in Kant, the imagination only synthesises and schematises under the legislation of the understanding. If Deleuze goes beyond Heidegger, it is because he shows that the 'source of time' (1997: 28) in Kant must be found, not in the activity of the transcendental imagination, but in the discordant relation between all the faculties (sensibility, imagination, understanding, reason) that are freed from the legislation of any particular faculty, and the theory of Ideas that grounds them. In the third *Critique*, Kant had analysed the *breakdown* of the activities of synthesising (in the sublime) and schematising (in symbolisation), recognising that there is a constant risk that something formless (time) will emerge from beneath the ground to break or dis-integrate the synthesis and schemata.[31] At such moments, there is *a presentation of Ideas in sensible nature*, of which Kant analyses four aspects: the sublime (a negative presentation), the symbol (a positive but indirect presentation), genius (a positive but secondary presentation, requiring the creation of an 'other' nature), and finally teleology (a positive presentation, primary as well as direct).[32]

Deleuze will carry this Kantian analysis in the *Critique of Judgment* a step further by inverting it: whereas for Kant, Ideas are totalising, unifying and transcendent, Deleuze will develop a theory of Ideas that are differential, genetic and immanent (this is the theme of the fourth chapter of *Difference and Repetition*).[33] As such, Deleuzian Ideas are pure forms of time, and conversely, the pure form of time is itself an Idea. As Deleuze will put it, time 'does not go from one actual term to another [chronology] ... but from the virtual [the Idea] to its actualization' (1994: 251). For Deleuze, the secret of time in Kant must be found neither in the transcendental aesthetic nor in the transcendental imagination, but in the doctrine of Ideas.

The Pure and Empty Form of Time: The Three Syntheses

1. The form of time as the idea of pure change (chaos)

In *What is Philosophy?* (1991), published more than two decades after *Difference and Repetition* (1968), Deleuze and Guattari proposed the concept of *chaos* to characterise the pure form of time, which might also be characterised as the Idea of pure change (as a differential and immanent Idea): 'Chaos is characterized less by the absence of determinations than by the *infinite speed* with which they take shape and vanish. This is not a movement from one determination to the other but, on the contrary, *the impossibility of a connection between them* since one does not appear without the other having already disappeared' (Deleuze and Guattari 1994: 42).[34] Chaos is a regime of *continuous variation* which retains determinations that nonetheless appear and disappear at an infinite speed with no relation to each other, neither temporally (no 'before' or 'after') nor spatially (no 'above', 'below', 'from', 'toward', 'between', etc.). There is no time – or more precisely, no modalities of time – but 'only its constantly aborted moment of birth' (Deleuze 1994: 70).

How can the modes of time be constituted within this chaos of pure change? Bergson had succinctly posed this problem in his 1922 book, *Duration and Simultaneity*, and outlined its solution:

> Consider a moment in the unfolding of the universe, that is, a snapshot that exists independently of any consciousness. Then we shall try conjointly to

summon another moment brought as close as possible to the first, and thus have a minimum of time enter into the world without allowing the faintest glimmer of memory to go with this. We shall see that this is impossible. Without *an elementary memory* that connects the two moments, there will be only one or the other, consequently a single instant, no before and after, no succession, no time. (Bergson 1965: 48)

In other words, for the modalities of time to appear, there must be *a third thing* that retains a 'first' determination when the 'second' determination appears – in other words, that *synthesises* the two determinations. In *Difference and Repetition*, Deleuze will outline three different syntheses of time, and it is this first synthesis that constitutes the *foundation* of time under the modality of succession.

2. The first synthesis: the variable present

For many philosophers, this 'third thing' is linked to the operations of the mind: for Kant, it is the faculty of the understanding that carries out the synthesis; for Hume, it is the imagination and habit. In appealing to an elementary memory, Bergson was willing to posit the existence of an elementary consciousness in matter itself.[35] Using a similar argument, Leibniz defined matter as a 'momentary mind' (*mens momentenea*) that retains one moment when the next one appears, although he considered this mind to be 'without consciousness, sense, or memory' (1976: 141).[36]

Deleuze, for his part, constructs two concepts to characterise the first synthesis of time: *contraction* and *contemplation*.[37] Both these terms emphasise the *passivity* of the temporal synthesis, that is, the fact it is not undertaken actively by the mind but rather is a synthesis that constitutes the body passively, as when we say the body 'contracts' a habit. Deleuze's concept of 'habit' here is derived as much from Samuel Butler as it is from Hume, and it refers less to the sensory-motor habits that we *have* than to the primary organic habits that we *are*: 'We are made of contracted water, earth light, and air . . . Every organism, in its receptive and perceptual elements, but also in its viscera, is a sum of contractions, retentions, and expectations' (Deleuze 1994: 73). Where Husserl spoke of the temporal retentions (past) and protentions (future) of consciousness, Deleuze points to the temporal syntheses of the organism: need is the organic form of expectation, just as cellular *heredity* is the retention of the past in the present. The contemporary discipline of chronobiology has gone far in exploring the complex coexisting contractions and rhythms that are present in living organisms: heartbeats, reproductive rhythms, sleep patterns, reaction times, migrations and so on (see Palmer 2002).

The first synthesis produces a *variable present* of which the past and the future are only dimensions. A teacher focused on an hour-long lecture inhabits a different present than the inattentive listener in the back row, and both their bodies integrate numerous rhythms. 'The duration of an organism's present, or of its various presents, will vary according to its natural contractile range' (Deleuze 1994: 77). Augustine suggested that it would be possible for the present to encompass the entirety of time, *a present of the future, a present of the present, and a present of the past*, all implicated in a single event ('the eternal now').[38] Although in *The Time-Image* Deleuze discusses cinematic explorations of what he calls 'peaks of the present' (*pointes de présent*), in *Difference and Repetition* he argues that a perpetual present or eternal now 'is not physically possible', since the present necessarily *passes*: fatigue and exhaustion are real components of an organism's present, marking the point where a contraction loses its capacity to sustain itself (1994: 76).

3. The second synthesis: the pure past

This leads to the second synthesis of time. If the present is the foundation of time, it does not provide us with the *ground* of time, since the present does not explain *why* the present passes. Indeed, Deleuze argues that the concept of the present is marked by a kind of illusion: we tend to think of the present as that which *is*, that which has being; and we think of the past as that which is no longer, that which has ceased to be, that which *is not*. But as Bergson showed, we have to reverse our ordinary determinations. It is the present which *is not*; it is pure becoming, always outside of itself, always passing, whether we consider the present as an instant or as the 'thick' present of lived experience. By contrast, it is the past which *is*, in the full sense of the word; the past is identical with being itself. 'Of the present, we must say of every instant that it "was", and of the past, that it "is", that it is eternally, for all time' (Deleuze 1988: 55). That Caesar crossed the Rubicon *is*, for all time. The *non-being* of the present implies the *being* of the past.

More profoundly, the past is the form under which being is preserved *in itself*. The question, 'Where are memories preserved?' is a badly posed problem, as if the brain were capable of preserving them. Bergson argued that memories do not have to be preserved anywhere other than 'in' duration: an ontological memory rather than a psychological memory (Deleuze 1988: 54). This claim is not as strange as it might initially seem.

In the realm of perception, we need to go to where things are in order to perceive them: to see the table in the next room, I do not need to look inside myself, but simply need to walk into the room. The same is true in the realm of memory: we have to look for memories, not in ourselves, but in the place where they are preserved – in duration. When we seek out a memory, we must first 'leap' into the being-in-itself of the past, and the recollection will gradually take on a psychological existence, passing from a virtual to an actual state. 'We should have no more difficulty in admitting the virtual insistence of pure memories in time', Deleuze writes, 'than we do for the actual existence of non-perceived objects in space' (1989: 80).

The notion that the past preserves itself entails three paradoxes, which Deleuze develops in *Difference and Repetition*. The first is the *contemporaneity* of the past with the present. 'If a new present were required for the past to be constituted as past, then the former present would never pass and the new one would never arrive. No present would ever pass were it not past "at the same time" as it is present' (Deleuze 1994: 81). The moment must be still present and already past, *at one and the same time*. This is what Deleuze considers to be the fundamental operation of time: 'since the past is constituted not after the present that it was but at the same time, time has to split itself in two at each moment as present and past, which differ from each other in nature' (1989: 81). The experience of *déjà vu* (paramnesia) makes this obvious point perceptible: there is a recollection of the present that is contemporaneous with the present itself, as closely coupled as a role to its actor.[39] In *The Time-Image*, Deleuze argues that, in film, it is 'the crystal-image' that makes perceptible this splitting or dividing of time in two: 'the actual image of the present which passes and the virtual image of the past which is preserved: distinct and yet indiscernible' (1989: 81).

A second paradox follows: the paradox of *coexistence*. 'If each past is contemporaneous with the present that it was, then *all of the past* coexists with the new present in relation to which it is now past' (Deleuze 1994: 81–2). Each present, in other words, is the entirety of the past in its most contracted state, although the concept of 'contraction' takes on a new sense here. In the first synthesis, the present is the contracted state of successive elements that are, in themselves, independent of each other. In the second synthesis, the present designates the most contracted state of the past, which is itself like a coexisting totality, though this totality itself is variable and open (the whole is the open) (Deleuze 1994: 82).[40] Genetics provides a concrete example of the coexistence of the past with the present: if my organism exists in the present, it is because there is a line of continuity between the first single-celled organism and myself, and that entire genetic history coexists with my present.

The final paradox completes the others: the paradox of *pre-existence*. The past does not cause one present to pass without bringing forth another, but the past itself does not pass: it is non-chronological. For this reason, we can say that the element of the past pre-exists the passing moment. Far from being merely a dimension of time, the past is the synthesis of all time, of which the present and future are only dimensions. This is what Deleuze will call the 'pure past', that is, a past that has never been present but rather forms a virtual coexistence, 'a pure, general, *a priori* element of all time' (1994: 82). What we live empirically as a succession of presents in the first synthesis is also the ever-increasing coexistence of the levels of the pure past in the second synthesis.

In the second synthesis, the non-chronological temporal mode of coexistence replaces that of succession. *Capitalism and Schizophrenia* provides the most obvious example of Deleuze's use of non-chronological time, since the typology of social formations that the book proposes – 'primitive' societies, States, capitalism and nomadic war machines – are not successive stages in a historical or evolutionary development, but concurrent formations that occupy a global field of coexistence. Deleuze's political philosophy turns the de facto problem of *chronological succession* into a de jure problem of *topological coexistence*, which becomes the condition for political transformation. This field of coexistence is what Deleuze would call the 'plane of immanence', a field where all the powers of the social machine coexist virtually, in constant becoming, enveloped and implicated in each other in a stratigraphic time.[41]

4. The third synthesis: the new (becoming)[42]

The third synthesis, finally, takes us to the heart of Deleuze's own philosophy. The modality of the third synthesis is no longer succession or coexistence but rather the *new*: it concerns the genesis of the heterogeneous or the production of difference. Deleuze tends to use the phrase 'the pure form of time' in two senses: often, he explicitly links the pure form of time to the third synthesis, but in many contexts he uses the phrase more generally to refer to the three syntheses taken together and to the conception of time introduced by the Kantian revolution.[43] But ultimately the two senses are the same, since it is the new (difference) that constitutes the 'essence' of time. As Bergson said, 'the more we study the nature of time, the more we shall comprehend that duration means invention, the creation of forms, *the continual elaboration of the absolutely new*' (1911: 13). The absolutely new entails what *Anti-Oedipus* calls 'a rupture with causality' (Deleuze and Guattari 1983: 377–8). If effects pre-exist in their causes, then causal processes can only give rise to things that are new in number, but not new in kind – the future is already contained in the past. The third synthesis, by contrast, requires a break with the past, since it concerns the conditions for the production of genuine *novelty* (Bergson) or *creativity* (Whitehead). The third synthesis constitutes a 'pure' future that breaks with its grounding in the past and its foundation in habit: Nietzsche's untimely or Butler's *erewhon* (Deleuze 1994: xx–xxi, 285).

Compared to the concise analysis of the second synthesis provided in the third chapter of *Difference and Repetition*, the discussion of the third synthesis can seem somewhat disjointed and unfocused, moving from Descartes and Kant to Hölderlin's analysis of Greek tragedy to Nietzsche's concept of the eternal return. But in fact it is the entirety of Deleuze's oeuvre that constitutes an analysis of the third synthesis. In *Difference and Repetition*, for instance, Deleuze argues that we need to replace the possible–real opposition with the virtual–actual couple in order to account for the form of time. In the possible, everything is already given, and the possible simply has existence added to it when it is 'realised': the real resembles the possible and does not produce the new. But the virtual is constituted by difference, and in becoming 'actualised' it differentiates itself: the actual differs from the virtual, and the actualisation of the virtual is the production of difference (Deleuze 1994: 211–12). What Deleuze calls *simulacra* are 'excessive systems' in which the different is linked to the different in order to produce the different (115). Similarly, *A Thousand Plateaus* is an analysis of manifolds or multiplicities, and Deleuze argues that it is the relation *between* manifolds that is an act of becoming that creates the new.[44]

Although Deleuze's entire philosophy can be seen as an exploration of the third synthesis of time, it is nonetheless worth examining the quite different presentations of the third synthesis that appear in *Difference and Repetition* and *The Time-Image* (the latter book does not in fact utilise the term 'synthesis').

5. *The third synthesis in* Difference and Repetition

In chapter three of *Difference and Repetition*, Deleuze initially explicates the third synthesis through an appeal to tragedy and a text by Hölderlin called 'Remarks on Oedipus' (Hölderlin 1988).[45] Hölderlin showed that, in Greek tragedy, Aeschylus' tragedies unfold in an *originary time* where the beginning and end 'rhyme' with each other, atoning for injustice, whereas Sophocles is the first tragedian to un-curve time in an *aberrant movement* in which the beginning and the end no longer rhyme but unravel in a straight line: Oedipus' long wandering is the incessant march of a slow death. But it is Shakespeare's Hamlet who is the first hero that truly needed the *pure form of time* in order to act: the action (avenging his father) marks a 'caesura' within the form of time between a before and an after that is productive of something new. The *before* appears in the form of an act that is 'too big' for Hamlet, and he remains in a past disconnected from the present (second synthesis); the *caesura* is the moment of metamorphosis, where Hamlet finally becomes capable of the act and equal to it (first synthesis); but the after (third synthesis) is revealed to be *the production of something new* that destroys both the condition (the past) and the agent (the present): Hamlet must die.[46]

Yet Deleuze, following Blanchot, notes that death has two aspects: the first is the disappearance of the person, but the second is 'the state of free differences when they are no longer subject to the form imposed on them by an I or an ego' (1994: 113). The latter 'death' is the object of the third synthesis: a domain of *singularities* and *events* that are both pre-individual and impersonal, and thus and irreducible to the self (Deleuze 1990: 177).[47] Life, in this sense, is coextensive with death: life is traversed by 'states of free differences' that destabilise the organisation of the organism as well as the identity of the self, while at the same time producing a new self and a new body (Deleuze 1994: 113; Somers-Hall 2013: 95–6). This 'death of the self' is the correlate to the 'death of God'. If the order of God can be defined in terms of the identity of God as the ultimate foundation, the identity of the world as the ambient environment, the identity of the person as a well-founded agent and the identity of bodies as the base, then the third synthesis entails the death of god, the destruction of the world, the dissolution of the self and the dis-integration of the body – but always in terms of a new self (affects and percepts), a new body (intensities and becomings) and ultimately the creation of a new world, a *chaosmos* (singularities and events) (Deleuze 1990: 292).[48]

Difference and Repetition presents Nietzsche's concept of the eternal return as the highest expression of the third synthesis, but Deleuze interprets the eternal return not as *a return of the same* but as the *repetition of the different*.[49] Zarathustra went through a transformation similar to that of Hamlet. In the *before*, Zarathustra is incapable of an act, the death of god ('The Convalescent'); in the *during* – or the *caesura* – he becomes equal to the act ('On Involuntary Bliss'), though he feels the hour has not yet come and still conceives of the eternal return as a return of the Same; but in the *after*, which would have been presented in the unwritten part of *Thus Spoke Zarathustra*, Zarathustra must die, because ultimately the eternal return only allows the return of differences, and mercilessly eliminates the identity of the hero (the second sense of death) (Deleuze 1994: 298–9).[50] In the third synthesis, the form of time is characterised by a *totality* that is divided into a *series* (before, caesura, after) that produces a pure *order* that is constitutive of the new. The eternal return, Deleuze writes, '*is present in every metamorphosis* . . . It is related to a world of differences implicated one in the other, to a complicated, properly chaotic world *without identity*' (1994: 57).

6. *The powers of the false in* The Time-Image

In *The Time-Image*, by contrast, the third synthesis appears in a chapter entitled 'The Powers of the False'. Though this chapter seems to bear little resemblance to the analyses in *Difference and Repetition*, Deleuze's definition of philosophy as 'the creation of concepts' (the production of the new) is an expression of the third synthesis in thought and is a direct consequence of the theme of the powers of the false.[51] If the discovery of originary time was one and the same as the discovery of the true, then the freeing of time puts the concept of truth in crisis and leads to the establishment of an autonomous and immanent concept of the false. But what does it mean to say that the liberation of time from its subordination to movement entails the liberation of the powers of the false from the form of the true?

Since Aristotle, the form of the true has meant *the universal and the necessary*: the true is that which is universal and necessary, always and everywhere, *in all times and in all places*. The false, by contrast, is effectuated in *error*. The false has no form, and error consists in giving the false the form of the true, although error itself does not itself affect the form of the true as universal. Deleuze's claim is that it is the form of time the puts the form of truth in crisis. A simplistic interpretation of this claim would be to say: truth changes with time. But the truth is never put in crisis if it is a question of a simple change in its *content*, since a change in content does not affect the *form* of the true. We can say that we once 'believed' that the sun revolves around the earth, but now we 'know' that the opposite is true *and has always been true*. Error affects the content of the true, but neither error nor changes in content affect the *form* of the true. Deleuze's thesis is that what puts the form of the true in crisis is the form of time *independent of its content*, independent of what is *in* time – that is, what is true at one moment and then ceases to be true the next moment. This is why Deleuze speaks of the form of time as being both pure and *empty*, 'having abjured its empirical content' (1994: 89). The form of time thus cannot be confused with chronology, which affects the content of what is in time. But what then is this 'non-chronological' form of time that undoes the concept of truth?[52]

Not surprisingly, the confrontation between the form of truth and the form of time had already taken place in antiquity under the classical form of the problem of *contingent futures*. This problem was encapsulated most succinctly in what came to be known as the 'Master Argument' of Diodorus Cronus.[53] The argument goes like this: If it is *true* that a naval battle *may* take place tomorrow, two logical paradoxes seem to follow. The principle of non-contradiction says that, of two contradictory propositions – 'there will be a naval battle tomorrow' and 'there will not be a naval battle tomorrow' – one is necessarily true and the other is necessarily false. If the naval battle indeed takes place, we can say that it was the first proposition, and *only* that proposition, that was true. But this is where the paradox emerges, in a double form. On the one hand, we began with two *possible* propositions, each of which changes modality once the event takes place: the first becomes necessary, while the second is now rendered impossible. In this case, the principle of non-contradiction is saved only at the price of contravening a second logical principle, namely, that the impossible cannot be derived from the possible. On the other hand, while the proposition 'there will be a naval battle tomorrow' was true yesterday, it was not necessarily true, since yesterday it was still possible that the naval battle could have not taken place. In this case, the principle of non-contradiction is saved by denying that a true proposition of the past is *necessarily* true.[54]

The paradox of contingent futures thus takes on two forms: *the impossible proceeds from the possible* and *what is true in the past is not necessarily true*.[55] It is easy to regard the paradox as a sophism, and philosophy has been marked by numerous attempts to resolve it.[56] It nonetheless shows the difficulty of conceiving a direct relation between truth and the form of time, which is what obliged philosophers to keep truth in the eternal rather than in time. But the Master Argument allows Deleuze to paint a picture of what he will call the 'falsifier' (*le faussaire*). If the 'truthful person', as a *conceptual persona*, is someone who allows their being to be *in*-formed by the form of the true, we could say that the falsifier is someone who, from the possible, makes the impossible emerge, or who, from the past, makes something that is not necessarily true.[57] The falsifier 'imposes a power of the false as adequate to time, in contrast to any form of the true that would control time' (Deleuze 1989: 132). Readers of Deleuze know the classic examples he provides of works that are, to a certain degree, 'falsifying' in this manner, such as Jorge Luis Borges' story 'The Garden of the Forking Paths', or Robbe-Grillet's screenplay for Alain Resnais' film *Last Year at Marienbad*, or even Leibniz's narration of the bifurcating possibilities in the life of Sextus in his *Theodicy* – all of which make a non-chronological time appear directly in the form *incompossible presents* and *not-necessarily-true pasts*.[58]

What prevented Leibniz's God from making all these possibilities, and even incompossibilities, pass into existence is the fact that such an operation would turn him into a mendacious God, a trickster God, a deceiving God, an 'evil genius' – something Descartes and Leibniz both saw very clearly, but shrank from with a kind of horror. For it is precisely here that the truthful God would be replaced by a *falsifying* God, and the concept of the false would achieve its *autonomy*. The false becomes independent and autonomous when it is no longer subject to the form of the true. In other words, *to say that something is false no longer means that it is 'not true'*. But when it is freed from the form of the true, the false takes on a *power*, which is the power of *metamorphosis*, that is, the power of creation. What stands opposed to the form of the eternal is the production of the new or the power of metamorphosis (becoming).

But to say that the concept of the false assumes an autonomy is not to say that 'everything is false'. Rather, what distinguishes the eternal form of the true from the temporal powers of the false is that the false always appears as a *plurality* or *multiplicity* of powers (x^1, x^2, x^3...). To ask 'What is a falsifier?' is a badly posed question, since the falsifier exists only within a series, in a plurality: behind every falsifier there is always another falsifier, like a mask behind every mask. But not everything is 'equal' in this chain of falsifiers. Even the truthful person is a falsifier: Plato was being a falsifier when he created the concept of an 'Idea', and one could say that the truthful person is the first of the powers of the false. Nietzsche called the powers of the false the *will to power*, though the will to power has two extremes, two powers: at one end, the falsifier is the 'higher man', the 'truthful person', someone who wants to judge life in the name of values higher than life; at the other end, the falsifier is a 'form of life' that is capable of changing itself, inventing, creating, where the powers of the false are no longer effectuated in 'judging life' but in 'assuring metamorphoses', in other words, creating the new.[59]

7. What is Philosophy? *The pure form of time in concepts*

As an example of the power of the false, we need look no further than to Deleuze's own philosophical concepts. One could say that the ultimate aim of the analytic of concepts developed in *What is Philosophy?* was to introduce *the pure form of time* into concepts, even though the word 'time' hardly appears in the book. To introduce time into concepts means that concepts do not have an *identity*, but they do have a *consistency*, that is, a *becoming* or a *metamorphosis*, but this consistency must have as its necessary complement the internal *variability* of the concept. Deleuze analyses these two temporal aspects of concepts under the rubrics of exo-consistency and endo-consistency: every concept links up with other concepts (exo-consistency) but each concept also has its own internal components (endo-consistency). Consider Deleuze's concept of intensity: in *Difference and Repetition*, the concept of intensity is primarily related to the dimension of depth, while in *The Logic of Sense* the concept of intensity is retained, but is now related primarily to the dimension of surface – same concept, different components. In *Anti-Oedipus*, the concept undergoes a third metamorphosis in which it is no longer related either to depth or surface; rather, rising and falling intensities are now events that take place on a body without organs.[60] Even within Deleuze's corpus, the concept of intensity has a temporal power that undergoes internal mutations and metamorphoses.

If *What is Philosophy?* is a book on time, or more precisely, a book on the third synthesis, it is because it a study of the determinations of thought that take place within the pure form of time. What Hume called the association of ideas (resemblance, contiguity, causality) links together our ideas in time with a minimum of constant rules, thereby forming a realm of *opinion* that protects us from chaos. But philosophy, science and art do more than this, and Deleuze describes their respective activities using his own (created) vocabulary. From the infinite and continuous *variability* of time (chaos), philosophers extract *variations* that converge as the components of a consistent concept; scientists extract *variables* that enter into determinable relations in a function; and artists extract *varieties* that enter into the composition of a being of sensation (Deleuze and Guattari 1994: 202).

The power of the false can thus be said to be creative. But creative of what? At this point, Deleuze suggests that there is no reason not to use the word 'truth': the power of the false is creative of truth. But this implies the creation of an entirely new concept of truth: the truth as something to be created (namely, the power of the false) has nothing to do with the truth of the truthful person, or with the form of the true. If one makes these modifications in the concept of the truth itself, one could say that philosophy, science and art, as powers of the false, are nothing other than enterprises in the creation of truth within the pure form of time.[61]

This is only a brief overview of the three syntheses that constitute the pure and empty form of time.[62] When time is freed from its subordination to movement, its *a priori* determinations of time are fixed or held, as though in a photo or freeze-frame. The first synthesis provides the *foundation* of time in the passing present, while the second synthesis provides its *ground* in the pure past. In the third synthesis, however, the ground is superseded by a groundlessness, a *sans-fond*, a universal un-grounding in which the freeze-frame begins to move once more. The extreme formality of the form of time, in other words, is there to produce the formless, that is, the new, difference-in-itself. The system of the future is 'the deployment and explication of the multiple, of the different, and of the fortuitous', it concerns 'excessive systems' (simulacra) that link the different with the different (Deleuze 1994: 115). But this is where time forms a circle again, for the third synthesis affects a world that has rid itself of the condition and the agent, a *chaos* – even if these singularities are taken up by the first two syntheses, and the singular is rendered regular and ordinary. 'This is how the story of time ends: by undoing its too well centred natural or physical circle and forming a straight line which then, led by its own length, reconstitutes an eternally decentred circle' (115).

Notes

1. Aristotle, *Physics*, Book 4, Chapter 11, 219b5–8: 'time is the number of movement in respect of before and after'.
2. See Leibniz, Letter to Arnauld, 30 April 1687, where Leibniz faults the ancients for substituting a concept of 'metempsychosis' for a 'metaschematism' [*metempsychosis pro metaschematismis*].
3. One of the classic analyses of intensive quantities is the 'Anticipations of Perception' section of Kant's first critique, which recapitulates a long tradition. See Kant 1929: 201–8, B207–18. Deleuze takes up the distinction in chapter four of *Difference and Repetition*, 'The Asymmetrical Synthesis of the Sensible' (1994: 222–61).
4. See Duhem 1954: 112. 'Diderot used to ask jokingly how many snowballs would be required to heat an oven.' Deleuze refers to this anecdote in his seminar of 20 March 1984. Deleuze's seminars can be accessed at 'The Deleuze Seminars' project, deleuze.cla.purdue.edu.
5. On the notion of an ideal fall, see Plotinus 1991: 236. 'Nature, asked why it brings forth its works, might answer (if it cared to listen and to speak): ... "Whatever comes into being is my vision, seen in my silence, the vision that belongs to my character who, sprung from vision, am vision-loving and create

vision by the vision-seeing faculty in me. The mathematicians from their vision draw their figures: but I draw nothing: I gaze and *the figures of the material world take being as if they fell from my contemplation*"' (emphasis added). The rejection of 'drawing' marks Plotinus' distance from Plato's dialectic, since the latter entails a 'real' fall of the intelligible into the sensible.

6. Deleuze discusses the Platonic and Neo-Platonic conceptions of time in a remarkable series of seminars from 7 February 1984 to 27 March 1984, which include analyses that have no correlate in Deleuze's published texts.

7. See Bergson 1965: 6. 'If we go looking in time for features like those of space [or movement] . . . we shall not have pushed on to time itself.'

8. See Gallison 2004, chapter 5, 'Einstein's Clocks'. Einstein's work in the Swiss patent office put him in a position 'to seize clock coordination as the principled starting point of relativity' (260).

9. Rovelli suggests that, in physics, it was general relativity that finally brought about 'the destruction of the notion of time' as a measure of movement in favour of pure change or pure 'events' (2018: 96–7).

10. Deleuze suggests that the entirety of Aristotle's corpus – metaphysics, physics, ethics and so on – could be read from the viewpoint of aberrant movements; see the seminar lecture of 28 February 1984.

11. For a helpful discussion, see Paul Krause, 'The Fall of the Soul from Plotinus to Augustine', online at *Voegelin View* (voegelinview.com/the-fall-of-soul-from-plotinus-to-augustine).

12. On Chinese conceptions of time, see Hui 2016: 210–11, and his references to the works of Marcel Granet and François Jullien.

13. In Catholic missals, the term 'ordinary time' (*tempus per annum*) refers to the part of the liturgical year that falls outside the two primary seasons of Christmastide and Eastertide, with their respective preparatory seasons of Advent and Lent.

14. Newton noted his own inversion of the movement/time relation: 'Absolute, true, and mathematical time, of itself, and from its own nature, flows equably without relation to anything external, and by another name is called duration: relative, apparent, and common time, is some sensible and external (whether accurate or unequable) measure of duration by the means of motion, which is commonly used instead of true time; such as an hour, a day, a month, a year' (1934: 6; 77 in the original Motte translation).

15. See Weber 2002, as well as Deleuze's seminar of 27 March 1984.

16. Deleuze, seminar of 7 February 1984.

17. Book Two of *Being and Time* recapitulates, in temporal terms, the analysis of 'everydayness' provided in Book One.

18. Deleuze elucidates these themes in his seminars of 17 April 1984 and 4 May 1984.

19. Deleuze's most complete analysis of Kant's contribution to the theory of time can be found in his seminar of 17 April 1984, to which the following analysis is indebted.

20. Shakespeare, *Hamlet*, Act 1, Scene 5.

21. For instance, the Gospel of Luke famously dates the beginning of the preaching of John the Baptist by contextualising it in a nexus of reigning officials in civil and religious institutions: 'In the fifteenth year of the reign of Tiberius Caesar, Pontius Pilate being governor of Judaea, and Herod being tetrarch of Galilee, and his brother Philip tetrarch of Ituraea and of the region of Trachonitis, and Lysanias the tetrarch of Abilene, Annas and Caiaphas being the high priests, the word of God came unto John the son of Zacharias in the wilderness' (Luke 3:1–2). In the 'Christian' calendar, time begins with the reign of Christ.

22. See Kosmin 2018. There were no 'end times' until the constitution of an ordinary linear time in the Seleucid empire (312 to 63 BCE), and Kosmin shows that apocalyptic eschatologies – such as the biblical Book of Daniel (c. 165 BCE), which was fiercely anti-Seleucid – can be seen as subversive attempts to contest the imperial institution of ordinary time.

23. Kant 1929: 76, A32/B48: 'The concept of motion, as alteration of place, is possible only through and in the representation of time.'

24. See Kant 1929: 214, A183/B226: 'If we ascribe succession to time itself, we must think yet another time, in which the sequence would be possible ... Without the permanent there is therefore no time-relation.'

25. See, for instance, Leibniz 1956: 15. 'I hold it [space] to be an order of coexistences, as time is an order of successions.'

26. See Kant 1929: 'Time cannot by itself be perceived' (213, A182/B225); 'time cannot be perceived in itself' (214, A183/B226; 219, A189/B233).

27. These three formulations of the disintegrating power of time appear in Deleuze's seminar of 14 April 1984.

28. Letter to Georges Izambard, 13 May 1871, letter to Paul Demeny, 15 May 1871.

29. Nonetheless, even Kant recognises that 'I cannot determine my existence as that of a self-active being; all that I can do is to represent to myself the spontaneity of my thought' (1929: 169, B158n). In other words, I can never truly recognise the spontaneity of thinking *as my own*: the passive self 'represents the activity of thought to itself *rather than enacting it*, it experiences its effect *rather than initiating it*' (Deleuze 1994: 86). For a penetrating commentary, see Kerslake 2005.

30. Bernard Stiegler, in his three-volume *Technics and Time* – especially in the third volume, *Cinematic Time and the Question of Malaise* – already went beyond Heidegger's analysis by rightly arguing that the temporal activity of schematisation, which Kant labelled a 'mystery', should be located in the 'tertiary retentions' of technics (the externalisation of memory) (see e.g., Stiegler 2011: 56–7).

31. For an analysis of the role of the formless in the third critique, see Smith 2012: 222–34, esp. 228–30.

32. We are here summarising Deleuze's important reading of Kant's *Critique of Judgment* in his 1963 article 'The Idea of Genesis in Kant's Aesthetics' (trans. Daniel W. Smith, in *Angelaki*, 5 (3), 2000, 57–70), which is an elaboration of themes developed in *Kant's Critical Philosophy*, published in the same year. See, for example: 'The theme of a presentation of Ideas in sensible nature is, in Kant, a fundamental theme. There are several modes of presentation ...' (Deleuze 1984: 66).

33. For an analysis of how Deleuze transformed Kant's theory of Ideas, see Smith 2012: 106–21.

34. In *Difference and Repetition*, the concept of the 'white nothingness' plays a similar role and is characterised by what Deleuze calls 'the rule of discontinuity or instantaneity in repetition': 'one instance does not appear unless the other has disappeared' (1994: 28, 70).

35. 'We place consciousness at the heart of things for the very reason that we credit them with a time that endures' (Bergson 1965: 49).

36. Though Leibniz held that the temporal synthesis of a body only lasts for a 'moment', he developed a theological theory of 'traduction' to account for the propagation of minds. See Mercer 2004: e.g., 163, 223. The quote, from a letter to Oldenburg, is cited in Mercer 2004: 164.

37. Deleuze would later speak of his affection for these analyses of fatigue and contemplation in *Difference and Repetition*. See Deleuze 2006: 65.

38. Augustine, *Confessions*, 14.17. See also Deleuze 1989: 100. Husserl knew Augustine well, and given his focus on the thickness of the present, Deleuze characterised Husserl as a 'theologian', a kind of 'church father'. See Deleuze, seminar of 27 March 1984.

39. See Bergson 1920: 109–51. 'Our actual existence duplicates itself all along with a virtual existence, a mirror-image. Every moment of our life presents two aspects, it is actual and virtual, perception on the one side and memory on the other' (135). See also Deleuze 1989: 79.

40. For an analysis of Bergson's claim that 'the whole is the open', see Smith 2012: 256–67.

41. On the role of the 'field of coexistence' in *Capitalism and Schizophrenia*, see Smith 2018: 232.

42. For an analysis of the components of the third synthesis as presented in *Difference and Repetition*, see Voss 2013.

43. For the first sense, see Deleuze 1994: 88: 'the pure form of time or the third synthesis'. For the second sense, see 299: 'What, however, is the content of this third time, this formlessness at the end of the form of time?' The phrase 'form of time' appears only three times in *The Time-Image* (1989: 130, 273, 274), and each seems to be used in the second sense.

44. See Deleuze and Guattari 1987: plateau 10, '1730: Becoming-Intense, Becoming-Animal, Becoming-Imperceptible . . .'.

45. Deleuze cites Jean Beaufret's influential commentary, 'Hölderlin and Sophocles', in Hölderlin, *Remarques sur Oedipe* (Paris: Union Générale d'Éditions, 10/18, 1965), which analyses Hölderlin's relation to Kant.

46. For analyses of Deleuze's use of Hamlet, see Somers-Hall 2011 and Plotnitsky 2015.

47. See Deleuze 1994: 6 on what lies beyond the laws of nature.

48. For an elaboration of these themes, see Smith 2012: 189–221.

49. See James Mollison's chapter in this volume.

50. The titles refer to the relevant sections in *Thus Spoke Zarathustra* (Nietzsche 1954): 'The Convalescent', III.13, 327–33; 'On Involuntary Bliss', III.3, 272–5.

51. To my knowledge, the phrase 'power of the false' appears once in both *Difference and Repetition* (1994: 128) and *The Logic of Sense* (1990: 263), but never in either *Anti-Oedipus* or *A Thousand Plateaus*. It is only in *The Time-Image* that Deleuze develops the theme of the power of the false in detail.

52. The term 'non-chronological time' appears throughout *The Time-Image*, usually with regard to the second synthesis (Deleuze 1989: 99), but in certain cases also with regard to the third (129, 181).

53. Deleuze, seminar of 29 November 1983, p. 7: 'The problem of contingent futures is the confrontation of the concept of truth with the form of time.' Jules Vuillemin, who taught at the Collège de France, wrote an important book on the Master Argument entitled *The Necessity of Contingency*, which Deleuze relies on.

54. For analyses of the Master Argument, see Vuillemin 1996 and Schuhl 1960. Vuillemin presents Epictetus' summary of the argument: 'It is contradictory to hold any two of the following propositions together with the third: "Every true proposition about the past is necessary. The impossible does not logically follow from the possible. What neither is presently true nor will be so is possible"' (1996: 3). For Deleuze's discussion, see the seminars of 8, 22 and 29 November 1983, as well as Deleuze 1989: 130–1.

55. See Deleuze, seminar of 29 November 1983, as well as Deleuze 1989: 130.

56. Aristotle, for instance, was a partisan of a solution which said that what is

necessary is only the *alternative* between the two propositions. See *On Interpretation*, 19a 24–25, 30–31: 'It cannot be said without qualification that all existence and non-existence is the outcome of necessity ... A sea-fight must either take place tomorrow or not, but it is not necessary that it should take place tomorrow, neither is it necessary that it should not take place, yet it is necessary that it either should or should not take place tomorrow.' Leibniz analyses the Master Argument in *Theodicy*, III, §§169ff. The problem is also taken up by Kierkegaard in *Philosophical Fragments*, in the 'Interlude' entitled '*Is the past more necessary than the future? Or, When the possible becomes actual, is it made more necessary than it was?*' (Kierkegaard 1936: 89ff.).

57. For analysis, see Deleuze, seminar of 29 November 198.
58. See Deleuze 1989: 130–1, as well as the seminar of 6 December 1983.
59. On these themes, see Deleuze, seminar of 12 June 1984.
60. See Deleuze 2006: 65–6. The concept of the 'affect' undergoes a similar metamorphosis. The concept first appears in Deleuze's work on Spinoza, where it designates the passage from one intensity to another in a finite mode that is experienced as a joy or a sadness. In *A Thousand Plateaus* and *What Is Philosophy?* the affect is no longer 'the passage from one lived state to another' but assumes an autonomous status – along with percepts – as a static becoming that exists between two multiplicities. 'The affect is not the passage from one lived state to another but the nonhuman becoming of humanity' (Deleuze and Guattari 1994: 173).
61. For further analysis, see Smith 2019.
62. The fullest analysis of the three syntheses can be found in Williams 2011.

References

Aveni, A. (1989), *Empires of Time: Calendars, Clocks, and Cultures*, New York: Basic Books.

Bergson, H. (1911), *Creative Evolution*, trans. Arthur Mitchell, New York: Henry Holt.

Bergson, H. (1920), *Mind-Energy*, trans. H. Wildon Carr, London: Macmillan.

Bergson, H. (1965), *Duration and Simultaneity*, trans. Leon Jacobson, Indianapolis: Bobbs-Merrill.

Crease, R. P. (2011), *World in the Balance: The Historic Quest for an Absolute System of Measurement*, New York: Norton.

Deleuze, G. (1984), *Kant's Critical Philosophy: The Doctrine of the Faculties*, trans. Hugh Tomlinson and Barbara Habberjam, London: Athlone Press.

Deleuze, G. (1988), *Bergsonism*, trans. Hugh Tomlinson and Barbara Habberjam, New York: Zone Books.

Deleuze, G. (1989), *Cinema 2: The Time-Image*, trans. Hugh Tomlinson and Robert Galeta, Minneapolis: University of Minnesota Press.

Deleuze, G. (1990), *The Logic of Sense*, trans. Mark Lester with Charles Stivale, New York: Columbia University Press.

Deleuze, G. (1994), *Difference and Repetition*, trans. Paul Patton, New York: Columbia University Press.

Deleuze, G. (1997), *Essays Critical and Clinical*, trans. Daniel W. Smith and Michael A. Greco, Minneapolis: University of Minnesota Press.

Deleuze, G. (2000), *Proust and Signs*, trans. Richard Howard, Minneapolis: University of Minnesota Press.

Deleuze, G. (2006), *Two Regimes of Madness: Texts and Interviews, 1975–1995*, trans. Ames Hodges and Mike Taormina, New York: Semiotext(e).

Deleuze, G. and F. Guattari (1983), *Anti-Oedipus*, trans. Robert Hurley, Mark Seem and Helen R. Lane, Minneapolis: University of Minnesota.

Deleuze, G. and F. Guattari (1987), *A Thousand Plateaus*, trans. Brian Massumi, Minneapolis: University of Minnesota Press.

Deleuze, G. and F. Guattari (1994), *What is Philosophy?*, trans. Hugh Tomlinson and Graham Burchell, New York: Columbia University Press.

Duhem, P. (1954), *The Aim and Structure of Physical Theory* [1914], trans. Philip Weiner, Princeton: Princeton University Press.

Gallison, P. (2004), *Einstein's Clocks and Poincare's Maps: Empires of Time*, New York: Norton.

Heidegger, M. (1962a), *Being and Time*, trans. John Macquarrie and Edward Robinson, New York: Harper & Row.

Heidegger, M. (1962b), *Kant and the Problem of Metaphysics*, trans. James S. Churchill, Bloomington: Indiana University Press.

Hölderlin, F. (1988), 'Remarks on "Oedipus"', in *Essays and Letters on Theory*, ed. and trans. Thomas Pfau, Albany: State University of New York Press, pp. 101–8.

Hui, Y. (2016), *The Question Concerning Technology in China*, Falmouth: Urbanomic.

Husserl, E. (1964), *The Phenomenology of Internal Time-Consciousness*, trans. James Churchill, Bloomington: Indiana University Press.

Kant, I. (1929), *Critique of Pure Reason*, trans. Norman Kemp Smith, London: Macmillan.

Kerslake, C. (2005), 'Transcendental Cinema: Deleuze, Time, and Modernity', *Radical Philosophy* 130: 7–19.

Kierkegaard, S. (1936), *Philosophical Fragments*, trans. David F. Swenson and Howard V. Hong, Princeton: Princeton University Press.

Knowles Middleton, W. E. (1966), *A History of the Thermometer and Its Uses in Meteorology*, Baltimore: Johns Hopkins University Press.

Kosmin, P. J. (2018), *Time and Its Adversaries in the Seleucid Empire*, Cambridge, MA: Harvard University Press.

Leibniz, G. W. (1956), *The Leibniz-Clarke Correspondence*, ed. H. G. Alexander, Manchester: Manchester University Press.

Leibniz, G. W. (1976), 'The Theory of Abstract Motion' [1671], in *Philosophical Papers and Letters*, ed. Leroy E. Loemker, Dordrecht: D. Reidel.

Mercer, C. (2004), *Leibniz's Metaphysics: Its Origin and Development*, Cambridge: Cambridge University Press.

Newton, I. (1934), *Philosophiae Naturalis Principia Mathematica*, Book 1 [1689], trans. Andrew Motte (1729), rev. Florian Cajori, Berkeley: University of California Press.

Nietzsche, F. (1954), *Thus Spoke Zarathustra*, in *The Portable Nietzsche*, ed. and trans. Walter Kaufman, New York: Penguin.

Palmer, J. D. (2002), *The Living Clock: The Orchestrator of Biological Rhythms*, Oxford: Oxford University Press.

Plotinus (1991), *The Enneads*, trans. Stephen MacKenna, London: Penguin.

Plotnitsky, A. (2015), 'The Calculable Law of Tragic Representation and the Unthinkable: Rhythm, Caesura and Time, from Hölderlin to Deleuze', in *At the Edges of Thought: Deleuze and Post-Kantian Philosophy*, ed. Craig Lundy and Daniela Voss, Edinburgh: Edinburgh University Press, pp. 123–45.

Proust, M. (1993), *In Search of Lost Time*, Volume VI, *Time Regained*, trans. Andreas Mayor and Terence Kilmartin, rev. D. J. Enright, New York: Modern Library.

Rimbaud, A. (1975), *Complete Works*, trans. Paul Schmidt, New York: Harper & Row.

Rovelli, C. (2018), *The Order of Time*, trans. Erica Segre and Simon Carnell, New York: Riverhead Books.

Schuhl, P.-M. (1960), *Le Dominateur et les possibles*, Paris: Presses universitaires de France.

Serres, M. (1994), *Atlas*, Paris: Julliard.

Serres, M. (2000), *The Birth of Physics*, trans. Jack Hawkes, Manchester: Clinamen.

Smith, D. W. (2012), *Essays on Deleuze*, Edinburgh: Edinburgh University Press.

Smith, D. W. (2018), '7000 B.C.: Apparatus of Capture', in *A Thousand Plateaus and Philosophy*, ed. Henry Somers-Hall, Jeffrey A. Bell and James Williams, Edinburgh: Edinburgh University Press.

Smith, D. W. (2019), 'The Pure Form of Time and the Powers of the False: Deleuze on Time and Temporality', *Tijdschrift voor Filosofie*, 81: 29–51

Somers-Hall, H. (2011), 'Time Out of Joint: Hamlet and the Pure Form of Time', *Deleuze Studies 5* (Supplement): 56–76.

Somers-Hall, H. (2013), *Deleuze's Difference and Repetition*, Edinburgh: Edinburgh University Press.

Stiegler, B. (2011), *Cinematic Time and the Question of Malaise*, trans. Stephen Barker, Minneapolis: University of Minnesota Press.

Voss, D. (2013), 'Deleuze's Third Synthesis of Time', *Deleuze Studies 7* (2): 194–216.

Vuillemin, J. (1996), *Necessity of Contingency: The Master Argument*, Stanford: Center for the Study of Language and Information Publications.

Weber, M. (2002), *The Protestant Ethic and the Spirit of Capitalism, and Other Writings*, London: Penguin.

Williams, J. (2011), *Gilles Deleuze's Philosophy of Time: A Critical Introduction and Guide*, Edinburgh: Edinburgh University Press.

PART II

HISTORY OF TIME

Chapter 4

Gilles Deleuze's Interpretation of the Eternal Return: From *Nietzsche and Philosophy* to *Difference and Repetition*

James Mollison

Deleuze famously describes his generation as 'more or less bludgeoned to death with the history of philosophy'.[1] His means of escaping this stifling atmosphere is infamous: 'The main way I coped with it', Deleuze writes, 'was to see the history of philosophy as a sort of buggery ... I saw myself as taking an author from behind and giving him a child that would be his own offspring, yet monstrous' (1995: 5–6). This provocative image makes it unsurprising if scholars working within the philosophical tradition tend to neglect Deleuze's readings of other philosophers. Respectable historians of philosophy seldom fraternise with monsters. But even if one adopts this dismissive view of Deleuze's historical commentaries, an exception would need to be made for his *Nietzsche and Philosophy*. For, in the same 'Letter to a Harsh Critic', Deleuze goes on to state: 'It was Nietzsche ... who extricated me from all this. Because you can't just deal with him in the same sort of way. He gets up to all sorts of things behind *your* back. He gives you a perverse taste for ... saying simple things in your own way.' Here, Deleuze indicates that his study of Nietzsche is not an instance of interpretive 'buggery'. In fact, reading Nietzsche relieves Deleuze's need for such an approach by enabling him to write in his 'own name' (6). Yet, there is a cost for attributing this catalytic function to Nietzsche. If we take Deleuze at his word when he describes *Nietzsche and Philosophy* as an attempt to pay his 'debts' to the history of philosophy (Deleuze and Parnet 2007: 16), then this early work seems vulnerable to the stifling interpretative demands that Deleuze otherwise seeks to abjure.

Deleuze's encounter with Nietzsche occurs at the boundary between the burdens of traditional interpretation and unabashed concept creation. This is perhaps best illustrated by Deleuze's interpretation of the eternal return. Nietzsche reveals the idea in a demonic declaration: 'This life as you live it now and have lived it you will have to live once again and innumerable times again; and there will be nothing new in it' (GS 341).[2] Notwithstanding the myriad controversies surrounding this idea, its central point seems obvious enough: each detail of our lives will repeat, endlessly and identically. Yet, in *Nietzsche and Philosophy*, Deleuze takes the eternal return to express the priority of becoming over being and to function as a selective ethical and ontological principle that eliminates all negativity. The claim that the eternal return eliminates all negativity is especially contentious among Nietzsche scholars. Some argue that a selective approach to ontology violates the doctrine's ethical aspiration of motivating an unconditional affirmation of existence.[3] Others argue that the elimination of negativity and reactive forces also eradicates affirmation and active forces.[4] And still others argue that the attempt to purge negativity and reactivity is ethically and politically dangerous.[5] While it is tempting to dismiss such arguments as hermeneutic concerns for which Deleuze has little patience, his claim that his reading of Nietzsche occurs *within* the history of philosophy suggests that things are not so simple. Nor are these concerns confined to *Nietzsche and Philosophy*. In the first work Deleuze authors in his own name, *Difference and Repetition*, the eternal return occupies a privileged place in Deleuze's theory of time, functioning as a transcendental synthesis of the *future*. Little wonder, then, that Deleuze is uncharacteristically defensive over his reading of the eternal return (1994: 297–302) – as his reading claims that the eternal return, which seemed to guarantee the past's endless and identical reappearance, is really a cypher for unbridled novelty. To Nietzsche scholars, the image of philosophical buggery could hardly seem more appropriate.

In this chapter, I examine Deleuze's interpretation of the eternal return and advance two claims about it. First, I suggest that much of the controversy surrounding *Nietzsche and Philosophy*'s appeal to the eternal return as a principle of selective ontology can be mitigated by attending to Deleuze's novel reading of the will to power as an evaluative typology that produces individuals' ontological commitments. The eternal return enacts an ontological selection, for Deleuze, by transforming the evaluative qualities of the will. Motivating this point takes some time, but it also sets the stage for the second claim advanced here – namely, that Deleuze's interpretation of the eternal return undergoes a significant shift in *Difference and Repetition*. In particular, I suggest that whereas *Nietzsche and Philosophy* hesitates over the metaphysical status of the eternal return, *Difference and Repetition* pursues an overtly metaphysical use of this idea as a principle of transcendental empiricism.[6] As a result, the eternal return ceases to denote the *present's* internal differentiation as simultaneously becoming-past and becoming-future, and comes to denote the priority of the *future* as a passive, temporal synthesis that grounds the present and past alike. In addition to revealing how the eternal return, in Deleuze's hands, comes to describe the future, I hope this discussion sheds light on Nietzsche's catalytic role in helping Deleuze develop his philosophy of time.

Deleuze's Will to Power

An evaluative typology

Deleuze describes *Nietzsche and Philosophy* by stating that 'this book sets out, primarily, to analyse what Nietzsche calls becoming' (1983: xii). It is thus unsurprising that he takes Nietzsche's world to consist of *forces* rather than beings.[7] Forces, for Deleuze, are essentially relational and plural (6). They are also necessarily unequal, such that whenever two forces relate, one is quantitatively superior. Deleuze analyses these quantitative disparities in terms of relations of 'command' and 'obedience', though he hastens to add that such quantitative differences produce *qualitative* differences, which he analyses in terms of 'activity' and 'reactivity' (40–3). Since Deleuze maintains that any relation among forces produces a body – whether chemical, biological, social or political – *Nietzsche and Philosophy* examines all phenomena by treating the active and reactive forces comprising them.

Deleuze distils Nietzsche's tendency to analyse allegedly primitive and simple concepts as products of dynamic principles down to a single concept – force. He also distils Nietzsche's tendency to explain divergences among individuals' outlooks in terms of qualitative differences in their constitutions down to a single qualitative distinction – active/reactive. But the active/reactive distinction cannot completely reduce to forces' quantitative differences. If it did, Deleuze could not explain Nietzsche's view that reactive forces can triumph over active forces while *remaining* reactive. Slave morality is exemplary in this regard. Nietzsche says of slave morality that 'its action is, from the ground up, reaction' (GM I.10). And while slave morality defeats master morality and shapes humanity today, it *remains* reactive (BGE 202; GM I.11–12). How does this occur? Nietzsche tells us that slave morality overthrows master morality by positing 'an indifferent substratum that is free to express its strength – or not to'. After likening this to misleading expressions such as 'lightning strikes' or 'force moves', which add an explanatorily otiose substratum behind activity, Nietzsche concludes:

'there is no "being" behind the doing, effecting, becoming; "the doer" is simply fabricated into the doing – the doing is everything' (GM I.13). The lesson Deleuze draws from this is that reactive forces triumph – not by forming a quantitatively superior force, but – by *decomposing* active forces (1983: 57). This decomposition is enabled by the fiction of a force separate from its expression.

If forces' qualities do not reduce completely to quantitative differences, then what else explains them? Deleuze answers that qualitative differences among forces trace to qualities of the will to power, *'the element from which derive both the quantitative difference of related forces and the quality that devolves into each force of this relation'* (1983: 50). In its affirmative dimension, the will to power is 'the power of transformation' (42). In its negative dimension, it is 'a will to nothingness' and 'a power of subtraction' (57). Deleuze observes a complicity between affirmative wills and active forces, on the one hand, and negative wills and reactive forces, on the other, but insists that affirmative/negative and active/reactive distinctions must not be conflated (53–4). The ability of these distinctions to come apart enables nuanced evaluations, such as the reactive affirmation of the ass and the negative action of priests. It also allows nihilism to be overcome via the *active negation* of reactive forces. Still, we must also resist distinguishing will from force too firmly, as this would make the will to power a 'metaphysical abstraction' that violates Nietzsche's rejection of transcendent principles. Deleuze accordingly analyses the will to power as 'an essentially *plastic* principle that is no wider than what it conditions, that changes itself with the conditioned and determines itself in each case along with what it determines' (50). Each change in relations among forces is thus accompanied by changes in the qualities of the will.[8]

Deleuze's interpretation of Nietzsche can be clarified by situating it among debates over how to reconcile the will to power with Nietzsche's perspectivism. In its least restricted form – as when Nietzsche claims that the world's 'essence is will to power' (BGE 186) – the will to power verges on a metaphysical concept that contradicts Nietzsche's claim that all knowledge is perspectival (GM III.12; GS 354). Some scholars address this tension by prioritising perspectivism over the will to power, for example, by taking the will to power to describe human psychology,[9] or by taking it to reflect Nietzsche's own, non-privileged perspective.[10] Other scholars opt to prioritise the will to power over perspectivism, for example, by interpreting the will to power as a metaphysical[11] or quasi-scientific hypothesis[12] that holds for all perspectives. Deleuze cuts between these extremes. He takes will to power to be a non-anthropomorphic notion, comparable to Schopenhauer's Will but distinguished by its affirmative and pluralist aspects (1983: 6–8; 82–4). While this much is common, Deleuze also claims that *evaluation* is non-anthropomorphic. 'To actualise the will under any quality whatever, is always to evaluate. To live is to evaluate' (184). Deleuze thus reconciles the will to power with perspectivism by pushing evaluation beyond human psychology. The will to power, understood non-anthropomorphically, is itself perspectival and evaluative.

The will to power's qualities, on Deleuze's reading, issue distinctive evaluations of the *differences* among forces in an ontogenetic field. Whereas an affirmative will to power celebrates these differences, a negative will to power opposes them. It is paramount to Deleuze's interpretation that affirmation and negation 'do not have a univocal relation'.[13] Whereas negation *opposes* affirmation, affirmation *differs* from negation. To illustrate such a relation of unilateral opposition, we might recall Socrates' opposition to the Sophists, which the Sophists deny. Another example of unilateral opposition is Nietzsche's view of the relation between mind and body. While the mind opposes the body, the body views the mind as a particular organic development. A third example might be a two-way mirror, which represents space as enclosed from one side and as continuous from the other. The import of this notion of unilateral opposition is seen in Deleuze's insistence that 'we cannot think of affirmation as "being opposed" to negation: this would be to place the negative within it' (1983: 188). The unilateral relation of the will to power's qualities thus allows Deleuze to avoid contaminating affirmation with negation. But it also allows him to maintain that the will to power is *fundamentally* affirmative, that '*the will to power is essentially creative and giving*' – *despite* its negative qualities (85; see also 53–4, 184–5). Negative wills to power also create interpretations and evaluations, and bestow these onto forces, though negative wills disavow this creative activity.

Images of thought

Nietzsche regularly explains individuals' perspectives in terms of their values – values which trace to psycho-physiological and socio-historical forces. For Deleuze, this explanatory strategy is emphatically non-reductive. Forces themselves carry evaluations, which emerge from still more fundamental, evaluative qualities of the will. Unflinching commitment to the view that values extend beyond the psychological domain reverberates in Deleuze's comparisons of Nietzsche with

Kant.[14] Notwithstanding Kant's 'genius' for conceiving of 'an immanent critique', Deleuze contends that Kant 'lacked a method which permitted reason to be judged from the inside without giving it the task of being its own judge'. If transcendental idealism safeguards reason, it is because it precludes the question of reason's genesis. Genealogy, by contrast, prompts us to ask, 'what is the will which hides and expresses itself in reason?' (Deleuze 1983: 91). Against Kant's critique of all *claims* to knowledge and truth,[15] Nietzsche criticises knowledge and truth *themselves* by tracing them to the evaluations of a will (89–90). It is worth dwelling on this aspect of Deleuze's interpretation, as it reveals how the will to power's qualities produce different accounts of the function of thought. How we construe the world, and the eternal recurrence, depends on the will's qualities.

Deleuze takes genealogy to reveal that the unconditional valuing of truth derives from a negative will to power (1983: 95–6). The belief that truth is always valuable could not arise from a will not to let oneself *be* deceived without assuming that truth is always beneficial. But some truths are useless and even harmful, and some illusions are life promoting. (To use one of Nietzsche's preferred examples, tragedy provides an artistic illusion that affirms the way life's exorbitant dynamism undermines individuation.) Hence the view that truth is unconditionally valuable must arise from a moral judgement never *to* deceive, not even oneself (GS 344). It is easy to see how the belief that truth is always valuable is life-negating in cases where truth is harmful or illusion is life-promoting. But Deleuze further claims that attributing anything other than instrumental value to truth is ascetic insofar as it leaves behind *life* as the ultimate arbiter of value (GM III.24–7). Even more strongly, Deleuze suggests that, if truth is valued as something that must be sought, this is because life is *already condemned* to mere appearance, because life and truth are already understood as *opposed*. Such oppositional thinking typifies a negative will to power.

A negative will which values truth as *opposed* to life yields a reactive image of thought as subordinate to *knowledge*. For Deleuze, knowledge is not only quantitatively reactive, in that it emerges from consciousness' reaction to forces superior to the body (1983: 39–41). Knowledge is also *qualitatively* reactive. 'Knowledge gives life laws that separate it from what it can do, that keep it from acting, that forbid it to act, maintaining it in the narrow framework of scientifically observable reaction: almost like an animal in a zoo' (100). Deleuze's claim that knowledge is paradigmatically reactive is bold, but it receives support from familiar features of Nietzsche's thought. Nietzsche not only explains the emergence of the self-conscious subject in terms of the herd's need to hold individuals accountable for their actions (GM I.13; GS 354). He also explains the notion of substance in these terms, analysing the concept of substance as a projection of the ego onto forces (TI III.5; VI.3; WP 485, 498). This, in turn, implicates causal categories – both because efficient causation is modelled on consciousness' *ex post facto* experience of 'willing' bodily actions (D 121; GS 127; BGE 21, 36) and because commonplace causal explanations posit discrete beings in place of continuums of forces (D 6; GS 112). This also undercuts the view of time as a series of discrete causally related moments (WP 520, 487, 545). Without belabouring the point, we can glimpse the reasoning behind Nietzsche's view that 'knowledge and becoming exclude one another' (WP 517), such that 'a world in a state of becoming could not, in a strict sense, be "comprehended" or "known"' (WP 520). And if knowledge categorically *opposes* the world's becoming, then we can also see the reasoning behind Deleuze's claim that 'the spirit of revenge is the genealogical element of *our* thought, the transcendental element of *our* way of thinking' (1983: 35). The basic categories humans use to make forces intelligible oppose life's dynamism.

Whereas negative wills oppose life's becoming and subordinate thought to knowledge, affirmative wills celebrate life's dynamism. An affirmative evaluation of becoming entails nothing less than a new image of thought, 'a thought that would *affirm* life instead of a knowledge that is opposed to life . . . Thinking would then mean *discovering, inventing, new possibilities of life*' (Deleuze 1983: 101). Here, Deleuze draws on Nietzsche's celebration of art as superior to knowledge for its ability to affirm life. Unlike Kant's approach to beauty from the perspective of observers' disinterested contemplation, Nietzsche approaches beauty from the perspective of the artist, who is overtly interested in selecting and amplifying active forces to stimulate further life-affirmation. If 'the activity of life is like a power of falsehood, of duping, dissimulating, dazzling and seducing', the artist doubles this power of falsehood in 'a *will* to deceive' (102–3). Deleuze describes this shift as one where the element of thought is no longer *truth*, but sense and value (104). Whereas the claimant of knowledge proceeds from a negative will that renounces thought's evaluative and creative qualities, the artist celebrates these, so that '*creation takes the place of knowledge*' (173).

At this point, it is important to recall Deleuze's notion of unilateral opposition. While claimants of knowledge *oppose* artists, artists do not reciprocate this opposition. Strictly speaking, in a world of becoming, *all* conceptual schemes are selective appropriations of forces based on the will's evaluative qualities. From an artist's vantage, those who pursue knowledge are merely conflicted artists, artists who select reactive forces, negate life's becoming and disavow thought's creative power. Affirmative artists, by contrast, select active forces, celebrate life's becoming and affirm the creative powers of the false. Whereas claimants of knowledge view truth and appearance as opposed, 'for the artist, *appearance* no longer means the negation of the real in this world but this kind of selection, correction, redoubling and affirmation. Then truth perhaps takes on a new sense. Truth is appearance' (Deleuze 1983: 103). For Deleuze, the difference between knowledge and art is not epistemological, since knowledge and art both selectively falsify becoming, but evaluative. Whereas the seeker of knowledge renounces thought's creative power, the artist celebrates thought's creativity to enable greater life affirmation.

Deleuze's Eternal Return

Physical, temporal and selective aspects

Since the will to power's qualities implicate our image of thought in the broadest sense, these qualities also inform our understanding of the eternal return. Nietzsche's best-known statement of the eternal return occurs in the following pronouncement, delivered by a demon:

> This life as you now live it and have lived it you will have to live once again and innumerable times again; and there will be nothing new in it, but every pain and every joy and every thought and sigh and everything unspeakably small or great in your life must return to you in the same succession and sequence . . . (GS 341)

Some scholars contend that this message is meant factually. On this 'cosmological reading', the eternal return describes the cyclical structure of time, which ensures that everything recurs in identical fashion *ad infinitum*.[16] Other scholars emphasise Nietzsche's discussion of how we might *respond* to the eternal return. The idea could 'possibly crush' us or, if we are sufficiently well disposed toward life, we might '*long for nothing more fervently*' than the eternal return (GS 341). On this 'hypothetical reading', the eternal return is not meant as an accurate piece of cosmology but as a thought experiment that diagnoses one's ability to affirm life.[17]

Deleuze cannot abide either of these interpretations of the eternal return, as he thinks that they fail to affirm life's becoming. Against the cosmological reading, Deleuze argues that if we resolve the prima facie tension between this view of the eternal return and Nietzsche's emphasis on becoming by making becoming a feature of limited perspectives within temporal cycles, then the eternal return would resemble ancient formulations of the idea that Nietzsche rejects (Deleuze 1983: 29).[18] Likewise, if the eternal return is a thought experiment that diagnoses one's ability to affirm life, then, insofar as life is characterised by *becoming*, the test's appeal to cyclical time is inconsistent with its aim. Both interpretations negate life by subordinating becoming to being via cycles of time. For Deleuze, the definitive formulation of the eternal return appears in Nietzsche's notes, where we read: 'That *everything recurs* is the closest *approximation of a world of becoming to a world of being*' (WP 617). Deleuze thus contends that '*return is the being said of that which becomes*' (1983: 24).[19] Similar to his extension of sense and value beyond the psychological domain to non-anthropomorphic forces and wills, Deleuze pushes the eternal return past its application to individuals' dispositions until returning characterises *becoming*.

By making return said of becoming, Deleuze can appeal to the eternal return as an explanation of time's passage. Here, he draws from notebook entries where Nietzsche argues against the possibility of equilibrium among forces and in favour of ceaseless becoming (WP 1062, 1067, 708). On the assumption that past time is infinite, Nietzsche reasons that if an equilibrium of forces was possible, it would have been achieved. Yet, the dynamism of the present shows that this has not occurred. Deleuze takes these reflections to further undermine cosmological readings of the eternal return, as the incompatibility between equilibrium and becoming raises questions about why a cycle of time would begin and why a completed cycle would give way to another (1983: 49). Deleuze then applies this reasoning about cycles' extreme states to the present moment. If time were a successive series of 'closed' moments, we could not explain why one moment gives way to the next. On pain of perpetual stasis, Deleuze concludes that 'the present must coexist with itself as past and yet to come' (48).[20] Becoming requires that the present is *internally differentiated*. Similar to how 'it is not being that returns but rather the returning itself that constitutes being insofar as it is affirmed of becoming', so the present does not return, for Deleuze. Rather, by affirming 'the synthetic relation of the moment to itself as present, past, and future', returning *constitutes* the present (48).

While Deleuze does not confine the eternal return to the psychological domain, he nevertheless considers its ethical application. He compares the eternal return to Kant's practical synthesis for action: '*whatever you*

will, will it in such a way that you also will its eternal return' (1983: 68).
This imperative eliminates all half-hearted willing. 'Laziness, stupidity, baseness, cowardice or spitefulness that would will its own eternal
return would no longer be the same laziness, stupidity, etc.', because
the practical thought of the eternal return pushes reactive forces to their
limit. Although this practical use of the eternal return 'makes willing
something whole', 'makes willing a creation', Deleuze thinks that this
is insufficient to overcome nihilism (69). Nietzsche describes the eternal
return as 'the most extreme form of nihilism' (WP 55) because reactive
forces *can* pass its practical test. This casts further doubt on hypothetical
readings of the eternal return, as the thought of life's identical replica-
tion fails to transform the Last Man content with a reactive life. Deleuze
infers from this that the eternal return must carry out a second selection,
one that 'involves the most obscure parts of Nietzsche's philosophy and
forms an almost esoteric element on the doctrine of the eternal return'
(1983: 69).

This second selection is ontological. Whereas the first selection concerns reactive forces, the second submits the *will to nothingness* to the
eternal return. This leads the will to nothingness to break its alliance
with reactive forces. As Deleuze puts the point, 'only the eternal return
can complete nihilism *because it makes negation a negation of reactive
forces*' (1983: 70). He illustrates this transition by distinguishing the
Last Man from the Man who actively destroys himself (69–70; 174). But
the details of this transmutation remain obscure. Inasmuch as the eternal
return forecloses the possibility of any life other than this, perhaps
it compels any evaluation which opposes life to confront its internal
contradiction, its use of life's creative powers to negate life itself. On
this suggestion, the eternal return forces the ascetic who denies life in
favour of heaven to either abandon asceticism or to affirm asceticism as
an active negation of life. Likewise, the eternal return forces those who
pursue truth in opposition to life to either question the value of truth or
to affirm the will to truth as an active negation of life. Generalising the
point: if one attempts to affirm the practical thought of the eternal return
under the sway of nihilism, negation is pushed to break its alliance
with reactive forces and to actively pursue the destruction of reactive
forces themselves. Unfortunately, though, I suspect that such an explanation of the eternal return's selective ontology remains all-too-human.
Throughout *Nietzsche and Philosophy*, Deleuze insists that the will to
power must not be confined to psychology – both because human psychology is categorically reactive (21, 34, 41, 64, 167–9) and because the
will produces forces more basic than individuals' psychological outlooks

(49–55, 84–6). The foregoing explanation of the eternal return's selective ontology is therefore in tension with Deleuze's reading, as it implies that the eternal return's selective ontology depends on the way the thought's practical application compels individuals to transform their values. Deleuze's claim that 'in and through the eternal return negation as a quality of the will to power transmutes itself into affirmation, becomes an affirmation of negation itself, it becomes a power of affirming', must somehow be understood non-anthropomorphically (72). The eternal return must compel negative wills to overcome their opposition to affirmation, if only to affirm themselves, and *without* making this transmutation pivot on human psychology.

Selective ontology

Despite my suspicion that the eternal return's selective ontology cannot reduce to individuals' reflection on its practical application, I'd like to ask whether the eternal return's ethical selection might yield a selective ontology. An affirmative answer to this question would amount to a general defence of Deleuze's reading, as scholars typically accept his claim that the eternal return functions as an ethical principle but resist his further claim about selective ontology.[21] Examining Deleuze's notion of selective ontology from this vantage also allows the distinctness of *Difference and Repetition's* interpretation of the eternal return to emerge in sharper relief.

The suggestion that the eternal return's ethical application *could* produce a selective ontology might seem ill formed. If ontology describes unalterable features of reality, and if the eternal return's ethical selection results from a psychological transformation, then one might think that the eternal return's ethical application cannot affect ontology, which is more fundamental than psychology.[22] However, at least in *Nietzsche and Philosophy*, Deleuze denies that ontology and metaphysics describe the ground floor of reality. 'According to Nietzsche the philosophy of the will must replace the old metaphysics: it destroys and supersedes it' (1983: 84; see also 35). Consistent with Nietzsche's explanations of individuals' ontological commitments in terms of their psychological constitutions, Deleuze maintains that the will to power's qualities produce our image of thought, including our ontological categories, such that 'metaphysics and the theory of knowledge themselves belong to typology' (145). Deleuze does not shrink before the consequences of this intrepid claim. He takes Nietzsche to replace the Platonic question of essence (*what is [x]?*) with questions of sense and value (*who wills [x]?*), and concludes that, 'truth, as a concept, is entirely undetermined. Everything depends on the value and sense of what we think. We always have the truths we deserve as a function of the sense of what we conceive, the value of what we believe' (104). Not only is it the case that, in a world of becoming, every phenomenon has multiple senses, such that there is no *one* way the world 'is'; even more to the point, in a world of becoming, *every ontology is selective*. Granted, a negative will to power leads thought to disavow its creative power, such that we mistakenly think that ontology circumscribes sense and value. But under an affirmative will, 'realist' ontologies are merely different modes of selection – to wit, selections of reactive forces. In *Nietzsche and Philosophy*, metaphysics is subordinate to typology. By transforming the evaluative qualities of the will, the eternal return transfigures everything.

Even if ethical selection can transform individuals' values and thereby produce a selective ontology, one might object that any selective ontology violates the eternal return's ethical aspiration. That is, if affirming the eternal return requires unconditional acceptance of the world as it is, then selective approaches to ontology might seem to express life-negation.[23] However, the suggestion that the eternal return inspires a global acceptance of the world is thoroughly at odds with Deleuze's account. To motivate this point, we can recall Deleuze's insistence that the world is irreducibly plural and dynamic, such that there is no *one* way that the world is for us to accept. Beyond this reply, we should also observe Deleuze's insistence that 'affirmation conceived of as acceptance, as affirmation of that which is, as truthfulness of the true or positivity of the real, is false affirmation' (1983: 184). Acceptance, according to Deleuze, is reactive. Affirmation differs from acceptance in compelling *creation*, and 'there is creation, properly speaking, only insofar as we make use of excess in order to invent new forms of life rather than separating life from what it can do' (185). For Deleuze, affirming the eternal return cannot entail *accepting* the world – even as pluralist and dynamic – because affirmation requires actively contributing to the world's becoming.

A third class of objections concerns Deleuze's view that the eternal return reveals that 'negation *sacrifices* all reactive forces' and that 'there is no return of the negative' (1983: 175, 189). Some object to this aspect of Deleuze's interpretation on the grounds that active forces require reactive forces for their distinction, such that eradicating reactive forces also eradicates active forces.[24] Others object that Deleuze's claims about elimination express a form of life-negation that is ethically or politically dangerous.[25] To address these concerns, recall Deleuze's insistence that the will to power's qualities are not univocal. Granted, from the perspective of a negative will, the eternal return is a kind of auto-destruction. To the extent that negative values define our human condition, affirming the eternal return is therefore difficult indeed.[26] But from an affirmative vantage, the eternal return does not require the elimination of negation or reactive forces; for, affirmation *does not oppose* negation or reaction. This affirmative perspective on the eternal return is reflected in Deleuze's descriptions of transmutation – not as a sacrifice, but – as revealing that negation *depends on* affirmation. The eternal return 'makes negation a power of affirming' (86), so that 'negation ceases to be an autonomous power' (191; see also 176–9). Similarly, reactive forces unilaterally *depend on* active forces (41). And insofar as Deleuze maintains that bodies in which active forces prevail are fundamentally active (86), there is a sense in which reactive forces need not be eliminated but only subordinated to active forces. Affirming the eternal return does not eliminate negation and reaction in some *physical* sense. Rather, it reveals that negation and reactivity *depend on* affirmation and activity. This is why the eternal return produces a double affirmation (186). Selective ontology does not select *some* phenomena as opposed to others; it affirms the affirmative wills and active forces that subtend *all* phenomena. Negation and reaction also rely on the affirmative powers of the false – the fiction of a will which does not create, or the fiction of forces separated from their expression, for example. The eternal return asks whether we can affirm such falsification to push the powers of the false still further.

Insofar as the practical thought of the eternal return forecloses the possibility of any life *other than this*, it compels individuals either to abandon life-negating values or to affirm these values as an active negation of the world. The ascetic deprived of the promise of heaven must either abandon asceticism or affirm asceticism as an active negation of life; the claimant of knowledge must either abandon their subordination of life to truth or affirm the will to truth as an active negation of becoming. Either response to the eternal return produces an ontological transformation. If the life-negating value of truth is replaced with the life-affirming value of artistic creation, our conceptualisation of the world becomes an artistic selection that contributes to the world's creativity. But if negative values are actively affirmed, instead of replaced, a profound conversion still unfolds. The ascetic who actively negates life is not the same as the ascetic who merely reacts to forces beyond their power. For, the active ascetic ceases to disavow the will's creativity and acknowledges that their will *evaluates* life but finds it wanting. Neither response to the practical thought of the eternal return – the replacement of negative with affirmative values, or the active affirmation of negative values – requires the physical destruction of negative wills or reactive forces. Rather, the transformation is evaluative. To affirm the practical thought of the eternal return, we must affirm the affirmative wills and active forces that subtend *all* phenomena, including the negative and reactive. Such a double affirmation actively contributes to the world's creative dynamism. To be clear: I am not suggesting that Deleuze's claim that the eternal return produces a selective ontology is beyond reproach, but that any *successful* reproach to this portion of Deleuze's reading must confront his interpretation of the will to power as a nonunivocal, evaluative typology that produces individuals' ontological commitments.

The Repetition of Difference

Transcendental empiricism

If the foregoing, sympathetic reconstruction provides a general defence of Deleuze's account of selective ontology, it does so by exploiting the puzzling position occupied by the will to power and the eternal return in *Nietzsche and Philosophy*. Insofar as Deleuze insists that these concepts are not confined to psychology but describe becoming, meta-physical interpretations of both notions seem invited. Yet *Nietzsche and Philosophy*'s discussions of metaphysics primarily aim at showing that metaphysics *in general* expresses a negative will to power. For Deleuze, 'Nietzsche ... makes nihilism the presupposition of all metaphysics rather than a particular metaphysics: there is no *metaphysics* which does not judge and depreciate life in the name of a *supra-sensible* world' (1983: 34; see also 195). But this only makes the status of affirmative wills and the return of becoming more perplexing. Are these not metaphysical? Sometimes, Deleuze seems to permit the possibility of an affirmative metaphysics – as when he claims that 'Nietzsche ... develops a philosophy which must ... replace the old metaphysics' (145, see also 84). Still, *Nietzsche and Philosophy* seems to vacillate before this pos-sibility, leaving us with an odd picture on which the phenomenal world is produced by non-anthropomorphic evaluations, which are affirmed non-anthropomorphically in the process of returning – and without any of this being metaphysical. If Deleuze wavers before the possibility of an affirmative metaphysics in *Nietzsche and Philosophy*, he overcomes this hesitation in *Difference and Repetition* by developing his method of transcendental empiricism.

For orientation purposes, it helps to very briefly consider Kant's transcendental idealism as Deleuze views it.[27] Deleuze takes Kant to advance beyond Descartes' *cogito* by realising, first, that determination (I think) implies an undetermined existence (I am) and, second, that determination cannot directly bear on the undetermined. Kant therefore introduces a third element, the form of determination, which is the form of time. As Deleuze puts it, 'my undetermined existence can be determined only *within time* as the existence of a phenomenon, of a passive, receptive phenomenal subject *appearing within time*', so that 'the spontaneity of which I am conscious in the "I think" cannot be understood as the attribute of a substantial and spontaneous being, but only as the affection of a passive self which experiences its own thought'. Deleuze celebrates this glimpse of the passive self, which fractures the I, as 'the discovery of the transcendental' (1994: 86). Nevertheless, he charges Kant with concealing this fracture with 'active synthetic identity' (87). Kant's active, *a priori* syntheses preserve the identity of the transcendental subject at the expense of making the unconditioned external to sensibility and of making the sensibility external to the understanding. Following Solomon Maimon, Deleuze contends that Kant's transcendental idealism only offers the conditions of *possible* experience, not those of *actual* experience.

Transcendental empiricism emerges against this background. Whereas Kant considers the difference between the undetermined and the determined an epistemological limitation of the transcendental subject, Deleuze considers this difference ontologically productive. He retains Kant's notion of the unconditioned but renders it *immanent to* phenomena. This 'noumenon closest to the phenomenon' is, of course, difference itself (1994: 222). Difference is 'not a sensible being but the being *of* the sensible. It is not the given but that by which the given is given' (140). Difference is thus a speculative concept that cannot be grasped empirically. It is not an *extensive* relation among sensible qualities, but an *intensive* relation that produces sensations. Such intensive differences produce ideas by *repetition*. Repeated variations among intensive differences in light, for example, communicate a kind of violence to the faculties, prompting the understanding to structure these intensive differences in an idea, say, of RED. Ideas are always actualised in unique ways; no two shades of red are identical. Like difference itself, repetition is a speculative concept, one that produces the ideas that structure sensations.

The concepts of difference and repetition allow Deleuze to remedy Kant's externalisation of the unconditioned from the given and of sensibility from the understanding. Difference in itself produces sensible qualities and 'forces us to think' by providing 'an object not of recognition but of a fundamental *encounter*' (Deleuze 1994: 139). As this description of thought as forced upon us suggests, transcendental empiricism remains faithful to Kant's discovery of the passive self. Beneath Kant's active synthesis of the present, Deleuze posits a prior, passive synthesis (habit) that makes corporeal receptivity possible. Beneath the active synthesis of the past, he posits a prior, passive synthesis (memory) which enables time's passage. Beneath the active synthesis of the future, he posits a prior, passive synthesis (the new) which makes the recognition of endurance possible. Without treating these syntheses in detail,[28] we can observe how they subject the Self and Ideas to the pure and empty form of time. Just as the I is fractured into undetermined being, the determinability of being and the process of determining being, so Ideas are 'undetermined with regard to their object, determinable with regard to the objects of experience, and [bear] the ideal of an infinite determination with regard to the concepts of the understanding' (169). The empty form of time fractures being and thought alike, revealing their emergence from the repetition of difference.

Far from being the form of the immutable and eternal, the pure and empty form of time, for Deleuze, is 'the form of change' itself. As the pure and empty form of time is a transcendental form that precedes all empirical content, Deleuze merely describes it as a 'caesura', which does not so much emerge *within* linear time as it *reorders* time as a whole, breaking time into the time before and the time after the emergence of the New (Deleuze 1994: 89–90). The consequences of this shift can hardly be overstated. Deleuze insists that 'there is nothing that does not lose its identity . . . when the dynamic of space and time in its actual constitution is discovered' (218). Indeed, insofar as philosophy traditionally defines truth as eternal and unchanging, the pure and empty form of time puts truth in crisis, revealing that concepts are not universal and necessary essences, but singular *creations* produced in response to shifting problematics.[29] Transcendental empiricism accordingly champions artists over truthful thinkers of common sense. Whereas the latter *judge* according to the eternal form of the true, the former *create* by deploying the powers of the false under the pure and empty form of time.

The eternal return of the new

Kant's transcendental idealism denounces the notions of the substantial self (the Soul), the totality of what exists (the World) and a first cause of this totality (God) as transcendental illusions produced by the unrestricted use of reason. Deleuze's transcendental empiricism attempts to go beyond Kant, however, by developing an account of the transcendental that actively *excludes* the coherence of the Self, the World and God. It is therefore fitting that *Difference and Repetition* makes much use of Nietzsche. For, already in *Nietzsche and Philosophy*, Deleuze claims that 'Nietzsche seems to have sought (and to have found in "the eternal return" and "the will to power") ... a re-invention of the critique which Kant betrayed at the same time as he conceived it' (1983: 52). Nevertheless, it is only in *Difference and Repetition* that Deleuze fully elaborates on the way the will to power and eternal return might yield a non-representational image of thought.

The notion of difference free from any dependence on identity is one of Deleuze's great philosophical achievements. If this concept resembles any from the history of philosophy, it is Nietzsche's will to power, as Deleuze understands it. Foreshadowing Deleuze's development of transcendental empiricism in *Difference and Repetition*, *Nietzsche and Philosophy* claims that 'the will to power manifests itself, in the first place, as the sensibility of forces and, in the second place, as the becoming sensible of forces', and that 'thinking depends on forces which take hold of thought' (1983: 63, 108). But in this early work, Deleuze is more concerned with analysing the image of thought produced by *negative* evaluations and *reactive* forces. In *Difference and Repetition*, by contrast, he dispenses almost entirely with negative wills and reactive forces to develop a thoroughly affirmative and active image of thought. *Difference and Repetition* thus describes the will to power as 'the world of flashing metamorphoses, of communicating intensities, differences of differences', and claims that 'difference in the will to power is the highest object of sensibility' (1994: 243). The first of these statements characterises the will to power as a theory of *singularities* that escape the notions of the Self, the World and God. The second characterises difference – which is celebrated under an affirmative will – as that which produces the given from the unconditioned. Difference in itself is a metaphysical concept appropriate to an affirmative will to power, a metaphysical notion free of transcendence and of the negative evaluations that characterise a representational image of thought.

The gap between sensibility and understanding is bridged by difference's repetition, which forces ideas to emerge as ways of structuring intensive variations. Deleuze claims, in *Nietzsche and Philosophy*, that 'we can only understand the eternal return as the expression of a principle which serves as an explanation of diversity and its reproduction, of difference and its repetition', and that 'the *thought* of the eternal return [as a selection of affirmative wills] goes beyond all the laws of our *knowledge*' (1983: 49, 108). While these cryptic claims foreshadow *Difference and Repetition*, they cry out for elaboration inasmuch as *Nietzsche and Philosophy* vacillates before the questions of what a non-anthropomorphic affirmation of the eternal return might entail and of how such an affirmation could be non-metaphysical. *Difference and Repetition* overcomes this hesitation. There, the eternal return 'is the only Same which can be said of this world and which excludes any prior identity therein', because the eternal return is a transcendental affirmation of difference itself. Insofar as the eternal return, as a double affirmation and a repetition of difference, marks the emergence of understanding from the given, Deleuze claims that 'repetition in the eternal return is the highest thought' (1994: 243). Just as *Difference and Repetition* dispenses with the will to power's negative qualities to focus on its affirmative aspect, Deleuze also dispenses almost entirely with the cosmological and psychological uses of the eternal return in favour of a transcendental use of the idea as an affirmation of difference. The eternal return ceases to describe a psychological transformation that induces a selective *approach to* ontology and becomes a properly *ontological selection*, one which ensures that only extreme intensive differences emerge in the understanding.

As the repetition of difference, the eternal return also marks the passive, temporal synthesis of the future. Deleuze is forthright about the speculative character of this portion of his interpretation of Nietzsche. He maintains that 'the Nietzschean doctrine of eternal return was never stated but reserved for a future work', and that 'Nietzsche gave no exposition of the eternal return' because '*Thus Spoke Zarathustra* is unfinished' (1994: 92, 297). While this gives Deleuze some reason to speculate about Nietzsche's ultimate formulation of the eternal return, such speculation is distinct from 'buggery'. Far from intentionally subverting Nietzsche's thought, Deleuze attempts to formulate what the eternal return would have become were it not for Nietzsche's collapse. Deleuze takes his conjectures on this score to be warranted by the way that the eternal return presupposes an absence of identity – the death of God and the dissolution of the Self. If what returns is *difference*, then sameness and identity only emerge as simulacra (126), 'as secondary powers' of difference (301). Strictly speaking, then, 'the eternal return affects only the new', since what repeats is always different (90). This view of the eternal return as a transcendental synthesis of difference entails a radical rethinking of time. While *Nietzsche and Philosophy* describes the eternal return's temporal consequence as the affirmation of the *present* as internally differentiated into a simultaneous becoming-past and becoming-future, *Difference and Repetition* appeals to the eternal return as the passive synthesis of the *future*. Deleuze describes this synthesis as 'the royal repetition', one which 'subordinates the other [passive temporal syntheses] to itself and strips them of their autonomy' (94). The emergence of the New constitutes the present and past alike, producing 'a universal ungrounding' (91). Everything that returns is new; only *creation* returns. Many Nietzsche scholars wrestle with the psychological consequences of the eternal return, asking how we might overcome the weight of the past in favour of the promise of the future. But Deleuze sidesteps these issues by making the present and the past *metaphysically* dependent on the future. He largely dispenses with the eternal return's psychological applications in favour of a transcendental use of the idea.

It might seem that Deleuze's ultimate appeal to the eternal return as an ontological selection of intensive differences leaves behind Nietzsche's preoccupation with the thought's ethical consequences. However, repetition is selective in the ontological and ethical senses. Repetition tests our ability to leave behind the illusions of being and identity, so that we might affirm a life of becoming and difference. In this sense, Deleuze remains committed to the eternal return's ethical challenge of demanding an affirmation of life's creative dynamism. He pursues an immanent ethics which encourages us to go to the limits of what we can do. While Nietzsche articulates the eternal return as a principle of the past (as cosmological condition) and present (as conditioning ethical transformation), his collapse prevented him from formulating the eternal return as a principle of the future (as the unconditioned, the repetition of difference). Deleuze attempts to complete Nietzsche's project, as he understands it, by transforming the eternal return's ethical imperative into a demand to be open to the new so that we might transform ourselves into extreme and singular forms and thereby discover who we might become.

Conclusion

Deleuze's interpretation of the eternal return develops at the threshold of the traditional demands of the history of philosophy. Attending to Nietzsche's views that evaluations subtend even the most banal descriptions of the world and that becoming exceeds all knowledge leads Deleuze to push the will to power's evaluative qualities and the eternal return's transformative effects beyond psychology, until they characterise the world's becoming. This makes *Nietzsche and Philosophy*'s claim that the eternal return produces a selective ontology more defensible than it might seem, as Deleuze holds that the eternal return selects *affirmative* wills and that the will to power is a non-anthropomorphic, nonunivocal evaluative typology that produces one's ontology. But this also prompts questions about the metaphysical status of affirmative wills to power and of a non-anthropomorphic affirmation of the eternal return. If these questions haunt *Nietzsche and Philosophy*, they are answered in *Difference and Repetition*, where Deleuze develops a transcendental account of the will to power as difference in itself and of the eternal return as the difference's repetition. This break from a psychological interpretation of the eternal return in favour of a transcendental interpretation of it also transforms the doctrine's temporal consequences. Whereas *Nietzsche and Philosophy* takes the eternal return to mark the present's internal differentiation as a simultaneous becoming-past and becoming-future, *Difference and Repetition* takes the eternal return to mark the priority of the *future* as a passive, temporal synthesis that constitutes the present and past alike. The consequences of Deleuze's admittedly speculative interpretation of the eternal return certainly merit closer examination. But hopefully the foregoing discussion clarifies Nietzsche's pivotal role in enabling Deleuze to develop his own theory of time, according to which all that returns is *new*.

Notes

1. Selected portions of this chapter are adapted from Mollison (forthcoming).
2. Citations from Nietzsche use abbreviations listed in the references. Arabic numerals refer to section numbers. Roman numerals to major divisions within works.
3. See Schrift 1995: 139 n.32; and D'Iorio 2011.
4. See Ansell-Pearson 1994: 114–16; Ward 2010: 106–10; and Woodward 2013: 134–7.
5. See Hallward 2006: 149–52; Malabou 2010; and Woodward 2013: 140–3.
6. This shift is concealed by the tendency to interchangeably cite *Nietzsche and Philosophy* and *Difference and Repetition* when examining Deleuze's reading of the eternal return. For examples, see Hallward 2006; Malabou 2010; Ward 2010; and, to a lesser extent, Woodward 2013. My developmental approach to this topic also distinguishes my discussion from those that only appraise Deleuze's interpretation *as* a reading of Nietzsche (e.g., Ansell-Pearson 1994; Malabou 2010; Ward 2010; D'Iorio 2011; and Woodward 2013) and those that grant Deleuze's interpretation to examine the use he makes of it (e.g., Williams 2011; and Voss 2013).
7. Deleuze's choice to draw from Nietzsche's *Nachlass* merits emphasising here. For while Nietzsche's publications provide some support for the claim that the

world is comprised of forces (e.g., BGE 12, 17; GM I.13), his notebooks provide drastically more support for it. The concept of force (*Kraft*) is used to analyse the world in general (WP 1064, 1062, 638, 1066), organic life (WP 641, 650, 647, 689, 702–3), human life (WP 686, 490, 660, 704), phenomenology and psychology (WP 664, 668, 568), value judgements (WP 260, 667, 781, 931, 386, 863, 576), social phenomena (WP 750, 762, 786, 784) and aesthetic activities (WP 852, 842, 809, 812, 815).

8. D'Iorio criticises Deleuze's interpretation of the will to power as entailing 'a form of dualism which Nietzsche's monistic philosophy strives to eliminate' (2011: 3). The portion of D'Iorio's argument concerning the legitimacy of the French translation of Nietzsche's notes that Deleuze uses is well-taken (see Montinari 1996). However, D'Iorio's accusation of dualism is complicated by Deleuze's analysis of the will to power as a plastic, empirical principle.

9. For examples, see Kaufmann 1956: 152–80; and Reginster 2006: 103–48.

10. For example, see Clark 1990: 205–44.

11. For example, see Richardson 1996.

12. For example, see Schacht 1985: 212–34.

13. On this aspect of Deleuze's reading, see Norman 2000.

14. On *Nietzsche and Philosophy*'s relation to Kant, see Marsden 1998.

15. This gloss is supported by Kant's description of his critical project as a 'ripened power of judgement, which will no longer be put off with illusory knowledge, and which demands that reason . . . institute a court of justice, [to] secure its rightful claims while dismissing all its groundless pretensions' (1998: Axi–xii).

16. For examples, see Kaufmann 1956: 274–86; Heidegger 1991; Loeb 2010; and D'Iorio 2011.

17. For examples, see Nehamas 1985: 141–69; Clark 1990: 245–86; and Reginster 2006: 201–27.

18. A similar argument motivates Deleuze's claim that the eternal return affirms chance (1983: 25–9).

19. D'Iorio argues that Deleuze's claim that *difference* eternally returns 'relies on one fragment by Nietzsche, and one fragment only' (2011: 1). The fragment in question results from Geneviève Bianquis' decision to combine two notes from Nietzsche's *Nachlass* and thereby obscure the fact that these notes criticise Johannes Gustav Vogt's rendering of the eternal return (D'Iorio 2011: 1–3; see also Woodward 2013: 128–9). D'Iorio is right to challenge Bianquis' rendering of these texts (see Montinari 1996), but I think he overstates his case against Deleuze. Nietzsche rejects ancient formulations of the eternal return as a cyclical hypothesis, insists on the priority of becoming over being, and argues that metaphysical notions of identity abstract from reality's complexity. Deleuze's claim that *difference* returns largely derives from *the cumulative force* that these themes exert on our understanding of the eternal return. Though, as we will see, Deleuze becomes more forthright about the speculative nature of his interpretation by the time of *Difference and Repetition*, where the return of *difference* is emphasised over the return of *becoming*.

20. This point bears a striking affinity with Deleuze's reading of Bergson – although, whereas Deleuze takes Bergson to claim that the present and past are contemporaneous (Deleuze 1988: 58–9), he takes Nietzsche to claim that the present, past and *future* are coeval. While Deleuze suggests that this point follows from Nietzsche's analysis of temporal cycles' extreme states, Borradori (1999) argues that Deleuze's earlier essay, 'Bergson's Conception of Difference', operates throughout much of *Nietzsche and Philosophy*. So, Deleuze may be perverting Nietzsche somewhat here.

21. For examples, see Ansell-Pearson 1994: 113–16; Schrift 1995: 139 n.32;

Malabou 2010; Ward 2010: 106–7; D'Iorio 2011; and Woodward 2013: 128–44. At the risk of seeming facile, I will not reconstruct and rebut specific objections raised against Deleuze's notion of selective ontology. Isolating any one objection strikes me as overly ad hoc and reconstructing all of the relevant arguments would take considerable time. Still, I think a broad defence of Deleuze's reading can be offered, at least insofar as one accepts that the eternal return carries ethical implications.
22. Ward seems to have something like this in mind when he accuses Deleuze of 'conflating two different notions of selection'. The first selection, according to Ward, operates 'purely as a thought, as something which forces us to think about existence in a particular way', whereas the second selection operates as 'a universal, cosmological process' (Ward 2010: 106).
23. For objections of this sort, see Schrift 1995: 139 n.32; Ward 2010: 106–10; D'Iorio 2011; and Woodward 2013: 134–7.
24. For examples, see Ansell-Pearson 1994: 114–16; and Ward 2010: 106–8.
25. For examples, see Hallward 2006: 149–52; Malabou 2010: 25; and Woodward 2013: 134–7, 140–3.
26. While Ward argues that Deleuze's selective ontology makes the eternal return 'something blandly cheering and optimistic' (2010: 106), I think this downplays Deleuze's insistence that humanity is categorically reactive. The elimination of the *ego*, for example, is neither comforting nor easily accomplished.
27. On *Difference and Repetition*'s relation to Kant, see Lord 2012.
28. For a detailed treatment of these syntheses, see Williams 2011.
29. On the relation between truth and the empty form of time, see Smith 2013.

References

Nietzsche's Works
BGE *Beyond Good and Evil*, trans. Judith Norman, Cambridge: Cambridge University Press, 2002.
  D *Daybreak*, trans. R. J. Hollingdale, Cambridge: Cambridge University Press, 1997.
GM *On the Genealogy of Morality*, trans. Maudemarie Clark and Alan J. Swensen, Indianapolis: Hackett, 1998.
 GS *The Gay Science*, trans. Josefine Naukhoff and Adrian Del Caro, Cambridge: Cambridge University Press, 2001.
 TI *Twilight of the Idols*, trans. Judith Norman, Cambridge: Cambridge University Press, 2005.
WP *The Will to Power*, trans. Walter Kaufmann and R. J. Hollingdale, New York: Vintage, 1968.

Other Sources
Ansell-Pearson, K. (1994), *An Introduction to Nietzsche as a Political Thinker*, Cambridge: Cambridge University Press.
Borradori, G. (1999), 'On the Presence of Bergson in Deleuze's Nietzsche', *Philosophy Today*, 43: 140–5.
Clark, M. (1990), *Nietzsche on Truth and Philosophy*, Cambridge: Cambridge University Press.
Deleuze, G. (1983), *Nietzsche and Philosophy*, trans. Hugh Tomlinson, New York: Columbia University Press.
Deleuze, G. (1988), *Bergsonism*, trans. Hugh Tomlinson and Barbara Habberjam, New York: Zone Books.

Deleuze, G. (1994), *Difference and Repetition*, trans. Paul Patton, New York: Columbia University Press.

Deleuze, G. (1995), *Negotiations 1972–1990*, trans. Martin Joughin, New York: Columbia University Press.

Deleuze, G. and C. Parnet (2007), *Dialogues* II, trans. Hugh Tomlinson and Barbara Habberjam, New York: Columbia University Press.

D'Iorio, P. (2011), 'The Eternal Return: Genesis and Interpretation', trans. Frank Chouraqui, *The Agonist*, IV (1): 1–43.

Hallward, P. (2006), *Out of this World: Deleuze and the Philosophy of Creation*, New York: Verso.

Heidegger, M. (1991), *Nietzsche*, trans. David Farrell Krell, New York: Harper Collins.

Kant, I. (1998), *Critique of Pure Reason*, trans. and ed. Paul Guyer and Allen Wood, Cambridge: Cambridge University Press.

Kaufmann, W. (1956), *Nietzsche: Philosopher, Psychologist, Antichrist*, New York: Meridian.

Loeb, P. (2010), *The Death of Nietzsche's Zarathustra*, Cambridge: Cambridge University Press.

Lord, B. (2012), 'Deleuze and Kant', in *The Cambridge Companion to Deleuze*, ed. Daniel W. Smith and Henry Somers-Hall, Cambridge: Cambridge University Press.

Malabou, C. (2010), 'The Eternal Return and the Phantom of Difference', trans. Arne De Boever, *Parrhesia*, 10: 21–9.

Marsden, J. (1998), 'Critical Incorporation: Nietzsche and Deleuze', *Journal of Nietzsche Studies*, 16: 33–48.

Mollison, J. (forthcoming), 'Deleuze's Nietzschean Mutations: From the Will to Power and the Overman to Desiring-Production and Nomadism', *Deleuze and Guattari Studies*.

Montinari, M. (1996), *'La volunté de puissance' N'existe Pas*, Paris: Éditions de l'éclat.

Nehamas, A. (1985), *Nietzsche: Life as Literature*, Cambridge, MA: Harvard University Press.

Norman, J. (2000), 'Nietzsche contra Contra: Difference and Opposition', *Continental Philosophy Review*, 33: 189–206.

Reginster, B. (2006), *The Affirmation of Life: Nietzsche on Overcoming Nihilism*, Cambridge, MA: Harvard University Press.

Richardson, J. (1996), *Nietzsche's System*, Oxford: Oxford University Press.

Schacht, R. (1985), *Nietzsche*, Boston: Routledge.

Schrift, A. (1995), *Nietzsche's French Legacy*, New York: Routledge.

Smith, D. W. (2013), 'Temporality and Truth', *Deleuze Studies*, 7 (3): 377–89.

Voss, D. (2013), 'Deleuze's Third Synthesis of Time', *Deleuze Studies*, 7 (2): 194–216.

Ward, J. (2010), 'Revisiting *Nietzsche et la Philosophie*', *Angelaki*, 15 (2): 101–14.

Williams, J. (2011), *Gilles Deleuze's Philosophy of Time: A Critical Introduction and Guide*, Edinburgh: Edinburgh University Press.

Woodward, A. (2013), 'Deleuze, Nietzsche, and the Overcoming of Nihilism', *Continental Philosophy Review*, 46: 115–47.

Chapter 5

Time and the Untimely: Deleuze, Foucault and the Production of the New

Strand Sheldahl-Thomason

> Untimely – that is to say, acting counter to our time and thereby acting on our time and, let us hope, for the benefit of a time to come (Nietzsche 1997: 60)
>
> Time is the most radical form of change, but the form of change does not change. (Deleuze 1994: 89)
>
> Once defined, a form is simultaneously too old and too new, too strange and too familiar, not to be instantly rejected . . . (Foucault 1998: 167)

Introduction: Time and History

The relationship between Gilles Deleuze and Michel Foucault was, if not untimely, then at least out of joint. Both thinkers acted counter to their time. Deleuze was an empiricist and a metaphysician in the time of phenomenology and structuralism. Foucault frequently shifted shape as he strove to develop a method for diagnosing the present. Deleuze and Foucault seemed to dance around each other on the margins of the intellectual stage that was France in the 1960s, '70s and '80s, coming closer to the centre as their disruptions came, perhaps inevitably, to define an age. Nietzsche deeply influenced both thinkers, but their respective uses of Nietzsche led them down quite distinct intellectual paths. Likewise, both frequently engaged the literary *avant-garde*, but Deleuze became a champion of Anglo-American literature while Foucault's tastes skewed continental. Both found fault with the dominant trends in psychology and medicine, which led Deleuze (and Guattari) to develop schizo-analysis, and Foucault into studies of madness, hermaphrodism and sexuality. Foucault rejected the term desire, while Deleuze made it a central concept of his philosophy. At the same time, Deleuze criticised Foucault's attempts to rehabilitate the notions of pleasure and truth. Their magnetic dance of attraction/repulsion led to a genuine friendship between the two, although collaboration between them was scant, and as their careers progressed their friendship cooled. Deleuze frequently wrote about and through other philosophers, but he wrote *Foucault* only after Foucault's untimely death in 1984. Foucault contributed a flattering preface to Deleuze and Guattari's *Anti-Oedipus: Capitalism and Schizophrenia 1*. The two collaborated in the Groupe d'Information sur les Prisons in the early 1970s, and they commented on one another from time to time in interviews and articles. Yet these encounters did not much lessen the gap between them. Deleuze said of Foucault, 'I do think there are a lot of parallels between our [Deleuze and Guattari's] work and his, although they're kept apart, as it were, by their widely differing methods, and purposes even' (1995: 85). The relationship between Foucault and Deleuze is a kind of missed encounter; one coming, one going; walking down different corridors of the same building; disjointed; discontinuous. It is perhaps unsurprising, then, that their approaches to time share a conceptual space but inhabit it quite differently.[1]

In comparing Deleuze and Foucault's views on time, a difficulty immediately presents itself. Deleuze is primarily a thinker of time, and to the extent that Deleuze and Guattari develop a philosophy of history, it grows out of this thought on time. Foucault is primarily a thinker of history, and his philosophy of history grows out of his reaction to transcendental philosophies of time. Received wisdom has it that, although Kant influences both Deleuze and Foucault, Foucault ultimately remains more Kantian than Deleuze. But when it comes to time, it is in fact Deleuze who is more Kantian. He borrows from Kant the notion of time as an empty form and puts it to work in his transcendental empiricism. Deleuze's philosophy of time is a philosophy of a network of temporal syntheses that make up a totality. Each synthesis of time is irreducible to any other synthesis, yet each remains inextricably linked to the others, and the pure, empty form of time stands out as the answer to Deleuze's guiding question of how novelty appears. In *Difference and Repetition* and to some degree in *The Logic of Sense*, it is the third synthesis of time, the future, or the pure, empty form of time, that appears as the engine that produces the new. What this engine runs on, so to speak, is the eternal return. What returns in the eternal return is difference, never the same, and this return affects everything, everywhere, all at once. The eternal return thus ungrounds what had become sedimented and reorders it. Deleuze and Guattari's positive remarks on the philosophy of history develop in relation to Deleuze's philosophy of time. History, of course, is not empty, but the content of history, namely dated events in a relation of succession, or systems of relations between ordinal points that are expressed as events, eras and epochs, becomes for Deleuze and Guattari something like the pure past (the second synthesis of time) that eternal return ungrounds and reorders. In keeping with Deleuze's totalising theory of time, all historical events coexist in a system that becoming criss-crosses. Just as eternal return affects the whole of time, so does it affect the whole of history, so that history itself is continuously undergoing change. What Deleuze's philosophy of time and Deleuze and Guattari's philosophy of history reject is homogeneous continuity. They preserve totality and universality.

At least when it comes to time and history, Foucault's Kantian inheritance extends to his retention of the term *a priori*, and his philosophy of history distinguishes between condition and conditioned. However, Foucault makes the *a priori* historical, and his move to history amounts to a rejection of transcendental philosophies of time. His analysis of Kant's *Anthropology* shows that the time of that work is a time of dispersion that is no longer subjectively contained. Nonetheless, he also argues that Kant never escapes the fundamental problem of transcendental philosophy: that of seeking an illusory, originary ground of finitude beyond or behind the field of experience. Foucault's positive philosophy of history emphasises the discontinuous. For Foucault, any notion of universal history goes by the wayside along with the founding subject. His discussion of the historical *a priori* and the archive shows that discursive proliferation and transformation cannot be reduced to a unified historical perspective. Foucault characterises his own work as a history of the present, but the point of such a history is not to justify or reify our forms of knowing. It is to reveal the groundlessness of that which grounds our ways of knowing and living, and to spur us to develop new ways of living that are not predicted or determined by the present, that cannot be articulated on the grounds of the present but rather transform those grounds. Foucault's philosophy of history rejects continuity, totality and universality.

Serious questions dog both thinkers. For Deleuze, the question becomes, is the empty form of time itself immune to becoming? For Foucault, the question is, can his philosophy of transformation remain coherent without metaphysical intervention? Yet these questions are unfair to both thinkers. Deleuze might respond: what sense does it make to speak of the transformation of that which is empty? Foucault might respond: why must I be consistent or coherent? Yet it may be that Foucault's refusal to engage in any attempt to trace a formal structure of time gives him the advantage when it comes to pushing us toward the genuinely new. As admirable and thorough as Deleuze's efforts to spell out a system of multiple, irreducible syntheses of time are, his adaptation of Kant's empty form of time undermines his own contention that 'form will never inspire anything but conformities' (1994: 134).

Deleuze's Metaphysics of Novelty

It may strike his readers as strange to hear Deleuze, the dedicated anti-Platonist, refer to 'the empty form of time' and 'an empty and pure form' (1994: 88). One might fairly ask why Deleuze would want to preserve any notion of form at all. The answer can be found in Kant's intervention in the conception of time. For Kant, time is the form of inner sense which renders undetermined subjective existence determinable. As Daniel W. Smith notes, Kant liberates time from subordination to movement, from cosmology, from psychology, and from the eternal (2012: 133). However, Deleuze is quick to point out that Kant immediately fills up this newly purified and emptied form of time with an active synthetic identity. Thus, whatever fracturing effect time has on the subject is papered over. Passivity is assigned only to receptivity, and synthesis to an active subject that seems to stand outside of time. Deleuze retains the notion of time as the empty form in which the undetermined is determinable, but he extends the fracturing effect of time's emptiness to being in general. Accordingly, time's emptiness is no longer filled by an active synthesis. Rather, Deleuze identifies three passive syntheses of time that are independent yet form a system in which no synthesis is reducible to any other. Neither is the system itself reducible to any synthesising activity that lies outside or escapes it. In the words of James Williams, what we get from Deleuze is 'a formal network of processes defining time as multiple' where 'any reduction of this multiplicity is disallowed' (2011: 3). Very briefly, the first synthesis is the living present, or the time of succession and bodily habit in which past and future appear as dimensions relative to the present. The second synthesis is the pure past, or 'the virtual co-existence of all time', and it is in the pure past that the living present passes (Lampert 2006: 13). The third synthesis of time concerns the appearance of the new. It is the instant 'without extension' that cuts time into past and future, or before and after (Deleuze 1990: 164). The living present retains successive particular events in an expectation of a general future, the pure past is the condition of possibility of time's passage in the present, and the third synthesis makes all of time again available for re-ordering.

The pure past is pure because it is not characterised by any set of particular presents. Rather, it is the *a priori*, general form of succession in the present. In terms of representation, the pure past is that 'in which' that allows a particular event in the living present to be represented as past and as a point in a succession of other events. While the pure past coexists with each passing present, it is itself unrepresentable. Yet the ability to represent events as past and as ordered successively in the present suggests a form that allows such representation. As Deleuze puts the point: 'It is with respect to the pure element of the past, understood as the past in general, as an *a priori* past, that a given former present is reproducible and the present present is able to reflect itself' (1994: 81). Although the pure past is a form of succession, and therefore not itself a successive series of presents, an appeal to history can shed some light on how the pure past functions. As Jay Lampert notes, 'when we experience something as belonging to the past, we experience it as part of a set of *histories of past elements* . . . In short, we experience a scene not as the present, but as an element in a scheme that has already been structuring the past' (2006: 44). The present gets its sense from these layered schemes that have already been structuring the past. Furthermore, these schemes are not themselves former presents but 'patterns that existed in their own right before a present is synthesized onto them' (44). If in the first synthesis of time succession occurs rhythmically or habitually, the pure past makes rhythm possible as its ground.

The pure past may be pure in the sense that it is not a set of particulars, but it is not exactly empty. It remains 'relative to what it grounds' (Deleuze 1994: 88). The characterisation of the pure past as a general patterning and structuring that allows a present to be synthesised on it reveals that the ground of succession and succession itself share elements. This opens even the second synthesis of time to a kind of circularity in which time remains subordinated to cardinal points through which it moves. Or, to put the point differently, the mutual structuring of pure past and living present do not on their own ensure that the past won't be represented according to the present passing present. Indeed, it always is so represented. Of the pure past Deleuze asks, 'how can we penetrate that in-itself without reducing it to the former present that it was, or to the present present in relation to which it is past?' (84). It is as if whatever emptiness the pure past suggests is immediately filled by the synthesis of the passing present. Deleuze calls for some further synthesis of time that goes beyond representation and any ground of representation and that disrupts the tight circuit between pure past and passing present. Something else is needed to break the rhythm.

It is the third synthesis of time that Deleuze identifies with the pure and empty form of time. If the traces of the subordination of time to movement remain from Plato even through to Deleuze's second synthesis of time, Deleuze's third synthesis of time achieves the promise glimpsed by Kant, but now freed of the Kantian baggage which takes synthesis as the province of an active subject. According to James Williams, 'the third synthesis of time is ... empty, in the sense of lacking cardinal numbering, and pure, in the sense of lacking hierarchies associated with numbering' (2011: 88). On the Platonic conception of time, time is measured according to the relation of points to the *cardo*, or the joint, hinge or astronomical pole which would serve as a ground for measurement, as in the measurement of revolutions of the earth. Even with the pure past, content remains that gives shape to the past and the present alike, and the passing present construes past events as cardinal points. With the third synthesis of time, 'Time itself unfolds ... It ceases to become cardinal and becomes ordinal, a pure *order* of time' (Deleuze 1994: 88). It is Shakespeare who gives literary expression to the third synthesis of time when Hamlet says, 'time is out of joint [*cardo*]'. Out of joint, time is purified of any relation to the notions of origin, copy and succession that are associated with cardinal numbers. The third synthesis of time is a pure ordering because it breaks the circle of time, or introduces a *caesura* in time, and in so breaking the circle orders time into a before and after, or a past and future. It is tempting to think of this ordering as an ordinal numbering (1st, 2nd, 3rd ...), but that would not be correct because, temporally speaking, such ordinal numbers are tied to cardinal points, as in the case of a line of kings. The third synthesis of time is a pure ordering because it is devoid of empirical content. Deleuze remarks that 'time is defined ... by a formal and empty order' because it has 'abjured its empirical content' (89). If the second synthesis of time grounds the ordering of events in the passing present, the third synthesis ungrounds the ground of that ordering and re-orders time as a whole. In other words, with the caesura, 'the whole of time is ordered, but it is ordered differently' (Williams 2011: 91). This formal ordering of the third synthesis of time therefore leads Williams to call it 'a speculative claim about time ... as condition for the new' (90). In order for the new to be genuinely new, as opposed to more of the same (the next king), it must stand out as new. That is, the new must be distinguished from the same-old. To be new the new breaks the circle of time and marks the before the new as past and the after the new as future. The caesura that accompanies the appearance of the new, then, touches the whole of time. This is why Deleuze says that the pure and empty form of time 'is defined . . . also by a totality' (1994: 89).

Deleuze's reference to the totality of time indicates that the caesura of the new cannot be the effect of some kind of blow from the outside of time. Accordingly, the last important ingredient of Deleuze's temporal recipe is something borrowed from Nietzsche: eternal return. In Williams's fine formulation, for Deleuze, eternal return is 'defined by the principle that only pure difference or difference in itself returns and never the same' (2011: 115). Deleuze is aware of the possibility of hearing eternal return as circular, and he points out Zarathustra's remark that we simplify the eternal return by relying upon the circle as its image. Yet the image of the circle is not entirely wrongheaded, so long as what circles back in eternal return is not understood as contents, events, identities or representations. Deleuze characterises time as an 'excentric circle', or a circle that is freed of the *cardo* (1994: 91). What returns in the eternal return is difference itself. In other words, the mistake that Zarathustra identifies is that of taking eternal return to mean the recurrence or recapitulation of a discrete passing present. When Deleuze calls forth the eternal return, he means the return of precisely that which differentiates passing presents. He therefore associates eternal return with ungrounding:

> The form of time is there only for the revelation of the formless in the eternal return. The extreme formality is there only for excessive formlessness (Hölderlin's *Unförmliche*). In this manner, the ground has been superseded by a groundlessness, a universal ungrounding which turns upon itself and causes only the yet-to-come to return. (Deleuze 1994: 91)

What returns in the eternal return is that groundlessness that accompanies any ground and allows it to function as ground.

If the question of what returns in the eternal return can be so answered, there remains the question of the meaning of *eternal* in eternal return. In fact, the language of the *eternal* return leaves Deleuze open to the charge that, by appealing to eternity, he undermines (so to speak) his own gesture toward groundlessness. In *The Logic of Sense*, Deleuze himself explicitly characterises the pure and empty form of time as 'the eternal truth of time' (1990: 165). Williams puts his finger on a possible problem with this characterisation when he asks, '*Is eternal return the time of a transcendent God outside the process of the world . . .?*' (2011: 125). The simplest response is that the word eternal here does not mean outside of time or process. As Smith notes, 'time has become the pure and immutable form of everything that moves and changes – not an eternal form, but precisely the form of what is *not* eternal' (2012: 133). Deleuze's adaptation of Nietzsche's eternal return is transcendental rather than transcendent, and it is here especially that the transcendental side of Deleuze's transcendental empiricism becomes apparent. The form of time is not separable from empirical contents but related to the new as its transcendental condition. It is also wrong to think of the caesura as 'taking time'. For the cut in time to itself take time, or be temporally measurable, would require another order of time, or a time of time, according to which the cut-event could be measured. However, the caesura does not work like this. Lampert provides a helpful summary of Deleuze's three syntheses of time that is illuminating here. He says, 'Just as the present *is* all of time in the sense of events in passage, and the past *is* all of time in the sense of events on record, so the future *is* all of time in the sense of events in play' (2006: 55). It is the third synthesis of time that returns all events to play, and in so doing it affects all events immediately. In other words, all processes of becoming are themselves part of a play that is not reducible to any particular move. Deleuze expresses this when he says, 'each event communicates with all others, and they all form one and the same Event . . . the Event for all events' (1990: 64). The eternal return is eternal in the sense that it does not change, and the caesura by which it reorders time does so immediately as the play that puts into play all events for (re)ordering.

The connection of Deleuze's philosophy of time to Deleuze and Guattari's philosophy of history is not as straightforward as it may seem. Deleuze and Guattari remain committed to a notion of universal history, or the notion that all events can be subsumed under a unifying interpretive framework, which is consistent with Deleuze's totalising temporal philosophy. For Hegel, contingency in history is subordinated to the necessity of universal reason. Deleuze and Guattari distinguish their notion of universal history from Hegel's when they say: 'universal history is the history of contingencies, and not the history of necessity' (1983: 140). According to Craig Lundy, Deleuze and Guattari's universal history is universal in the sense that 'the present forms a heterogeneous continuity with the past, and it is this continuity *as a whole* that continuously undergoes change' (2016: 73). Deleuze and Guattari see history not only as a series of contingent events retrospectively posited by the present, but as a totality of relations that are contingent everywhere all the time. For Lundy, this 'continual contingency' is enough to reconcile the appearance of the new with a history that is genuinely universal (71). Yet a familiar problem arises again. If the connection between the living present and the pure past devolves into one of representation and its ground in Deleuze's philosophy of time, Deleuze and Guattari's philosophy of history similarly faces the problem that even a continually contingent history is not separable enough from the present's retrospectivity without some further, fracturing element.

Whether history is universal or not, time is not reducible to history, and while it may encompass all relations between events, history cannot for all that account for the appearance of new events. Deleuze and Guattari themselves ask rhetorically, 'How could something come from history?' (1994: 96). They deploy the language of becoming to contrast the new with historical events. As Deleuze says in a 1990 interview, 'What history grasps in the event is the way it's actualized in particular circumstances; the event's becoming is beyond the scope of history' (1995: 170). It may seem that the third synthesis of time would function here much as it does for the other two syntheses of time, with the difference that now the pure past and the living present are layered over by the particular circumstances of historical events. However, Deleuze and Guattari instead turn to Nietzsche's notion of the untimely (*unzeitgemäss*) for an explanation of the appearance of the new. Where Nietzsche diagnoses history as it was practised in his time as working against life, and therefore advocates untimeliness, or acting counter to the time of this excessive historical sense, Deleuze and Guattari make untimeliness a crucial element of becoming in relation to history. Thus Deleuze says, 'history amounts only to the set of preconditions, however recent, that one leaves behind in order to . . . create something new. This is precisely what Nietzsche calls the Untimely' (171). Yet the historical past is not simply erased in becoming. Here eternal return tacitly returns in connection to becoming. In *Difference and Repetition*, Deleuze immediately moves from his discussion of the third synthesis of time to a discussion of history and historical figures. He notes: 'Historical actors or agents can create only on condition that they identify themselves with figures from the past' (1994: 91). This is a jarring formulation given Deleuze's own denial that what returns in the eternal return is 'the identical, the similar, and the equal, in so far as these constitute the forms of indifference' (243). However, the identification that Deleuze has in mind here is not indifferent but precisely different. That is, historical agents create by taking on historical roles that they re-write through re-playing. As Lampert puts the point, 'The earlier event has to be made earlier by the force of its successor's attempt to resist identifying with it' (2006: 94). It is not only that the historical agent acts against the past, but that the historical agent brings a past event into play again as past event. Thus 'historical transition goes beyond the limits of what it surpasses by introducing a new sense of history along with a new social order' (123). To put past events in play again is not to inaugurate a free-for-all that destroys the past, but to free past events for re-grounding or re-ordering. Lundy claims, 'if the past is contingent then this is ... because it itself continues to be contingent through its continual participation in the emerging whole that is reality' (2016: 74). The untimely is the force through which the past, as contingent, continues to participate in the emerging whole that is reality. Untimeliness revitalises historical relations and makes them circulate in new ways.

Foucault's Histories of the Present

Unzeitgemäss is usually translated into French as *inactuel*. It would therefore appear to be opposed to *actuel*, or the present or current. Thus it would seem that untimeliness is opposed to one of the abiding aims of Foucault's work: to write a 'history of the present' (Foucault 1995: 31).[2] Yet, as Deleuze and Guattari point out, Foucault's interest in the present is not an interest in idly describing an age or a passing present, and his interest is even less a performance of retrospectivity in which the past is interpreted according to the present. What writing a history of the present means is to diagnose what we are already ceasing to be in order to invent new forms of life (Deleuze and Guattari 1994: 112–13). The question, 'What are we now?' is the question, 'What may we become?' For Deleuze and Guattari, then, Foucault is as untimely a thinker as Nietzsche, and his relationship to history parallels Nietzsche's. This is borne out in Foucault's own resistance to totalising philosophies of history à la Hegel's. Speaking of himself and Foucault, Deleuze says in one interview, 'We weren't looking for origins, even lost or deleted ones, but setting out to catch things where they were at work, in the middle, breaking things open, breaking words open. We weren't looking for something timeless, not even the timelessness of time, but for new things being formed, the emergence of what Foucault calls "actuality"' (1995: 86). As we have seen, Deleuze's philosophy of time does in fact appeal to a certain timelessness of time insofar as the third synthesis of time is the form of change that does not change. Even Deleuze and Guattari's philosophy of history and becoming, in its appeal to Deleuze's metaphysical reading of the eternal return as the force behind untimeliness, tends toward abstraction. Foucault's search for new things being formed leads him away from time as either abstraction or ideal form and into history as the site of the emergence of new forms of life.

Foucault's most sustained discussion of time as such appears in his minor thesis, *Introduction to Kant's* Anthropology. In Kant's *Anthropology from a Pragmatic Point of View* Foucault sees a solution to a problem that Deleuze's philosophy of time also solves. That is the problem, which emerges from Kant's critical works, of associating synthesis with the activity of a subject while associating passivity with mere receptivity. According to Foucault, 'the time of the Anthropology is assured by a dispersion which cannot be contained, for it is no longer that of the given and passive sensibility; we are dealing with a dispersion of the synthetic activity with regard to itself – dispersion with which it can "Play" as it were' (2008: 89). On Foucault's reading, Kant's *Anthropology* dissociates synthetic activity and the unity of a subject, so that synthesis is itself fractured. Foucault continues, 'The synthetic activity is not contemporaneous with itself in the organization of multiplicity; it never fails to follow on from itself, thus laying itself open to error, and all the other unsettling slippages' (89). In other words, in Kant's *Anthropology* the subject is returned to time and time seems to fracture the subject yet again, which is what time does in Deleuze as well.

However, even Kant's *Anthropology* does not escape what Foucault identifies as a major problem with transcendental philosophy in general, which in *The Order of Things* he comes to call the analytic of finitude. By making *anthropos* the object of his later study, Kant maintains the link between philosophy and subjectivity. The re-opening of the fracture in subjectivity is filled, after Kant's *Anthropology*, with a search for the ground of humanity's finitude that remains always out of reach. Foucault says, 'all knowledge of man is presented as either dialecticized (*dialectisée*) from the start or fully dialecticizable (*dialectisable*) – as always invested with a meaning which has to do with the return to the origin, to the authentic, to the founding activity, to the reason why there is meaning in the world' (Foucault 2008: 123). From one side, in Kant's *Anthropology*, and from the other side, in Kant's critical works, 'man appears in his ambiguous position as an object of knowledge and as a subject that knows' (Foucault 1994: 312). It is this ambiguity that transcendental philosophy finds untenable and tries to resolve into a unity. Thus, rather than freeing philosophy for the new and freeing thought for play in its temporal dispersion, the reintroduction of the fracture in the subject in Kant's *Anthropology* sends thought on an endless search for an elusive ground.

Foucault sees Nietzsche as pointing a way out of this anthropological circle. In *History of Madness* he takes a broadly Nietzschean approach to history, which is to say that he writes against the transcendental, historical sensibility that seeks unity in history. Foucault argues that reason itself is articulated against the background of unreason. Ascendant reason comes to isolate unreason within itself as madness, but it cannot fully conquer this necessary, threatening double that unpredictably erupts into history and contests the stability of its development. It is transcendental philosophy and the philosophy of history that grows out of it that Foucault has in mind when he says, 'The plenitude of history is only possible in the space . . . of all the words without language that appear to anyone who lends an ear, as a dull sound from beneath history, the obstinate murmur of a language talking *to itself*' (2006: xxxi). His claim is that reason, with the communication and recognition that accompany it, needs to define itself against what it is not. Reasonable language therefore demarcates itself and excludes from itself whatever is left over, which becomes not only not reason but not even language. If time is reason's form of determination, and history is a condition of possibility of recognition, both time and history are also secondary to the cut by which reason inaugurates itself as opposed to unreason. Therefore Foucault says, '*The necessity of madness* throughout the history of the West is linked to that decisive action that extracts a significant language from the background noise and its continuous monotony, a language which is transmitted and culminates in time; it is, in short, linked to *the possibility of history*' (xxxii). His history of madness is the history of reason's ongoing relation to that which it is not. It is the history of reason's attempt to engulf unreason by making it an object of knowledge and fold it into the natural history of *anthropos*. Madness is not unreason, or rather madness is unreason transformed into a knowable, treatable pathology. For all that, unreason remains at the limit of reason, and continues to contest rational history's necessity and inevitability. As Foucault says, 'the experience of unreason, such as is evident in Hölderlin, Nerval, and Nietzsche, always leads back to the roots of time – unreason thereby becoming the untimely (*contretemps*) within the world *par excellence*' (363). Foucault's *History of Madness* can only be a history of madness, and not a history of unreason, because unreason has no history. What a history of reason's relation to unreason can do is show, at least, that a particular human science, psychology, is not a route to the elusive unity of the subject-object that is *anthropos*. At most it shows the contingency and arbitrariness of the very rationality, along with its time and history, that presents itself as necessary.

These achievements are chiefly negative, and they call for a reconsideration of history as it is practised. The question becomes, if hope for the unity that reason's time promises has to be given up, what becomes of time and history? Foucault's response to this question is to develop his archaeology, which takes discontinuity as its theme and studies discontinuous modes of knowing, or 'epistemic formations', that engender their own temporalities. In Foucault's words, 'One of the most essential features of the new history is probably this displacement of the discontinuous: its transference from the obstacle to the work itself; its integration into the discourse of the historian, where it no longer plays the role of an external condition that must be reduced, but that of a working concept' (2010: 9). Where Kant's *Anthropology* fails to deliver on the promise of freeing thought for the new, archaeology may succeed by dissociating time and subjectivity and hewing closely to time's uncontained dispersion. The work of the archaeologist is to look at statements as they appear and isolate those rules that allow them to appear, to make sense as knowledge claims, and to relate to other statements. In other words, to do archaeology is 'to deal with a group of verbal performances at the level of the statements and of the form of positivity that characterizes them' (125). The form of positivity that allows statements to emerge does not find its ground somewhere beyond itself. As Foucault says, 'The time of discourse is not the translation, in a visible chronology, of the obscure time of thought' (122). Rather, forms of positivity and the statements that they condition are immanent to each other.

To account for the grounding function of what is ultimately ground-less, and to explain the discontinuities that separate epistemic formations, Foucault historicises the *a priori*. Where a formal *a priori* is one 'whose jurisdiction extends without contingence', the historical *a priori* functions only in a limited capacity, and only over a certain domain of statements (Foucault 2010: 128). It is historical in one sense because it is intimately connected to what is actually said and known, not to what is only possibly said or known. In fact, it is more empirical than transcendental, but Foucault retains the language of the *a priori* to explain what allows statements to appear with a regularity that relates them and makes them mutually intelligible. The historical *a priori* is historical in the further sense that it is transformable. According to Foucault,

> these rules (making up an historical *a priori*) are not imposed from the outside on the elements that they relate together; they are caught up in the very things that they connect; and if they are not modified with the least of them, they modify them, and are transformed with them into certain decisive thresholds. The *a priori* of positivities is not only the system of a temporal dispersion; it is itself a transformable group. (Foucault 2010: 127)

There are in fact two levels of temporality at play here. On one level, there is the temporality of the appearance of statements that contribute to an epistemic formation. On another level, there is the temporality of the rules that govern those statements. Not every statement inaugurates a new historical *a priori*, but statements bend and distort the rules of what may be said as they accumulate, until statements produced according to one iteration of the historical *a priori* are no longer intelligible to statements produced according to a different iteration. In fact, Foucault refers to plural historical *a prioris*. What distinguishes his notion of history from Hegelian universal history is both that there is no dialectic in Foucault, only subtle transformations of relations between statements that affect neighbouring relations, and that events are *not* all contained in a single context susceptible to a unifying interpretive framework. History in Foucault is not universal. There is not yet a third level of time that would unite incommensurable historical *a prioris*.

Foucault's discussion of the archive makes this last point plain. The archive is the most general discursive feature that Foucault discusses in *The Archaeology of Knowledge*. In that book, he spells out a certain hierarchy of generality that extends from statements to discursive formations to *epistemes*. The term *episteme* refers to the relations that give rise to formal sciences. The archive is more general still because it is that collected or sedimented background out of which any *episteme* can emerge. Foucault describes the archive as 'a complex volume, in which heterogeneous regions are differentiated or deployed, in accordance with specific rules or practices that cannot be superposed' (2010: 128). The materiality of the archive has often been noted, but it is more than a collection of records. It is not something inert like the 'library of all libraries', but a living system that is the invisible underside of those statements that actually appear (130). Foucault distinguishes between the archive, the corpus and language. The corpus is that inert collection of what has been said. Language governs possible sentences that, while grammatically correct, may not function as statements in a particular discourse. The archive lies between the corpus and language as that which makes what is said neither dead nor disconnected. Lynne Huffer characterises the archive as 'the abstract and unseen operating system Foucault describes . . . as an episteme's condition of intelligibility' (2020: 7). Yet the archive is more like the computer code that flows into the motherboard of words, powered by the electricity of language, on which the operating system of the historical *a priori* runs to organise information. It is that unsaid system of relations out of which the historical *a priori* extracts rules that in turn make statements intelligible. Perhaps the best technological metaphor for how the historical *a priori* and the archive work together is that of machine learning. As discourse proliferates and statements build up an archive, the historical *a priori* refines its rules to retain certain statements and exclude others. The archive thus allows for discursive transformation and discontinuity, or the new, rather than reducing all that is said to one grand discourse. Foucault says 'it is that which differentiates discourses in their multiple existence and specifies them in their own duration' (2010: 129).

The archive generates incommensurable historical *a prioris*, which in turn give rise to overlapping discourses which nonetheless do not share the same duration. Since archaeology displaces continuous history and the subjectivity and philosophies of experience that undergird continuous history, history as a general term no longer makes sense except as 'a multiplicity of time spans that entangle and envelop one another' (Foucault 1998: 430). In fact, Foucault suggests that the archive itself, however general, is multiple. As a ground, the archive is something like a floating foundation or a tectonic plate, which is to say it is itself unstable and itself roiled by the transformations that it enables. From the perspective of the present, the ground is shifting under our feet, as it is always shifting, but such that, while we may be able to more or less trace previous shifts, we cannot predict the specific character of shifts that are happening now, just as nobody can predict when and where an earthquake will happen or how powerful it will be. Hence Foucault says: 'it is not possible for us to describe our own archive, since it is from within these rules that we speak' (2010: 130). The rules that allow us to speak as we do are being rewritten as we speak, and because we are speaking. As diagnostician of the present, the archaeologist will study the archive in its close proximity to us and isolate those rules that mark us in our difference from what we can no longer say.

Deleuze characterises Foucault's discontinuous history as a Markov process, a random process in which only the current state of a system in flux can be used to assign the probability of what the next state will be (Deleuze 1988: 86). This is an apt characterisation, and it points to the difference between Deleuze and Foucault concerning time and history. Markov processes do not have a memory, so while on the one hand it might be said that the discontinuities that archaeology identifies order time into a before and after, or that the archive is like the event for all events, it is on the other hand true that the archive is not a totality, and that once-active relations can become inert, forgotten or put out of play as the archive transforms. One of Foucault's main purposes in writing *The Archaeology of Knowledge* was to show how sciences both ground themselves and transform. He therefore focuses on a specific type of verbal or linguistic performance that is not merely casual. The archive is the system of relations between these types of performances – statements – that operate in one or another scientific discourse. Archival transformation does not affect all verbal performances, which are governed by other rules that Foucault does not excavate. Thus, as epistemically jarring as discursive transformations may be, they do not inaugurate a total reordering of experience – other continuities surrounding the discourses in question may persist. Of course, Foucault's work goes on to cover non-discursive relations and their production of our experience, as well as the self's relation to the self and its potential to modify our experience, and an emerging consensus in Foucault scholarship is that the archaeological model of transformation is not so much abandoned as modified or extended in Foucault's later work (see for example Thompson 2016). Yet even the broader transformation of experience is in Foucault a painstaking transformation that calls for granular attention to multiple processes. The appearance of the new is not, in Foucault, a decisive cut that affects everything, everywhere, all at once. Lastly, Foucault is clear that even what he is able to say about the archive depends on 'the archive system that makes it possible today to speak of the archive in general' (2010: 130). Perhaps tomorrow one will no longer be able to speak of the archive. That is, even Foucault's philosophy of history is contingent as philosophy. By contrast, because he speaks of the pure and empty form of time that does not change, and because he and Guattari rely on a metaphysical interpretation of Nietzsche's eternal return to explain historical change, Deleuze speaks from within the present about the present, or from within becoming about the becoming that is becoming, at least on these points. This may be enough, though, to threaten Deleuze's edifice of becoming for the simple reason that transcendental or metaphysical explanation bears with it the residue of homogeneous continuity that Deleuze otherwise wishes to reject.

Conclusion: An Untimely Symmetry

Does 'untimely' describe any god better than Hermes? Hermes with his caduceus, patron of outlaws, herald of the dead? In their sometimes mirroring philosophies of time, history and the new, may we not see Deleuze and Foucault as the two snakes on Hermes' staff? On one side a philosophy of time that gives way to a philosophy of becoming. On the other side a philosophy of history that departs from time's formalisation.

Untimeliness draws them together into a symmetry. Both thinkers resist the sedimented, the continuous, the transcendent and the eternal. Both seek the new, and grasp novelty's complicated, fractured relation to time. Deleuze works from a formal account of time down to the point where its very form becomes the possibility of its formlessness. Foucault adherence to the practice of discourse in its positivity points out the malleability of that which grounds our experience. They do not quite meet in the middle. Deleuze remains committed to metaphysics, Foucault to diagnosis. Yet reading Deleuze and Foucault together reveals the extent to which each thinker is invisible in the other's work. What is most interesting is not so much who has the explanatory, theoretical or practical advantage, but how reading them now might spur our becoming.

Notes

1. For two nice synopses of the relationship between Deleuze and Foucault, see Nicolae Morar, Thomas Nail and Daniel W. Smith, 'Introduction: Between Deleuze and Foucault', and François Dose, 'Deleuze and Foucault: A Philosophical Friendship', in Morar et al. (eds) 2016.
2. This well-known quote from *Discipline and Punish* is a translation of the French *l'histoire du présent*. Foucault sometimes seems to conflate *actualité* and *présent*, as when he says in a 1981 interview that one task of philosophy is to 's'interroger sur ce que nous sommes dans notre présent et dans notre actualité' (Berten 1988: 10). However, Deleuze and Guattari interpret him as differentiating between *présent* and *actualité* in *L'archeologie du Savoir*, as when he says, 'L'analyse de l'archive comporte donc une région privilégiée: à la fois proche de nous, mais différente de notre actualité, c'est la bordure du temps qui entoure notre present' (Foucault 1969: 172). On the basis of this passage Deleuze and Guattari claim that *actualité* corresponds to Nietzsche's untimely while *présent* refers to what we are, and therefore what we are in the process of no longer being.

References

Bell, J. A. and C. Colebrook, eds. (2009), *Deleuze and History*, Edinburgh: Edinburgh University Press.

Berten, A. (1988), 'Entretien avec Michel Foucault', *Les cahiers du GRIF*, 37–38: 8–20.

Deleuze, G. (1983), *Nietzsche and Philosophy*, trans. Hugh Tomlinson, New York: Columbia University Press.

Deleuze, G. (1988), *Foucault*, trans. Sean Hand, Minneapolis: University of Minnesota Press.

Deleuze, G. (1990), *The Logic of Sense*, trans. Mark Lester and Charles Stivale, New York: Columbia University Press.

Deleuze, G. (1994), *Difference and Repetition*, trans. Paul Patton, New York: Columbia University Press.

Deleuze, G. (1995), *Negotiations: 1972–1990*, trans. Martin Joughin, New York: Columbia University Press.

Deleuze, G. and C. Parnet (2007), *Dialogues II*, trans. Hugh Tomlinson and Barbara Habberjam, New York: Columbia University Press.

Deleuze, G. and F. Guattari (1983), *Anti-Oedipus*, trans. Robert Hurley, Mark Seem and Helen R. Lane, Minneapolis: University of Minnesota.

Deleuze, G. and F. Guattari (1994), *What Is Philosophy?*, trans. Hugh Tomlinson and Graham Burchell, New York: Columbia University Press.

Foucault, M. (1969), *L'Archéologie du savoir*, Paris: Gallimard.

Foucault, M. (1994), *The Order of Things: An Archaeology of the Human Sciences*, New York: Vintage Books.

Foucault, M. (1995), *Discipline and Punish*, trans. Alan Sheridan, New York: Vintage Books.

Foucault, M. (1998), *Aesthetics, Method, and Epistemology: The Essential Works of Michel Foucault, 1954–1984*, trans. Robert Hurley and others, New York: The New Press.

Foucault, M. (2006), *History of Madness*, trans. Jonathan Murphy and Jean Khalfa, New York: Routledge.

Foucault, M. (2008), *Introduction to Kant's* Anthropology, trans. Roberto Nigro and Kate Briggs, Los Angeles: Semiotext(e).

Foucault, M. (2010), *The Archaeology of Knowledge*, trans. A. M. Sheridan Smith, New York: Vintage Books.

Huffer, L. (2020), *Foucault's Strange Eros*, New York: Columbia University Press.

Lampert, J. (2006), *Deleuze and Guattari's Philosophy of History*, New York: Continuum.

Lundy, C. (2016), 'The Necessity and Contingency of Universal History: Deleuze and Guattari contra Hegel', *Journal of the Philosophy of History*, 10: 51–75.

Morar, N., T. Nail and D. W. Smith, eds. (2016), *Between Deleuze and Foucault*, Edinburgh: Edinburgh University Press.

Nietzsche, F. (1997), *Untimely Meditations*, trans. R. J. Hollingdale, Cambridge: Cambridge University Press.

Smith, D. W. (2012), *Essays on Deleuze*, Edinburgh: Edinburgh University Press.

Thompson, K. (2016), 'From the Historical A Priori to the Dispositif: Foucault, the Phenomenological Legacy, and the Problem of Transcendental Genesis', *Continental Philosophy Review*, 49: 41–54.

Williams, J. (2011), *Gilles Deleuze's Philosophy of Time: A Critical Introduction and Guide*, Edinburgh: Edinburgh University Press.

Chapter 6

Kant, Merleau-Ponty, Deleuze and the Constitution of Experience

Henry Somers-Hall

In this chapter, I want to explore the relationship between Kant's account of the constitution of experience and the accounts developed by Merleau-Ponty and Deleuze. Merleau-Ponty and Deleuze both hold ambivalent attitudes toward Kant's account of how experience is to be understood. It is Kant who places synthesis at the centre of the constitution of the world, and who discovers the concept of a transcendental illusion, a concept central to the thought of both Merleau-Ponty and Deleuze.[1] Kant holds that basic ontological concepts such as that of an object are simply ways of organising experience, rather than fundamental structures given in space and time. Furthermore, Kant breaks with the metaphysical tradition in recognising that time itself has a positive existence outside of categorial thought.[2] 'Time is not a discursive, or what is called a general concept, but a pure form of sensible intuition' (Kant 1929: A32). Both Merleau-Ponty and Deleuze argue, however, that Kant leaves unexamined the nature of the world which is to be explained through the transcendental idealist method. Similarly, both seek to replace the notion of synthesis as a process that takes place from nowhere with one that unfolds within the temporality of the world. Perhaps Merleau-Ponty expresses this most clearly when he writes that:

> We must make this notion of the world, which guides the whole transcendental deduction of Kant, though Kant does not tell us its provenance, more explicit. 'If a world is to be possible', he says sometimes, as if he were thinking before the origin of the world, as if he were assisting at its genesis and could pose its *a priori* conditions. In fact, as Kant himself said profoundly, we can only think the world because we have already experienced it; it is through this experience that we have the idea of being, and it is through this experience that the words 'rational' and 'real' receive a meaning simultaneously. (Merleau-Ponty 1964: 16)

Now, there are a number of key claims in this passage that will be central to both Deleuze and Merleau-Ponty's readings of Kant. First, we can note that Merleau-Ponty makes a distinction here between thinking and experience. As we shall see, this distinction introduces two different ways of understanding what it is for something to have a determination, and has affinities with Deleuze's own distinction between representation and intensity. Second, Merleau-Ponty here implies that Kant presupposes experience, but that he does not provide a proper analysis of it. In Deleuze too, we shall find that for every synthesis Kant proposes, Deleuze will argue that there is a passive synthesis that makes it possible. Third, Kant illicitly assumes that the kind of determination that we find in thinking or representation is prior to the genesis of the world, and is responsible for it. Once again, this will be disputed by both Deleuze and Merleau-Ponty, and here we can find an unlikely parallel between Deleuze's claim of a continuing 'psychologism' (1994: 135) in the second edition of the *Critique of Pure Reason* and Merleau-Ponty's claim that Kant mischaracterises experience as 'mutilated thought' (1968: 35) in the *Critique*. For Deleuze, psychologism relates to a model of the subject already overrun by representation, and Merleau-Ponty's mutilated thought is one that similarly understands experience from the point of view of the categories of judgement.

I want to begin by looking at Kant's account of synthesis in the first *Critique*. We will focus on the transcendental deduction, but the aim will be to look at what Kant takes synthesis to be. We will then explore how this ties in to his account of determination as he sets it out in the transcendental ideal, since it is this account that Deleuze takes up explicitly. Following that, we will turn to Deleuze and Merleau-Ponty's accounts of synthesis. I will argue that Merleau-Ponty's influence on Deleuze's account of synthesis is significant, despite the paucity of explicit references to Merleau-Ponty in most of Deleuze's work. We will see how Deleuze's account of determination as a lightning flash can be understood in both Deleuzian and Merleau-Pontian terms. Having seen how Deleuze and Merleau-Ponty's accounts of determination differ from Kant's, we will then explore how this difference in determination leads both philosophers to a radically different notion of synthesis.

Kant on Synthesis and Determination

Given Kant's claim that time is not conceptual, his account of synthesis is integral to his project. For pre-Kantian philosophers, a key problem was justifying the correspondence of our concepts to objects in the world. Kant solves this problem but in turn opens up a novel problem of how concepts are to be related to our intuition of time, given their difference from each other. The heart of Kant's solution to this problem is found in the *Critique*'s transcendental deduction, where he shows the role of synthesis in bridging the gap between the faculties. Now, the essential move Kant makes in the *Critique* is to argue that rather than objects making representations possible, representations make objects possible. In order to make this move, Kant asks what concepts allow us to understand the world in terms of objects. The key concept that makes this understanding possible is the concept of an object itself: 'Now all experience does indeed contain, in addition to the intuition of the senses through which something is given, a *concept* of an object as being thereby given, that is to say, as appearing. Concepts of objects in general thus underlie all empirical knowledge as its *a priori* conditions' (Kant 1929: A93/B126). Since the concept of an object is not given in intuition, the aim of the deduction becomes to show how we are able to understand experience in terms of objects rather than simply the flux of intuition. Ultimately, Kant's claim will be that we can only understand experience as experience of a world of objects insofar as we see the subject as introducing the concept of an object to experience, and this in turn is only possible through the application of the categories of the understanding to the manifold of intuition.

Kant substantially rewrites the transcendental deduction between the first and second editions of the *Critique*, but what is central to both editions is the notion of synthesis. In the deduction in the second edition, Kant begins with the claim that 'It must be possible for the "I think" to accompany all my representations; for otherwise something would be represented in me which could not be thought at all, and that is equivalent to saying that the representation would be impossible, or at least would be nothing to me' (1929: B132). Without being able to see all representations as mine, we would just have a series of fragmented impressions with no unity. Kant notes that even if representations are already united, then we still require a moment of synthesis here to recognise the unity within representations. Kant's claim is that this unity of apperception, the 'I think', is analytic, and presupposes a prior synthetic unity that is actually responsible for unifying representations. Since this transcendental unity is what makes experience possible, it itself falls outside of experience, and therefore cannot be determined in the way we determine empirical phenomena. It is this synthetic activity that allows us to understand the subject as unified:

That relation comes about, not simply through my accompanying each representation with consciousness, but only in so far as I *conjoin* one representation with another, and am conscious of the synthesis of them. Only in so far, therefore, as I can unite a manifold of given representations in *one consciousness*, is it possible for me to represent to myself the *identity of the consciousness in [i.e. throughout] these representations*. In other words, the *analytic* unity of apperception is possible only under the presupposition of a certain *synthetic* unity. (Kant 1929: B133)

What allows us to relate these representations together in one consciousness is that these representations are understood as representations of an object. The object therefore provides a point of reference to allows us to refer the manifold given by intuition to a point of unity. Seeing representations as referring to an object is also a requirement for being able to distinguish representations from the self. Just as the subject is not given in experience, so the transcendental object is simply a way of organising what is given in experience, and hence has to be understood as 'something in general = x' (Kant 1929: A104).

Understanding what Kant takes synthesis to be is complicated by the side-lining of his account of the three syntheses in the second edition of the *Critique*, and by the identification in that edition of the imagination and the understanding. For our purposes, it is important to note that Kant's general definition of synthesis is as 'the act of putting different representations together, and of grasping what is manifold in them in one [act of] knowledge' (1929: A77/B103). In the first edition of the *Critique of Pure Reason*, and more briefly in the second, Kant gives an account of experience in terms of synthesis. This account, which Kant labels a subjective deduction, involves three syntheses that together organise intuition and relate it to the categories. First, in what he calls the synthesis of apprehension in intuition, Kant claims we need to take what is given as an indeterminate intuition of time, and organise it into both individual elements and a unity of these elements as a sequence. 'Every intuition contains in itself a manifold which can be represented as a manifold only insofar as the mind distinguishes the time in the sequence of one impression upon another' (A99). This synthesis which creates the manifold is followed by a second synthesis, the synthesis of reproduction in imagination, which holds that if experience is to be understood as ordered – as, for example, we find in the empiricist claims that laws of association can make sense of experience – then appearances must be 'actually subject to such a rule' (A100). Similarly, if we are to draw a line, we need to be able to relate not just present impressions, but also prior impressions in order to be conscious of a sequence. Finally, Kant's account of the third synthesis holds that in order to understand a sequence as a whole, we do not need to simply have the consciousness of the elements themselves, but require a consciousness that the elements relate together into a unity. Such a unity of a manifold of representations under a generic identity is a conceptual unity, and such a conceptual unity requires consciousness of the identity of the various elements that make it up. This unity is in turn supplied by relating all representations to the transcendental object, and this in turn relies on synthesising representations according to the categories, which are transcendental forms of the functions of judgement, which we use to make logical claims.

This account raises a number of questions about the nature of the syntheses involved. As we have seen, Kant defines synthesis at one point as 'the act of putting different representations together, and of grasping what is manifold in them in one [act of] knowledge' (1929: A77/B103). How are we to understand this in terms of determination? When we look at the third synthesis, which is explicitly conceptual, we can note that since it is categorial, it has its roots in the way in which we determine concepts in judgement. Kant is explicit, for instance, in noting that it is the same faculty at work in unifying representations into a judgement and unifying representations into objects. As such, it operates by attributing properties to objects. We will return to the implications of this in a moment, but first, let's consider the first and second syntheses. In the A deduction, these two syntheses are attributed to the imagination, but by the time we reach the B deduction all synthesis is seen as a product of the understanding:

> all combination – be we conscious of it or not, be it a combination of the manifold of intuition, empirical or non-empirical, or of various concepts – is an act of the understanding. To this act the general title 'synthesis' may be assigned, as indicating that we cannot represent to ourselves anything as combined in the object which we have not ourselves previously combined. (Kant 1929: B130)

Kant argues that '[i]t is one and the same spontaneity, which in the one case, under the title of imagination, and in the other case, under the title of understanding, brings combination into the manifold of intuition' (1929: B162n). The situation is more complicated in the A deduction, though Longuenesse suggests that the imagination should be taken in the A deduction simply as a non-reflective operation of synthesis according to rules provided by the understanding, in contrast to the reflective operation of the understanding proper.[3] Regardless of whether we accept Longuenesse's account here, we can note that Kant's account of the imagination sees it as operating in terms of the combination of determinate representations into unities. As such, whichever faculty is responsible for the various syntheses of experience, it fulfils the definition that Kant adopts, namely of 'putting different representations together, and of grasping what is manifold in them in one [act of] knowledge' (A77/B103).

If synthesis involves conceptual determination, then what does Kant take conceptual determination to involve? Kant's claim is that in order to be able to understand the world in conceptual terms, we need to be able to assume that phenomena are so constituted that for any property of an object, it either holds of that object or does not. Without this claim, we won't know when we pose a question about the nature of an object in the world whether an answer could, even in principle, be given. The basis for this principle is the notion of opposition:

> The proposition, *everything which exists is completely determined*, does not mean only that one of every pair of *given* contradictory predicates, but that one of every [pair of] *possible* predicates, must always belong to it. In terms of this proposition the predicates are not merely compared with one another logically, but the thing itself is compared, in transcendental fashion, with the sum of all possible predicates. (Kant 1929: A573/B601)

Kant combines this with a further claim that, for transcendental logic, one of the opposed predicates must be understood as primary, and one has to be understood as a limitation of it through the introduction of a negation:

> If, therefore, reason employs in the complete determination of things a transcendental substrate that contains, as it were, the whole store of material from which all possible predicates of things must be taken, this substrate cannot be anything else than the idea of an *omnitudo realitatis*. All true negations are nothing but limitations – a title which would be inapplicable, were they not thus based up on the unlimited, that is, upon 'the All'. (Kant 1929: A575–6/B603–4)

Now, we can note that for Kant this notion of complete determination is a transcendental idea, which means that we need to assume it in order for reason to investigate the world (if we do not assume that objects are completely determined, then the law of excluded middle would not hold, since it would be possible for an object to not have a particular determination or its negation), but that its truth goes beyond the limits of possible experience. As such, we can see that Kant's account of the synthesis of experience draws together two claims here. First that at heart all synthesis operates in categorial or at least quasi-categorial terms, and second that such a mode of synthesis is completely determining of the nature of objects we find in the world.

Deleuze and Merleau-Ponty on Symmetrical Synthesis

For Kant, therefore, experience is constituted through the synthesis of representations into unities on a model that is analogous to the synthesis of representations into a judgement. Now, at the heart of the critique of Kant developed by both Merleau-Ponty and Deleuze is the claim that Kant illegitimately holds that all synthesis needs to be understood in these terms – as operating on a manifold of discrete moments in order to constitute it as a unity open to discursive thought. For Merleau-Ponty, Kant understands synthesis 'in a style that is not the sole possible one' (1968: 32), illegitimately equating synthesis with categorial synthesis, and hence presupposing a vision of the world as fully amenable to judgement. Similarly, Deleuze takes the view that 'representation is the site of a transcendental illusion' (1994: 265), this illusion being that all determination operates in terms of opposition and limitation. For both, therefore, at the heart of their criticism is the claim that Kant extends judgement beyond its legitimate domain of operation, thereby falsifying his account of the genesis by forcing it into a juridical account. For the rest of this chapter, I want to look at how Merleau-Ponty and Deleuze respond to this account of synthesis. In the present section, I will consider their accounts of the traditional model of synthesis before turning to their alternative accounts in the next section. As we shall see, both see the model of synthesis as a surface effect of a deeper process.

There is a passage in *Difference and Repetition* that offers up both a Deleuzian and a Merleau-Pontian reading. What is shared by both these readings is an attempt to develop a new account of synthesis and determination that moves beyond our traditional understanding of them. What Deleuze is addressing here is the traditional model of determination that sees it as operating in terms of a relationship between elements that share the same nature, and that are each fully determinate. Deleuze here opposes this model to an account of determination that sees determinations as emerging against a background that escapes from the structure of determination. It is this claim, and the way it plays out in relation to Kant's transcendental deduction, that I want to explore. I will present the passage here, then we will look at how these two readings tie into Deleuze and Merleau-Ponty's work:

Difference is the state in which one can speak of determination as such. The difference 'between' two things is only empirical, and the corresponding determinations are only extrinsic. However, instead of something distinguished from something else, imagine something which distinguishes itself – and yet that from which it distinguishes itself does not distinguish itself from it. Lightning, for example, distinguishes itself from the black sky but must also trail it behind, as though it were distinguishing itself from that which does not distinguish itself from it. It is as if the ground rose to the surface, without ceasing to be ground. There is cruelty, even monstrosity, on both sides of this struggle against an elusive adversary, in which the distinguished opposes something which cannot distinguish itself from it but continues to espouse that which divorces it. Difference is this state in which determination takes the form of unilateral distinction. We must therefore say that difference is made, or makes itself, as in the expression 'make the difference'. (Deleuze 1994: 28)

What does it mean here to talk about a unilateral distinction? Normally, we understand determination in terms of elements that are all equally determinate, or at least are determined equally through their interaction. We see this in terms of the difference between things, as Deleuze puts it. For Deleuze, Merleau-Ponty, and for Kant, the archetypal model of this account of determination is judging. Deleuze and Merleau-Ponty both understand this in terms of an *extensive* account of relations,[4] where we take extensity to be the kind of model of space found in Euclidean geometry, which is so central to Kant's model of space in the *Critique of Pure Reason*. Deleuze names an account of the world that operates in these terms a sedentary distribution.[5] In characterising how determination operates in extensity, he explicitly takes up the two functions of limitation and opposition.[6] We need to bear in mind that Deleuze's concepts often have multiple sources, but we can note that one aspect of extensive determination is the model of determination found in Kant's thought. Deleuze defines it as follows:

We must first of all distinguish a type of distribution which implies a dividing up of that which is distributed: it is a matter of dividing up the distributed as such. It is here that in judgement the rules of analogy are all-powerful. In so far as common sense and good sense are qualities of judgement, these are presented as principles of division which declare themselves the best distributed. A distribution of this type proceeds by fixed and proportional determinations which may be assimilated to 'properties' or limited territories within representation. (Deleuze 1994: 36)

Merleau-Ponty foreshadows Deleuze's notion of a sedentary distribution with what he calls 'objective thought', which he defines as 'thought applied to the universe and not to phenomena' (2012: 50). Here too, we have the assumption that our basic categories of understanding involve an extensive view of the world, and rely on judgement and conceptual determination. What are the basic characteristics of the sedentary model, or the model of objective thought?

First, we can note that both objective thought and the sedentary distribution deal with the existence of a field of 'ready-made things' (Merleau-Ponty 2012: 99). As Deleuze similarly puts it, 'extensity does not account for the individuations which occur within it' (1994: 229). In effect, for Kant, synthesis involves taking elements that already exist, and synthesising them into unities. This allows us to see the world as 'an invariable system of relations to which every existing thing is subjected if it is to be known . . . like a crystal cube, where all possible presentations can be conceived by its law of construction and that allows its hidden sides to be seen in its present construction' (Merleau-Ponty 2012: 342).

Second, the world for Kant is understood as composed of representations that themselves are all fully determinate. We have seen this already in Kant's notion of determination outlined above. There is thus a symmetry, or, as Kant argues in the Analogies, a reciprocity, between the elements that make up the world around us. As Merleau-Ponty notes, this model rests on an idea of temporality as a series of instantaneous 'now's, in which 'every "elsewhere" is given as another here' (2012: 348) such that everything can in principle be given at once as determinate in perfect simultaneity.

Third, such a synthesis presupposes the notion of a self as the source of the synthetic activity that relates together the representations. Kant notes that even when the self isn't clearly represented, it is still present in our synthesis of the world:

> that all the variety of *empirical consciousness* must be combined in one single self-consciousness is the *absolutely* first and synthetic principle of our thought in general. But it must not be forgotten that the bare representation 'I' in relation to all other representations (the collective unity of which it makes possible) is transcendental consciousness. Whether this representation is clear (empirical consciousness) or obscure, or even whether it actually occurs, does not here concern us. But the possibility of the logical form of all cognition is necessarily conditioned by relation to this apperception *as a faculty*. (Kant 1929: A118n)

Fourth, and following from all of the claims we have looked at so far, ultimately synthesis takes as its model the synthesis of judgement, with its concomitant claims to subsumptive relations between determinate representations. It is judgement that gives us an account of fully determinate properties that are related together in terms of an underlying unity, and that pushes us to ground our account of determination in terms of the relations of a subject to an object.

Fifth, both Deleuze and Merleau-Ponty follow Kant in arguing that at the heart of this model is the ideal of God's view of the world.[7] Even if the world is not a completed synthesis for Kant, it is still the case that the categorial nature of the world precludes an encounter with a genuine moment of indeterminacy in the world. This is the root of Deleuze's claim: '[f]inite synthetic Self or divine analytic substance: it amounts to the same thing' (1994: 58).

Finally, and following from all of these claims, both Merleau-Ponty and Deleuze hold that the traditional account of synthesis is based on an understanding of the subject that places it in the universal, and denies it particularity. For both, this claim is associated with common sense, and involves a transcendental illusion. We also find the claim that such an account represents 'the dogmatism of common sense'. As such, it provides the basis for traditional scientific and philosophical enquiry by guaranteeing a common objective framework that is 'the same for everyone, valid for all times and for all places' (Merleau-Ponty 2012: 73–4), independent of the changes in perspective. The determinate model of the world allows for clear and distinct temporally invariant dichotomies in our characterisation of it (50), and hence makes possible traditional models of philosophy or science.[8] In effect, once we separate our perception of things from things themselves, we are able to place all of the indeterminacy we find in perception onto perception itself, and thereby grant to the world outside of us a fully determinate nature. Even in the case of Kant, therefore, time tends toward a medium within which determinations are discovered rather than created. 'The world, in the full sense of the word, is not an object, it is wrapped in objective determinations, but also has fissures and lacunae through which subjectivities become lodged in it or, rather, which are subjectivities themselves' (349).

Deleuze's Asymmetrical Synthesis

Before going through the differences between the characteristics of symmetrical and asymmetrical syntheses, I want to give a brief outline of what asymmetrical synthesis itself is. In the passage quoted above, Deleuze characterises this in terms of 'lightning, [which] distinguishes itself from the black sky but must also trail it behind, as though it were distinguishing itself from that which does not distinguish itself from it' (1994: 28). What would it mean for determination not to operate reciprocally? Deleuze's alternative to the sedimentary distribution is the nomadic distribution. He describes this a situation where 'there is no longer a division of that which is distributed but rather a division among those who distribute themselves in an open space – a space which is unlimited, or at least without precise limits' (36). We can see that this also gives an account of synthesis, but not of the synthesis of a field of elements by a subject, but rather of a field that synthesises itself. Rather than diversity, which Deleuze associates with extensity, the nomadic distribution instead operates in terms of difference. 'Difference is not diversity. Diversity is given, but difference is that by which the given is given, that by which the given is given as diverse' (222). Deleuze's claim is that this field of difference gives rise to the kinds of extensive properties that Kant talks about in terms of intensity.

Deleuze takes as his model here embryogenesis, with the egg as a qualitatively indeterminate field that determines the development of the embryo within it. Deleuze argues that the development of an embryo is a process whereby determinate features emerge from an apparently homogeneous field. We can see the egg as a field that appears homogeneous, but which is composed of gradients of intensities. The embryo develops through an unfolding through velocities and distances that are governed by these gradients. In effect, therefore, the egg is for Deleuze a field of forces that determines the transformations of the embryo as it develops. Now, Deleuze argues that 'the world is an egg' (1994: 251), thereby suggesting that these processes can be generalised to everything that exists:

> Here too, however, the positive element lies less in the elements of the given symmetry than in those which are missing. An intensity forming a wave of variation throughout the protoplasm distributes its difference along the axes and from one pole to another. The region of maximal activity is the first to come into play, exercising a dominant influence on the development of the corresponding parts at a lower rate: the individual in the egg is a genuine descent, going from the highest to the lowest and affirming the differences which comprise it and in which it falls. (Deleuze 1994: 250)

We can note a number of key features that emerge from this account of the embryo. First, the space of the embryo cannot be understood as a simple extensive space. Rather, the development of the embryo takes place through processes of folding the structure of space itself: 'Embryology shows that the division of an egg into parts is secondary in relation to more significant morphogenetic movements: the augmentation of free surfaces, stretching of cellular layers, invagination by folding, regional displacement of groups' (Deleuze 1994: 214). These transformations cannot be properly understood in metric terms, as 'the destiny and achievement of the embryo is to live the unliveable, to sustain forced movements of a scope which would break any skeleton or tear ligaments' (215). The claim here is therefore that intensity operates topologically, and hence is not determined in terms of a uniform metric.[9] Second, to talk about intensive space is in fact a simplification which emerges quite naturally from the reference to topology. The development of the embryo could equally be understood as a process, with the emergence of the 'differential rhythms' that characterise the organism. In fact, the intensive is neither purely spatial nor temporal, and these two terms can only be separated once explicated in extensity: 'the distinction is obviously relative, for it is clear that the dynamism is simultaneously temporal and spatial – in other words, spatio-temporal . . . The duality does not exist in the process of actualisation itself, but only in its outcome, in the actual terms' (217).

Deleuze provides a model for how to think the relation between metric and non-metric spaces with an example from mathematics. We can begin by taking the series of cardinal numbers, 1, 2, 3, . . . Now, we can note that in some cases, such as 7 divided by 5, we can only divide this sequence of numbers by introducing a further set of numbers: the fractions. These allow us to take a difference which cannot be resolved and resolve it in a new domain. We can in turn discover within the domain of fractions a set of numbers, namely the irrational numbers, that cannot be determined within the domain of fractions, but can be determined, once again, in their own domain. We have seen briefly that the space of intensive transformations cannot be understood in terms of precise measurements, but rather is defined by topological transformations. Deleuze notes that what makes the arithmetical relations within the series of natural numbers possible, and similarly measurement within space, is that both of these presuppose a basic metric unit between elements. Just as there is a difference in natural numbers that cannot be resolved without the introduction of a new series, Deleuze asks if there is a series that is itself resolved into the natural numbers, and argues that this series is the ordinal numbers (first, second, third). Here, we have a series which contains an order, but without the idea of a shared metric (the difference between first and second does not need to be the same as that between second and third). Deleuze takes this lack of a metric to explain how the genesis of systems can involve transformations that seem impossible from the point of view of fully constituted systems.

As well as understanding the genesis of space from a field which is indeterminate from the perspective of Euclidean space, Deleuze also argues that the notion of properties as determinations is secondary to processes. We have just seen that intensive space involves a difference that cannot be reduced to an identity except by explicating it in an extensive space. Deleuze takes as his model temperature, which is not a quality, but rather a measure of the difference in heat between different bodies. As such, rather than a self-identical quality, temperature is a difference. Deleuze generalises from this to argue that 'qualities are signs which flash across the interval of a difference' (1994: 223), and thus that qualities are a misrepresentation of an inherently processual model of the world. As such, qualities are a way of representing in extensity something that cannot be given in extensity. For Deleuze, therefore, Kant fails to recognise that synthesis can operate in a manner that constitutes the basic elements of extensity and quality, rather than simply operating through a transposition of them. Before looking at the implications of this model, I want to turn to Merleau-Ponty's model of asymmetrical synthesis.

Merleau-Ponty's Asymmetrical Synthesis

At the heart of Merleau-Ponty's criticisms of Kant is a similar recognition that there is a necessary moment of indeterminacy to the world. Merleau-Ponty claims that we tend to fall prey to what he calls the 'experience error', wherein 'we immediately assume that what we know to exist among things is also in our perception of them' (2012: 5). As such, we tend to attribute the kind of complete determination we think applies to objects to our field of perception itself:

> Through optics and geometry we construct the fragment of the world whose image can, at any moment, form upon our retina. Anything outside of this perimeter – not reflecting upon any sensitive surface – no more acts upon our vision than does light falling upon our closed eyes. We ought to thus perceive a sharply delimited segment of the world, surrounded by a black zone, filled with qualities without any lacunae, and subtended by determinate size relations like those existing upon the retina. But experience offers nothing of the sort, and we will never understand what a visual field is by beginning from the world. Even if it is possible to trace a perimeter around vision by beginning at the centre and gradually approaching lateral stimuli, the results of such a measurement nonetheless vary from one moment to the next, and the precise moment at which a previously seen stimulus ceases to be seen can never be identified. The region surrounding

the visual field is not easy to describe, but it is certainly neither black nor grey. (Merleau-Ponty 2012: 6)

As Merleau-Ponty notes, given that our understanding of the world is itself grounded in perception, there is a complex circularity in under-standing the nature of perception in terms of a field of objects, since perception is the way in which we encounter those objects in the first place.

Merleau-Ponty argues that this claim about the borders of our visual field is not an accidental aspect of our perception, but rather is tied to the fundamental nature of perception itself. If perception is understood on the model of the world, then it is a short step to seeing the basic unit of perception as being the correlate of a point on the retina, effectively the kind of atomic sense-datum we find in Hume's empiricism. Merleau-Ponty instead argues that '[a] figure against a background is the most basic perceptual figure that can be given' (2012: 4). Now, by this he does not simply mean that our perception is contextual but that perception has a necessarily complex structure which involves the interrelation of a moment of determinacy and one of indeterminacy. This immediately pushes Merleau-Ponty's account of perception away from the notion that synthesis involves the interrelation of determinate elements. Rather, for Merleau-Ponty, perception is an autochthonous mode of organisa-tion. As such, perception, and with it the world, involves the interplay of figure and background, which highlights its inherently perspectival nature. When we look at extensity, according to Merleau-Ponty, we cannot understand how basic categories such as up and down are to be understood without presupposing a perspectival engagement with the world. The key idea here is that attending to the world involves a constitution of categories, rather than simply an inessential indetermi-nacy that belongs purely to perception itself. Merleau-Ponty writes: 'the act of attention is ... at least rooted in the life of consciousness, and we can finally understand that it emerges from its indifferent freedom to give itself a present object. The passage from the indeterminate to the determinate, this continuous taking up again of its own history in the unity of a new sense, is thought itself' (33). Here, then, just as the flash of lightning distinguishes itself from its background without the background itself becoming distinguished, we find for Merleau-Ponty that the figure emerges from a field of indeterminacy without itself deter-mining its constituting field. 'Psychological atomism is but a particular case of a more general prejudice: the unquestioned belief in determinate being and in the world' (510).

Asymmetrical Synthesis

Merleau-Ponty is not mentioned in the long bibliography at the end of *Difference and Repetition*, and is barely mentioned within the text itself. Nonetheless, we find that Deleuze's account of the three syntheses in chapter five of *Difference and Repetition* makes clear the importance of Merleau-Ponty's work for Deleuze. Here, the concern is with space rather than time, but 'we should not be surprised that the pure spatial syntheses repeat the temporal syntheses previously specified' (Deleuze 1994: 230). In the syntheses of time, we begin with the structure of habit and discover that habit could only be understood in terms of an ontologically prior field of memory. Here, Deleuze begins with three oppositions: 'up and down, the right and the left, and the figure and the ground' (229, translation modified).[10] Each of these oppositions is dealt with in detail by Merleau-Ponty in relation to his discussion of extensity, and in each case he argues that the opposition can only be properly understood if we assume that our relation to space is perspectival. As such, we can see here Deleuze recognising Merleau-Ponty as a precursor, implicitly arguing that Merleau-Ponty's discussion of perspective can be understood as an analysis of intensity in another element.

So how do these asymmetrical syntheses differ from the symmetrical synthesis of Kant's philosophy? Let us return to the six characteristics of the symmetrical synthesis, and see how they compare to those of the asymmetrical synthesis.

First, as we saw, the symmetrical synthesis involves a combination of ready-made representations. Now, Kant's account is constitutive of experience, in that the transcendental unity of apperception is outside of time. As such, it is a synthesis of constitution from nowhere in that it precedes space and time, and it operates in terms of ready-made elements. For Deleuze, synthesis operates between two levels, and is a continuous process of communication between these two levels: 'In reality, the individual can only be contemporaneous with its individuation, and individuation, contemporaneous with the principle: the principle must be truly genetic, and not simply a principle of reflection. Also, the individual is not just a result, but an *environment* of individuation' (Deleuze 2004: 86). This process of movement between intensity and extensity is precisely what constituted the qualities taken up by representation, not as states, but rather themselves as processes of difference. For Merleau-Ponty too, we saw that through the process of attention we did not simply have the illumination of the world, but rather the constitution of properties. Just as for Deleuze synthesis is a continual process of generation, for Merleau-Ponty synthesis operates by transition from one perspective to the next, providing an account of constitution without presupposing a moment outside of time.

Second, we saw that symmetrical synthesis operated in terms of determinate properties. As we have seen, for Deleuze, synthesis is instead constitutive of properties, as properties are a well-founded illusion generated by intensive processes of difference. For Merleau-Ponty too, the key element in Kant's account, the representation, is a falsification of our notion of perspectival experience. For Kant, perception occurs through the organisation of representations in relation to the concept of an object. For Merleau-Ponty, while we might say that synthesis operates through the movement between perspectives, in fact this characterisation of a movement between perspectives is an artifice of our reflection on the constitution of experience. Instead, perspectives are not individuated, and 'the diversity of points of view is only suspected through an imperceptible slippage, or through a certain "indeterminacy" of the appearance' (Merleau-Ponty 2012: 344). Perspectivism here operates in a smooth space of transition that carries with it the unquantifiable nature of the intensive.

Third, we saw that for Kant synthesis required the notion of a self to organise experience, by analogy with judgement, which involves the manipulation of representations by a subject. Once we see experience itself as a process, we open up the possibility of synthesis giving rise to the subject, rather than being a consequence of it. For Deleuze, 'time itself unfolds . . . instead of things unfolding within it' (1994: 88). In this sense, the self for Deleuze is an organisation of intensity into a set of rhythms and differences that in turn determine it with particular characteristics. What we normally take to be the self is merely the representational reflection on this process of individuation: 'Psychology regards it as established that the self cannot contemplate itself. This, however, is not the question. The question is whether or not the self itself is a contemplation, whether it is not in itself a contemplation, and whether we can learn, form behaviour and form ourselves other than through contemplation' (73). We find a similar claim in Merleau-Ponty's work, where perception constitutes the subject and object. This is the meaning of his famous claim of the primacy of perception:

[Bergson] evokes, beyond the 'point of view of the object' and the 'point of view of the subject', a common nucleus which is the 'winding' [serpentement], being as a winding (what I called 'modulation of the being in the world'). It is necessary to make understood how that (or any Gestalt) is a perception 'being formed in the things'. This is still only an approximative expression, in the subject-object language (Wahl, Bergson) of what there is to be said. That is, that the things have us, and that it is not we who have the things. (Merleau-Ponty 1968: 194)

Fourth, and as a direct consequence of rejecting the notions of self, determination and the ready-made, we open up the possibility of synthesis that doesn't operate in terms of judgement. 'Here there is, prior to objective relations, a perceptual syntax that is articulated according to its own rules: the breaking up of previous relations and the establishing of new ones – judgment – only express the outcome of this deep operation and are its final report' (Merleau-Ponty 2012: 38).

Fifth, rejecting judgement involves rejecting the ideal of God. As we saw, God is the model of complete determination for Kant. As such, in rejecting complete determination, we reject the notion that there could be a view from nowhere. 'Intellectualism and empiricism do not give us an account of the human experience of the world; they say of human experience what God might think of the world' (Merleau-Ponty 2012: 266–7). 'The oneness and identity of the divine substance are in truth the only guarantee of a unique and identical Self, and God is retained so long as the Self is preserved' (Deleuze 1994: 58).

When we take these claims together, we find an account of synthesis that captures the particularity of our relationship with the world. We no longer need to understand constitution in terms of judgement, but can instead see it in terms of the genesis of a field of determinations from a field that, in respect to them, remains indeterminate.

Conclusion

I want to conclude this chapter by considering two questions. First, why does Kant fall into the errors that he does? And second, how do we distinguish Merleau-Ponty and Deleuze? The response to the first question is that it is by understanding time in terms of moments that we fall into error, and that so long as we understand synthesis to operate in relation to judgement, we cannot help but fall into this error. Time cannot be reconstituted once it has been broken up into discrete atomic elements. 'It thinks it can comprehend our natal bond with the world only by *undoing* it in order to *remake* it, only by constituting it, by fabricating it' (Merleau-Ponty 1968: 32). The ultimate implication of this for both Deleuze and Merleau-Ponty is that traditional accounts of synthesis are unable to explain our experience within time without recourse to paradox. Merleau-Ponty puts the point as follows:

The definition of time, which is implicit in the comparisons made by common sense and which could be formulated as 'a succession of nows', does not merely commit the error of treating the past and the future as presents: it is in fact inconsistent since it destroys the very notion of the 'now' and the very notion of succession. (Merleau-Ponty 2012: 435)

Deleuze extends this point in *Difference and Repetition*, where he also develops a series of paradoxes that emerge from attempting to constitute time through a succession of nows: 'It is futile to try to reconstitute the past from the presents between which it is trapped, either the present which it was, or the one in relation to which it is now past' (1994: 81).[11]

Both Deleuze and Merleau-Ponty hold that the paradoxes within the representation of synthesis lead us to recognise the unsustainability of traditional accounts of synthesis. Judgement fails to explain constitution, and instead 'prevents the emergence of any new mode of existence. For the latter creates itself through its own forces, that is, through the forces it is able to harness, and is valid in and of itself inasmuch as it brings the new combination into existence' (Deleuze 1998: 135). Deleuze and Merleau-Ponty recognise that synthesis does not have to be understood as categorial synthesis, and so they are able to develop an alternative model of the structure of the world which allows us to understand it as indeterminate, but not as thereby indifferent. How do their alternative accounts differ? Both see asymmetrical syntheses as operating between determinacy and indeterminacy, but perhaps the fundamental difference lies in the interrelation between these fields. For Deleuze, synthesis happens between two levels, with each being complete, even if it is not whole.[12] For Merleau-Ponty, determination and the indeterminate are related in an asymmetrical intertwining that holds both on the same plane. We will leave a discussion of how we distinguish between these models for a later work.

Notes

1. For both, transcendental illusion is a key methodological discovery that is not taken far enough by Kant himself. Merleau-Ponty explicitly takes Kant's account of the antinomies into his own methodology, noting that 'One of Kant's discoveries, whose consequences we have not yet fully grasped, is that all our experience of the world is throughout a tissue of concepts which lead to irreducible contradictions if we attempt to take them in an absolute sense or transfer them into pure being, and that they nevertheless found the structure of all our phenomena, of everything which is for us. It would take too long to show (and besides it is well known) that Kantian philosophy itself failed to utilise this principle fully and that both its investigation of experience and its critique of dogmatism remained incomplete' (1964: 18–19). Deleuze takes

Kant's discovery of the paralogisms to be likewise both pivotal but underexploited by Kant (Deleuze 1994: 86).

2. Kant distances himself from the 'intellectualised appearances' (1929: A271/B327) of Leibniz's account of space and time. For the radicality of Kant's departure from prior philosophers (and Plato in particular), see Deleuze 1978.

3. See Longuenesse 2001: 63–4 for her account of the interrelation of the understanding and imagination.

4. 'Thus, the positing [position] of a single object in the full sense of the word requires the composition [or co-positing] of all of these experiences in a single, polythetic act. Therein it exceeds perceptual experience and the synthesis of horizons – just as the notion of a universe (a completed and explicit totality where relations would be reciprocally determined) exceeds the notion of a world (an open and indefinite multiplicity where relations are reciprocally implicated). I take flight from my experience and I pass over to the idea. Like the object, the idea claims to be the same for everyone, valid for all times and for all places, and the individuation of the object at an objective point of time and space appears, in the end, as the expression of a universal positing power' (Merleau-Ponty 2012: 73–4).

5. Deleuze sees a sedentary distribution as a set of transcendental claims about the rules for understanding how experience is organised. The assumptions behind sedentary distributions are discussed in more detail in chapter three of *Difference and Repetition*. See Williams 2004: 65–7; Somers-Hall 2012: 38–42 for more on the interrelation of sedentary and nomadic distributions.

6. Cf., for instance, Deleuze 1994: 52.

7. While Kant posits the transcendental ideal of God as a condition for determination, it is important also to recognise that Kant breaks with what Allison calls the 'theocentric' model of thought that we find in pre-Kantian metaphysics (cf. Allison 2004: 27–34). He does so by positing a difference between the intuitive thought of an infinite being and the discursive thought of a finite being. For an analysis of the ambivalences this generates in Merleau-Ponty's reading of Kant, see Somers-Hall 2019.

8. Deleuze defines traditional metaphysics and transcendental philosophy as holding to the claim that one must have '*either* an undifferentiated ground, a groundlessness, formless nonbeing, or an abyss without differences and without properties, *or* a supremely individuated Being and an intensely personalized form' (1990: 106). This is in effect once again the claim that all determination must related to a central unity, with the only alternative being a lack of determination (in effect, either being or nothingness). Deleuze and Merleau-Ponty both seek a new form of thinking that will be adequate to thinking the genesis of form itself.

9. Deleuze is here breaking with much of the philosophical tradition by seeing time as independent of measure. He will argue that, from Plato, time has been understood simply as the medium through which causal or logical relations are expressed, such as in Plato's notion of the world as the 'moving image of eternity', or Leibniz's account of well-founded phenomena. Deleuze calls this notion of intensity separated from measure the pure form of time. For Deleuze, it is Kant who inaugurates a break with the metaphysical tradition by determining time independently of rational categories. While he recognises this difference in kind, Kant goes wrong by understanding time as purely passive rather than generative. See Somers-Hall 2011.

10. Patton here translates *le haut et le bas* as 'high and low', which obscures the connection with Merleau-Ponty's discussion of up and down in the *Phenomenology of Perception*.

11. Cf. Ansell-Pearson 2001: 185–91 for a discussion of these paradoxes.
12. Deleuze takes this distinction from Descartes. Cf. Deleuze 1994: 209.

References

Allison, H. (2004), *Kant's Transcendental Idealism: An Interpretation and Defense*, New Haven: Yale University Press.

Ansell-Pearson, K. (2001) *Philosophy and the Adventure of the Virtual*, London: Routledge.

Deleuze, G. (1978), 'Cours Vincennes: Synthesis and Time', trans. Melissa McMahon, at <https://www.webdeleuze.com/textes/66>.

Deleuze, G. (1990), *The Logic of Sense*, trans. Mark Lester with Charles Stivale, London: Athlone Press.

Deleuze, G. (1994), *Difference and Repetition*, trans. Paul Patton, New York: Columbia University Press.

Deleuze, G. (1998), 'To Have Done with Judgment', in *Essays Critical and Clinical*, trans. Daniel W. Smith and Michael A. Greco, London: Verso.

Deleuze, G. (2004), 'On Gilbert Simondon', in *Desert Islands and Other Texts 1953–1974*, ed. David Lapoujade, trans. Mike Taormina, Los Angeles: Semiotext(e).

Kant, I. (1929), *Critique of Pure Reason*, trans. Norman Kemp Smith, London: Macmillan.

Longuenesse, B. (2001), *Kant and the Capacity to Judge: Sensibility and Discursivity in the Transcendental Analytic of the* Critique of Pure Reason, trans. Charles T. Wolf, Princeton: Princeton University Press.

Merleau-Ponty, M. (1964), 'The Primacy of Perception', in *The Primacy of Perception*, ed. James M. Edie, Evanston: Northwestern University Press.

Merleau-Ponty, M. (1968), *The Visible and the Invisible*, ed. Claude Lefort, trans. Alphonso Lingis, Evanston: Northwestern University Press.

Merleau-Ponty, M. (2012), *The Phenomenology of Perception*, trans. Donald A. Landes, Abingdon: Routledge.

Somers-Hall, H. (2011), 'Time Out of Joint: Hamlet and the Pure Form of Time', *Deleuze Studies*, 5 (supplement): 56–76.

Somers-Hall, H. (2012), *Deleuze's* Difference and Repetition: *An Edinburgh Philosophical Guide*, Edinburgh: Edinburgh University Press.

Somers-Hall, H. (2019), 'Merleau-Ponty's Reading of Kant's Transcendental Idealism', *The Southern Journal of Philosophy*, 57 (1): 103–31.

Williams, J. (2004), *Deleuze's Difference and Repetition: A Critical Introduction and Guide*, Edinburgh: Edinburgh University Press.

Chapter 7

Disjoint and Multiply: Deleuze and Negri on Time

Peter Trnka

> The joint, *cardo*, is what ensures the subordination of time to those properly cardinal points through which pass the periodic movements which it measures ... By contrast, *time out of joint* means *demented time* or *time outside the curve* which gave it a god, liberated from its overly simple circular figure, freed from the events which made up its content, its relation to movement overturned; in short, time presenting itself as an empty and pure form. Time itself unfolds ... instead of things unfolding within it ... It ceases to be cardinal and becomes ordinal, a pure *order* of time. (Deleuze 1994: 88; emphasis added)

Preamble

In the spirit of Gilles Deleuze and Félix Guattari's collaboration, or deindividuated authorial coupling 'between you and me', we speak together (or not at all) as a fused reader-writer becoming-couple; a reader reading written signs of some writer(s) is the minimal threshold or condition.

In the imperative mode: disjoint, multiply, time or times, that is. An imperative, however, of exhortation, not command. We speak together, for the displacement and disjointing of unitary imposed time, that is, work time.

Presuming for now, at least at the limit (and the limit is, as we shall see below, the measure of the gradient or scissor angle between formal and real subsumption), more and more, all time is work time, as if all digital clocks had hidden punches. Work time is the marching time of 'one-two-three-four-one-two-three-four': regular, automatic, endlessly repetitive, instituting fast grooves to follow-fill. So on and so on and so on and so on.

Dis-joint, de-couple, dis-place. Favour, instead, multiplication. Love multiplies. Add and add and then take adding to the next power. Increase and fold over the increases to increase faster and at different scales. Release the folds of plural times, bloom a hundred flowers, explicate a thousand plateaus or levels.

Practice over theory, action over representation, knowing full well that as we use the technology or machine of language, the name of the thing tends to insist it is done and finished, pushing any dynamic tendencies, flows and fluxes of time to the margins, peripheries, and dumping lots of error.[1]

As if time does not infect all things. *As if* names as fixed identities do not always fail. *As if* we had some continued interest in thingifying, reifying, fetishising, idolising.

The practical mode is the futural mode of what is to be done: what is to be made, to-come to-be. Revolutionary communism[2] is futural and in the infinitive: live to multiply futures. At times these futures are exclusively micropolitical, molecular, micro-futures (a shared glance across a room), but there are also rarer molar shifts, revolutions in fundamental modes of being. Futures, of course, come with things, whole worlds of things in each and every new time.

Our method is to read Deleuze, his work alone and in collaboration with Guattari, through his friend and comrade Negri. This serves the purpose of a clear political line, to Marx that is. We begin, then, in the next section, with Negri's reading of Marx, and of Marx's theory of time. The third section features Deleuze's thought of time, in his singularly authored works and with Guattari in *A Thousand Plateaus* (oddly, for philosophy, many authorial couples in these territories: Marx-Engels, Deleuze-Guattari and Negri-Hardt). Section four on the time-image is something like an example of a collective phenomenological constitution of new machines and new experiences of time. The differences between Deleuze and Negri on time appear to centre on their differential appraisals of Spinoza's thought of time, duration and eternity, which we will tease out at some length in section five, with the help of Spinoza scholars Samuel Alexander, H. F. Hallett and David Savan.

When Negri speaks of a 'communist idea of time', and specifies that '[r]evolution is born from the pathways of a constitutive phenomenology of temporality' (2003: 21), he is putting the politics of time, its production, control, circulation, distribution and exchange, at the heart of liberation struggles. Time is not money. Time is living labour. Time is life.

Translate academic vocabularies and grammatologies. Believe that you can do something to change the fucked-up world. Update the eleventh thesis on Feuerbach: 'The philosophers have hitherto only interpreted the world in various ways, the point, however, is to change it.'

Negri on Marx and Time

The Marx that inspires Negri is the later or latest Marx, the Marx of *Capital* but more so the *Grundrisse*, most fully expressed in Negri's *Marx Beyond Marx*, the title of which signals the central point, namely, that the name 'Marx' here means the procedure of thinking through the temporally dynamic historical situation with regard to desired futures-to-come (and as such denotes a movement always and essentially beyond any existing configuration).

Negri, in two remarkable texts written while in prison in Italy on two different, long 'occasions' (first, 'The Constitution of Time' and, second, 'Kairos, Alma Venus, Multitudo', collected in English and published under the joint title *Time for Revolution*), takes guidance primarily from Marx and Deleuze in writing a political ontology, or radical historical materialist dialectic, of time. Tensed and dated, subjective and objective, time A and time B: polar oppositions in the flow and experience of time. Oppositions often hypostatised into categories, separate realities, which Negri seeks to coordinate, under a narrative explanation of the generative constitution of molar capital command time, and its corollary, and antithetical, profusion of molecular times.[3]

Hence Negri is able to consider 'time as its own essence, as immanent, as human . . .' (2003: 34) without denying or diminishing time. Instead, the details, styles, fashions, particular ways or modes of thinking-feeling-experiencing-living time(s) are to be thought as historical modes of the production, distribution and circulation of time, as of anything else (notably space, including floors, ceilings, sitting and standing areas, lunchrooms, and so on and so on and so on, as well, of course, as all the minutiae that go along with spacetimes, namely, ways of shaping and doing things). There is not but one Time, there are many – perhaps discrete, potentially mutually exclusive – times, in the emphatic plural.

Consider two faces of human time, two faces of the lived constitution of time, temporally distinct: living labour and dead labour,[4] in other words, wages and capital, humanity split and fighting against itself, in its division into classes and times – people of the past and people of the future-to-come. The struggle between classes, between living labour and dead labour, proletarian and bourgeois, Marx expresses as 'subsumption' – that is, total control and possession – of 'labour by capital', in two phases or modes: formal (potentiality, as authority, allowance, contract) and real (the actuality, as developed, extensively and intensively). The two phases are scissored or related as poles on a continuum, such that the movement from formal to real is quantitative, intensive and expressive of the measure of class exploitation and domination. To be really fully subsumed is the limit of one's suffering and plasticity under capital control. As subsumption extends and intensifies, working time becomes constitutive of life, or, in other words, the difference between the time (and place) of work and the time and place for life (free of work) fades and disappears.

Time for Marx becomes 'the tautology of life' (Negri 2003: 34–5). Real subsumption of labour by capital is a subsumption into labour time, a molar absolute closed time that operates on molecular, open multiple constitutions of time. Real times have a *'positive entropy'*, writes Negri, that 'is richly described in that beautiful tract of the phenomenology of time and times that is Deleuze's and Guattari's *A Thousand Plateaus*' (41). The multiplication of new times is the creation of new forms of becoming, hence new forms of time, continually (as an expanding spiral, not an enclosing circle). Real subsumption, he continues, 'produces and displays a *complete transcription of the real relations* (individual, of class, of force)', i.e., the ground and shape of things and persons and activities and relations has shifted, with real difference; real subsumption 'introduces a maximum of plurality and dynamism. Antagonistic *dispositifs* open up and consolidate themselves starting precisely from a new irreducibility of action to average value, or to unified time' (41).

Plural times conflict with the 'real time' of production, the specular spectacular time of global universal command. Each is a construction: *'capital constructs time as collective substance'* (Negri 2003: 41). Construction is here real material process, the making of the objective conditions that make lives and activities this way rather than that. Remembering, if we can, that the constructive moment does little to dampen the hypostatising tendencies of language, that is to say, there is always it seems the implication that the thing is in the same way that the word is appearing fixed on its location on the page.

The logic of placing and conjoining, of displacing and disjoining, unsettles and perturbs: 'In my *Marx Beyond Marx* I demonstrated in depth how the mechanism of *displacement* dominates Marx's logic', Negri writes, specifying that by Marx's logic he means

the scientific standpoint of class. When real subsumption is reached through the development of productive forces and of the relations of production, the displacement of all the constitutive parameters is thereby determined.

The synchronic rules are modified within the framework of the diachronic transition. (Negri 2003: 42)

Ontological figures are subject to diachronic displacement. The molar organisation of unified time finds its ontological basis in a molecular multitude. Negri defines multiplicity 'in materialist terms . . . as irreducibility of the many to the one, *time* conceived in its founding dynamic – and therefore, molecular *reality* as against any molar projection' (2003: 43). The single unitary Time of Capital and Dead Labour coexists in tension with the Many Times of the Resistance of Living Labour; as Negri explains:[5] 'in the hysteresis of the dissociation of multiple times we find opposed tendencies, material tendencies constituting themselves as the negation of command, and therefore as logics of liberation' (43).[6]

Real subsumption describes the average condition of social labour in real crisis, where real crisis means irreversible time; real subsumption is founded on the contradiction between the 'plural substantial times of subjects', on the one hand, and the 'analytic of command', on the other (Negri 2003: 55). It is not a question of subjective versus objective senses of time, as the subject here is as objective as objective, and subjective, get. It is a question of the conditions of genesis (the production by capital, in many current cases, of the antinomies and the need to solve them) (101–2). Liberated time is omnilateral, universally versatile, and productive subjectivity. 'Liberation occurs in the form of subjectivity, from the refusal to work to the rediscovery of productive rationality, from self-valorization to auto-determination, from spontaneity to unfolded collective consciousness'; Negri continues to define liberated time as collectivity itself, or the life of such, in a 'time that cannot be measured, precisely because liberation consists in the destruction of the structural dimensions of time-as-measure. The one schema of organization of liberated time is thus rediscovered in terms of a phenomenology of collective praxis' (120–1). Materialist phenomenology means here a historico-genetic and critical-descriptive analysis of forms of making and creating: 'Liberated time is a *machine* of constitution' (21).

An interrelation of procedure, subjectivity, time and machine, or machinic assemblage or apparatus. Subjects, subject-types, move in social alliances. Negri writes of a manuscript Deleuze worked on:

In the period of *La Grandeur de Marx*, Gilles Deleuze spoke of the common notion (in the case in point, of communism) as the possibility of translating the community of the *episteme* into an ontological common. The common name is the teleological trace (a teleology of the instant, the *telos* of the event) that unites the events in the construction of a community: it is thus the ontological composition of the events that expresses itself as power and imagines itself as reality *to-come*. (Negri 2003: 157)

The expression of power is at one and the same time an act of imagination: an imagining, in the full concrete desiring aching sense; imagining, wanting, demanding and making what is to-come. Imagination is here Hume's constructive power, as affirmed in the mad, fabulous sense of Deleuze's *Empiricism and Subjectivity* (see Trnka 1997). Such a positive and absolutely free imagination is far from the tamed Kantian faculty. As constructive, in Negri's terminology, constitutive power, imagination is an ontological force; it is real and makes things real. Subjectivity has real forms and real effects.

Unitary command time and the multitudes of liberated times are opposed and co-implicated; Negri claims that '[w]ith these two references (to Marx and Deleuze) before us, we find ourselves introduced to the full experience of the power of the *Kairos*' (2003: 158). What is *Kairos*? It is 'the power to observe the fullness of temporality at the moment it opens itself onto the void of being, and of seizing this opening as innovation. The common name is situated in the passage (*Kairos*) from fullness to the void: it is a common and imaginative act of production' (158). It is not a decision, in some Schmittian-Hobbesian possessive individualist nominalist ontology, but a collective historical work of the multitudes of intellectual and manual workers, in the broadest sense of those subjectivities who think, feel and move. The common name, such as, for example, 'communism', 'democracy', 'freedom', 'is not only the sign of the singular existent in the instant that links the act of naming to the thing named, nor is it solely the seeking of multiplicity in *surveying* over the edge of time. Situated within the power of the production of being, it is also the construction of the *telos* of generation' (158), the tendency of the striving and work of the collective: 'It is this production, that is to say this generation, which we call *praxis*' (158). Praxis is collective goal-oriented practical activity. Praxis makes what is to come.

What was to come and did, of course, has constituted us and our situations, tools and weapons. To the draw of the future over the push of the past Negri 'give[s] the name of "*to-come*" ... the horizon of experimentation of the adequation of the name and the thing, and to the imaginative perspective that – in realizing itself – presents itself as new being' (2003: 163). This is a perspective in accord with ordinary experience:

The everyday sense of life confirms the definition of that 'which is coming' as *to-come*, rather than as future. It is ... in the struggle for the free appropriation of the present that life opens itself to the *to-come*, and desire perceives – against the empty and homogeneous time in which all is equal (including, and in particular, the future) – the creative power of *praxis*. (Negri 2003: 163)[7]

Real subjectivity as embodied material historical subjectivity lives. It lives in individuals and groups; in the many forms of global social multiples, of groupuscules, cells, assemblies, associations and institutions; in multiple aggregates and assemblages of imaginative acts of person-types, aka, individuals and groups. Real subjectivity and real subjects live in uncountable times: 'To be in the eternal means to be in "production" . . . If the "before" is eternal and the "after" is *to-come*, time – in the arrow that constitutes it – is the immeasurableness of production between this "before" and this "after"'(Negri 2003: 167).

Negri thinks through the character of productive or constituent power as procedure. That is, procedure is the way of creation, the manner of world making. In his work *Insurgencies*, on political revolutions – the British, French, American and Russian, primarily – and their transformative and emergent contribution to the historical production of collective social imaginary forms of being, he brushes off the surface similarities between Marx's and Heidegger's criticisms of clock time. Heidegger's mystification of time, as Negri puts it, is not the same as Marx's identification with time: 'temporality can be grounded in human productive capacity, in the ontology of its becoming – an open, absolutely constitutive temporality that does not disclose Being but instead produces beings' (1999: 30). As offering such a constitutive, productive view, 'Marx's metaphysics of time is much more radical than Heidegger's', he claims; 'Marx frees what Heidegger imprisons.' How so? 'Heideggerian time is the form of being, the indistinctness of an absolute foundation.' In contrast to the mystical opaqueness of Heidegger's Being, 'Marxian time is the production of being and thus the form of an absolute procedure' (30). An absolute procedure is one which is totally adequate for its task, it is all there is and all that is needed, and it knows itself as such and acts as such. Absolute procedure expresses its power: 'Marxian temporality represents the means by which a subject formally predisposed to being adequate to an absolute procedure becomes a subject materially capable of becoming part of this process, of being defined as constituent power' (30). Formal to material, like virtual to actual, is a transformation and intensification of power. Negri sums up the passional and imaginative social character of this power: 'Every human drive in search of the political consists in this: in living an ethics of transformation through a yearning for participation that is revealed as love for the time to constitute' (335).

Deleuze and Guattari on Time

Deleuze's works of the late 1960s, *The Logic of Sense* and *Difference and Repetition*, each disjoint and multiply unitary Time. The time of Chronos is the time of chronological series, hence the time of measure and order and work. The time of Aion, 'the unlimited Aion, the becoming which divides itself infinitely in past and future . . . always eludes the present' (Deleuze 1990: 5). The splitting into past and into future, this infinite constant splitting into an ever anew generated past and ever anew generated future, is the transcendental apparatus of Aion. Chronos is the ordering of the moments of the expressed or generated series. Aion is the self-renewing reservoir of time and time-production, always has just been and about to be:

> time must be grasped twice, in two complementary though mutually exclusive fashions . . . entirely as the living present in bodies which act and are acted upon . . . [and] entirely as an entity infinitely divisible into past and future, and into the incorporeal effects which result from bodies, their actions and their passions. Only the present exists in time and gathers together or absorbs the past and future. But only the past and future inhere in time and divide each present infinitely. (Deleuze 1990: 5)

It just has, it is just about to, but it is not now. 'The infinitely divisible event is always *both at once*', Deleuze writes. 'It is eternally that which has just happened and that which is about to happen, but never that which is happening' (1990: 8). The vein of paradox, which Deleuze affirms positively, is appropriate to the attempt to think time.

The logic of the time of the event is posited in a counter-actualised Stoic ontology of sense, filled with bits of Bergsonian *durée*. Events are typically out of reach, on stage, separated from the limit of one's powers, out of bounds, spectacularised, as in Hollywood. Desiring[8] to become an actor of one's own events, 'the actor delimits the original, disengages from it an abstract line, and keeps from the event only its contour and its splendor, becoming thereby the actor of one's own events – a *counter-actualization*' (Deleuze 1990: 150).[9] As I've shown elsewhere (Trnka 2001: 56), Deleuze's 'ultimate sense of counter-actualization' brings together the time of the infinitive with the construction of a concept and the notion of an event, such that an individual involved would 'grasp the event actualized within her as another individual grafted onto her'

(Deleuze 1990: 178). (How Spinoza trumps Bergson on duration, and how Negri takes Spinoza and Marx further in and on time than does Deleuze, is still to come. Deleuze's time constructions, in the cinema books and with Guattari in *A Thousand Plateaus*, are fully consonant with Negri. Deleuze's major difference from Negri in the ontology of time lies in his reliance on a Stoic logic of the event of sense and on Bergson's *durée*. Negri expands the love of immanence and univocity in Spinoza which he shares with Deleuze, to encompass what many have found difficult, if not impossible, namely, a Spinoza who is a friend of real, new time.[10])

Untimely opposition to the commanding flow of time disjoints the cardinal and institutes the ordinal intensive; counter-actualisation proceeds thus through the time of Aion, or, rather, Aion is populated by the events of counter-actualisation, infinitely into the past and infinitely into the future to come.

The Logic of Sense and *Difference and Repetition*, together with the Bergson book and the Bergson sections in the Cinema books, lay out the transcendental dimension of Deleuze's thinking of time. The later, collaborative *Capitalism and Schizophrenia* volume II, *A Thousand Plateaus*, is the practice of that theory. We prefer the practice. It is the work pointed to by Negri: 'We like Deleuze and Guattari because they immerse temporality in the autonomy of a thousand plateaus of creativity' (Negri 2003: 134). Brian Massumi, in his 'Translator's Foreword' to *A Thousand Plateaus*, explains the dating of the plateaus: 'The date corresponds to the point at which that particular dynamism found its purest incarnation in matter, the point at which it was freest from interference from other modes and rose to its highest degree of intensity' (1987: xiv). The experience of each and every plateau and the sequence taken from one to another to another is not linear, if the user instructions are to be followed, but more in the mode of listening to a vinyl record player, which allows placing the needle here and there, breaking from ordered arborescence and constructing rhizomatic extensions. The rhizomatic sequencing concerns the rhythms and cadences of time and social life.

Rhizomatics is non-linear, non-arboreal, positive expression: free line drawing, free lines of flight. Taking a thin line through rhizomatics, a free-form point-line diagrammatics and machinic construction. Collective human creation in and of times, by way of an interrelation of procedure, subjectivity, time and machine or machinic assemblage. Apparatuses for the capture of times in Work Time and Trading Time. Apparatuses for the liberation and proliferation, disjunction and dislocation of times.

The contrast between arborescent and rhizomatic forms of growth, becoming and organisation is a question of purpose: for what end? Because we desire to do what? Muck around, play in the most serious and most fun of senses, make different: 'The rhizome is ... a *map and not a tracing* ... What distinguishes the map from the tracing is that it is entirely oriented toward an experimentation in contact with the real. The map does not reproduce an unconscious closed in upon itself; it constructs the unconscious' (Deleuze and Guattari 1987: 12).

Actual, virtual, real. The actual is real and so is the virtual. There is an interplay between virtual and actual. Rhizome maps out the interplay. Actuality is derivative, not primary. Aion is a virtual set of forms, like but unlike in Plato (see Appendix I to *The Logic of Sense*, 'The Simulacrum and Ancient Philosophy').

Rhizomes lie on the practical terrain of getting somewhere and getting something done, ready to go in whichever direction is fruitful: 'A rhizome has no beginning or end; it is always in the middle, between things, interbeing, *intermezzo*. The tree is filiation, but the rhizome is alliance, uniquely alliance. The tree imposes the verb "to be," but the fabric of the rhizome is the conjunction, "and ... and ... and ..."' (Deleuze and Guattari 1987: 25). Conjoining, disjunctively synthesising, stitching an alliance, drawing a bridge, the rhizome maps territories and courses of activity.

Mapping of the rhizome is a machinic diagrammatics:

> *diagrams* must be distinguished from *indexes*, which are territorial signs, but also from *icons*, which pertain to reterritorialization, and from *symbols*, which pertain to relative or negative deterritorialization. Defined diagrammatically in this way, an abstract machine ... plays a piloting role. The diagrammatic or abstract machine does not function to represent, even something real, but rather constructs a real that is yet to come, a new type of reality. (Deleuze and Guattari 1987: 142)

Cinema as a new type of reality, a new type of temporal reality, is the example or paradigm we examine in our soon to come next part, on the time-image.

To draw an abstract line, to diagram, to make a machine, we are propelling arrows into the future, breaking up the stasis of points: 'The line-system (or block-system) of becoming is opposed to the point-system of memory', argue Deleuze and Guattari. 'Becoming is the movement by which the line frees itself from the point, and renders points indiscernible: the rhizome, the opposite of arborescence; break away from arborescence. *Becoming is an antimemory*' (1987: 294). Chronological point order is disrupted, forgetting displaces memory, the abstract line of pure imagination is freed to wander. Aion generates live possibilities for Chronos. The liberated line in nomadic distribution runs across the infinities of Aion for times to come: 'There is no act of creation that is not transhistorical and does not come up from behind or proceed by way of a liberated line. Nietzsche opposes history not to the eternal but to the subhistorical or superhistorical: the Untimely, which is another name for haecceity, becoming . . .' (296).

Time-Image Paradigm

A paradigm of the historically dynamic constitution of a machinic assemblage of subjectivity, one that allows us to imagine time as never before: cinema, and, more specifically, its later 'time-image' (which Deleuze distinguishes in historical and formal ways from the original 'movement-image'). Procedure led to a course of machines, producing generations of subjectivities and multiplications of times. In the second volume of his *Cinema: The Time-Image*, the machinic assemblage concerns the future to come:

> The French school never lost its taste for clockwork automata and clock-making characters, but also confronted machines with moving parts, like the American or Soviet schools. The man-machine assemblage varies from case to case, but always with the intention of posing the question of the future. (Deleuze 1989: 263)

The human-machine assemblage, the historical subject, that is, as prosthetically extended by the history of labour and technology. Deleuze does not overextend his analysis of the human-film camera-movie theatre to the televisual or videodromic scenes, which are newer still: 'Clockwork automata, but also motor automata, in short, automata of movement, made way for a new computer and cybernetic race, automata of computation and thought, automata with controls and feedback' (Deleuze 1989: 264–5). The technology and collective nature and phenomenological feel of these media all differ: 'The electronic image, that is, the tele and video image, the numerical image coming into being, either had to transform cinema or to replace it, to mark its death. We do not claim to be producing an analysis of the new images' (265).

Cinema already transforms the rules of the game in terms of erasing any distinction between real and imaginary, between past, present and future, and so between memory and anticipation:

For the time-image to be born . . . the actual image must enter into relation with its *own* virtual image as such; from the outset pure description must divide in two, 'repeat itself, take itself up again, fork, contradict itself'. An image which is double-sided, mutual, both actual and virtual, must be constituted. (Deleuze 1989: 273)

The image has two sides or faces at one and the same time:

We are no longer in the situation of a relationship between the actual image and other virtual images, recollections, or dreams, which thus become actual in turn: this is still a mode of linkage. We are in the situation of an actual image *and* its own virtual image, to the extent that there is no longer any linkage of the real with the imaginary, but *indiscernibility of the two*, a perpetual exchange. (Deleuze 1989: 273)

The two are one and yet differ in a perpetual relay of exchange. At the late capitalist postmodern moment of spectacularised society, we affirm the pre-eminence of imagination and the early affirmation of time and social constitution in David Hume: '*Repetition changes nothing in the object repeated, but does change something in the mind which contemplates it*. Hume's famous thesis takes us to the heart of a problem' (Deleuze 1994: 70). So Deleuze situates in relation to Hume his own work on repetition in *Difference and Repetition*. Deleuze glosses Hume's thesis as follows: 'Time is constituted only in the originary synthesis which operates on the repetition of instants. This synthesis contracts the successive independent instants into one another, thereby constituting the lived, or living, present' (70).

Imaginative constructive habit à la Hume is the basic psychic machine, the free productive agency which gives birth to memory and reason:

The passive synthesis of habit [first] in turn refers to . . . [a] more profound passive synthesis of memory: Habitus and Mnemosyne, the alliance of the sky and the ground. Habit is the originary synthesis of time, which constitutes the life of the passing present; Memory is the fundamental synthesis of time which constitutes the being of the past (that which causes the present to pass). (Deleuze 1994: 79–80)[11]

Hence the subject's creation in and of time, by way of the capacity of synthesis, of holding things together.

The time-image extends our account of Deleuze's theory and practice of temporal constitution, and also exemplifies an emergent quality, a new experience and collective constitution of time that is cinema.[12] Temenuga Trifonova begins her 'A Nonhuman Eye: Deleuze on Cinema' by linking Deleuze to the Sartre of *Imagination* and *The Psychology of Imagination* and characterising their joint venture (with Bergson) as one of plumbing the heights and depths of times or durations: 'Deleuze's task in the two volumes of *Cinema* is to demonstrate how modern cinema in particular has made it possible to surpass the human condition by abolishing subjectivity as a privileged image' (Trifonova 2004: 134). The time-image expresses a new collective experience and constitution of time, and as such, a transformation of subjectivity (by a new human-machine hybridity). This transformation is a liberation: subjectivity expresses itself more and more in pure time (leaving space behind, so to speak): 'when duration dictates what is happening, rather than events determining time, the subject has restored its independence from the world' (135). The coincidence of actual and virtual image in the time-image forms its self-referentiality: 'The self-referentiality of the image consists in the indistinguishability of the true and the imaginary within the image', as we saw above; 'Time (but not spatialized time, which is always referential and thus measurable) is self-referential in nature: the time-image does not describe a certain state of things but is itself that state of things' (146). The cinematic time-image allows us to live more in the future.

Beginning in the one and the many, the jointed and out of joint, we have moved through living labour to dead labour and back again, and to the future of machines, and subjective collectivities. The three syntheses of time in *Difference and Repetition* will be our closing note on Deleuze, one which allows us to express a discontent at his associating eternity and dislocated time with the death instinct:

> The first passive synthesis [of time], that of Habitus, presented repetition as a binding, in the constantly renewed form of a living present . . . The second synthesis, that of Eros-Mnemosyne, posits repetition as *displacement* and *disguise*, and functions as the ground of the pleasure principle . . . When the narcissistic ego takes the place of the virtual and real objects, when it assumes the displacement of the former and the disguise of the latter, it does not replace one content of time with another. On the contrary, we enter into the third synthesis. It is as though time had abandoned all possible mnemonic content, and in so doing had broken the circle into which it was lead by Eros. It is as though it had unrolled, straightened itself and assumed the ultimate shape of the labyrinth . . . Time empty and out of joint, with its rigorous and formal and static order, its crushing unity and its irreversible series, is precisely the death instinct . . . If there is an essential relation between eternal return and death, it is because it promises and implies 'once and for all' the death of that which is one. If there is an essential relation with the future, it is because the future is the deployment and explication of the multiple, of the different and of the fortuitous, for themselves and 'for all times'. (Deleuze 1994: 108–15)

Instead of Nietzsche's eternal return and Freud's death instinct, we go back to Spinoza and the positive affirmation of life, but we need to sort out some problems first.

Spinoza's Duration Between Deleuze and Negri

Why is there almost no mention of time in Deleuze's big book on Spinoza? Deleuze, unlike Negri, is nervous at the end of the day concerning Spinoza's monism and expressivism; as Robert Piercey writes: 'Deleuze thinks that although Spinoza is *the* philosopher of immanence, his treatment of substance still contains a residue of transcendence or emanation. Spinoza, in Deleuze's view, privileges substance over mode' (1996: 280). Piercey cites *Difference and Repetition*: 'With Spinoza . . . there still remains a difference between substance and the modes: Spinoza's substance appears independent of the modes, while the modes are dependent on substance, as though on something other than themselves' (Deleuze 1994: 40). Negri is a more consistent or fully immanent interpreter of Spinoza than Deleuze, as we shall see below.

What is the relation or situation between substance and its modes? The immanent expressivism of Spinoza takes some wrangling to sort out. Samuel Alexander's Deleuzian-type reading of Spinoza against Spinoza gives us an inkling of what this position might be. This inkling is fattened up by Negri's consistent affirmation of Spinoza from a future-oriented point of view. Negri's minor position is supported, as we shall see, by H. F. Hallett and David Savan. This reading solves some riddles of the substance–mode situation, and, hence, of the thought of change, transformation and revolution.

Alexander is close to Deleuze in taking up the latter's rude form of philosophical commentary that turns the subject monstrous (see Trnka 2001). Accordingly, Alexander 'propos[es] to explain what difference it would make to Spinoza's philosophy if, to make an impossible hypothesis, he had treated Time as an attribute of God' (1939: 353). Alexander is wrong that his is an impossible hypothesis and wrong to 'locate' Time in the attributes, as opposed to where Spinoza put it himself, namely, in substance (or God or Nature) in its active, creative, expressive aspect (or face), that is, as *Natura naturans*, rather than in its more passive, created, expressed face (or aspect), that is, as *Natura naturata*. Naturing nature is substance in its more fully substantival, that is acting, creating role. Natured nature is substance in its substantial but now passive, exhausted, if you will, role, showing its fruits.

Let us take our bearings from the *Ethics* itself at two points, a random couple from Spinoza's admittedly few explicitly positive mentions of time in the work. Consider, first, this temporal qualification of the nature of individuals, from IIIP8: '*The conatus with which each single thing endeavors to persist in its own being does not involve finite time, but indefinite time*' (Spinoza 1982: 110). And consider this with the later claim, at VP29, wherein Spinoza is developing his understanding of the most virtuous form of conatus or striving, i.e., the drive to know and love God or Nature: '*Whatever the mind understands under a form of eternity it does not understand from the fact that it conceives the present actual existence of the body, but from the fact that it conceives the essence of the body under a form of eternity*' (218). The Proof is expansive on the relation between time as measure, the felt experience of duration, and the eternal point of view:

> In so far as the mind conceives the present existence of its body, to that extent it conceives a duration that can be determined by time, and only to that extent does it have the power to conceive things in relation to time . . . But eternity cannot be explicated through duration . . . Therefore to that extent the mind does not have the power to conceive things under a form of eternity. But since it is the nature of reason to conceive things under a form of eternity . . ., and since it belongs to the nature of mind, too, to conceive of the essence of the body under a form of eternity . . . and since there belongs to the essence of mind nothing but these two ways of conceiving . . ., it follows that this power to conceive things under a form of eternity pertains to the mind only in so far as it conceives the essence of the body under a form of eternity. (Spinoza 1982: 218)

We will not explicate the full sense of this passage but only note the differentiation between measurable and hence unreal time, on the one side, and real duration, on the other; and, second, the possibility, as well as the limitation and warning concerning, the movement from duration to eternity. Alexander's critical dismissal of Spinoza on time is precociously quick. 'Time has been slipped', he alleges, 'into Extension out of the undefined activity of God' (1939: 359). He continues on to explain that while we contemporaries 'might be tempted to say that extension includes not only extension in space but duration in time' and that such a supposition would 'solve Spinoza's problem', yet 'there is no word of it in Spinoza and could not be'. It is our contention that there indeed could be and was. Alexander makes the implausible assumption that Spinoza simply misconceives motion: 'The truth appears to be that Spinoza could pass so easily from extension to motion because motion was conceived as it were statically' (359).

Not so, we shall show; rather, substance is conceived by Spinoza as essentially moving or dynamic.

Alexander then goes on to construct his time attribute 'gloss' (rather than commentary) on Spinoza, which he sums up as follows: 'In our gloss upon Spinoza the ultimate reality is full of Time, not timeless but essentially alive with Time, and the theatre of incessant change. It is only timeless in the sense that, taken as a whole, it is not particularised to any one moment or duration but comprehends them all' (1939: 361). It follows then that '[t]he grades of modal perfection are no longer a "static" series of forms, but a hierarchy produced in the order of time' (365); accordingly, 'nature infected with Time . . . does not stop, but pushing on, evolves out of these stable forms fresh distributions and a new order of beings with their specific character and their own conatus to persevere in their type'. Alexander gives the name *nisis* (over *conatus*) to this 'striving of Space-Time' (380) and defines it as 'the impulse of the world towards new levels of existence (as well as towards new kinds of being within any one level), and the guarantee that the particular distribution of motion attained shall not be permanent as a whole' (382).

Deleuze grants Spinoza an originality in the theory and practice of expressivism: 'The significance of Spinozism seems to me this: it asserts immanence as a principle and frees expression from any subordination to emanative or exemplary causality. *Expression itself no longer emanates, no longer resembles anything.* And such a result can be obtained only within a perspective of univocity' (1992: 180). Deleuze takes immanence and univocity from Spinoza but not the thinking of duration and eternity, or these, at least, not so much as from Bergson. Perhaps it is not so obvious that for Spinoza substance dominates the modes and time is an illusion. Might Spinoza be read in a more time-friendly way?

Let us go further back in time to the great 1930 work on Spinoza which is Hallett's *Aeternitas*. The immanence of which Deleuze is fond Hallett connects to the matter of the totality and its completeness or perfection:

> Only where the condition is completely fulfilled is there real process in the sense of *production* as distinct from conditioning, and here transiency gives place to immanency. The perfection of the whole, therefore, must already contain all the stages of its achieving . . . *sub specie aeternitatis*, and after the manner in which premises are contained in their explained conclusion: i.e., as constituting, not an identity in *mere* difference, or *symmetrical* difference, but an identity uniting and retaining the difference of the logically prior and the logically posterior. (Hallett 1930: 59)

Perfection and the expression of the totality are seen as productive and differentiating, not representative or copying. Hallett is clear on the real qualitative felt character of duration in distinction from time as measure: 'Spinoza's theory of joy ... must be taken as his recognition that the finite mind perceives duration, not as separated *puncta*, but as quality. Pure externality belongs only to time and measure, and these are unreal' (1930: 59). Duration, in distinction, is process; it is qualitative, not quantitative; 'and the essence of existence, even of enduring existence, is that very qualitative growth through which we escape the "absolute relativity" of mere time (and the self-contradictory phrase exactly describes the logical vice of both time and measure)' (59). Hallett argues that Bergson's 'intensive quantity, i.e., a quality' (59), is not a refutation of Spinoza but 'a partial and inadequate Spinozism; for it is not, strictly speaking, the past as past that permeates the present, but only the past as the given, and therefore as our main source of creative essence' (60). What is creative production?

> The creativity of duration is one with the determination of the temporal occurrence of individual things and minds, and this again with the production by the eternal whole of its own finite expressions or partial content. It is the nature of the whole so to express itself and, in expressing, to constitute itself; and since 'matter was not lacking to him for the creation of everything from the highest down to the lowest degree of perfection' [*Ethics* I, Appendix], the expressions are of every degree of completeness, and cannot but appear, therefore, to the finite expressions themselves as incomplete and successive, i.e., as involving limited duration. The creativity of duration is thus but a finite extract of real creativity, which is eternal and constitutive. (Hallett 1930: 61)

And if that is not clear enough, the footnote spells it out: 'All existence is, in a sense, miraculous: that is the significance of the term "creation"; but there is nothing in "emergent qualities" more demanding of natural piety than in the constitution of Space-Time itself. My thesis is that Space-Time and its so called "emergent" qualities should never have been divorced' (Hallett 1930: 61).

The new, emergent, positive quality is a part of the whole, expressive and expressed, and as such, eternal in its formal essence:

> positive quality is caught up into eternity, while its externality and limitation, its negativity, is lost ... Joy is the realizing of perfection in its degrees, its temporal achieving; *acquiescentia* is the realization of a perfection already achieved; blessedness is the realization of perfection and its eternal achievement; it is the ideal limit of both desire and joy as they constitute a being for whom transformation involves no succession. (Hallett 1930: 61–2)[13]

For Hallett, as for Negri and, as we shall see shortly, David Savan also, the distinction between *Natura naturans* and *Natura naturata* is real and explanatory of Spinoza's doctrine of creation, implying 'an eternal act': 'Substance as *Natura naturans*, in expressing itself in the complete modal system, *Natura naturata*, in the same eternal act recreates itself with infinite degrees of perfection, and thereby creates the nature which it expresses, and which expresses it' (Hallett 1930: 206).[14]

Qualitative, intensive synthesis, that is the character, according to Hallett, of the movement in and to eternity. 'Time is the phenomenon of eternity', he claims, and 'eternity the infinite existence that determines and comprehends all existence in time, and partly expresses itself in the duration of things. Eternity at once transcends and pervades its finite expressions' (1930: 228). Such an eternity is 'full' or 'purely intensive'; it is qualitatively transforming but not successive.

A similar corroborating reading may be found in David Savan's 'Spinoza on Duration, Time, and Eternity', which he begins by noting his major presupposition – which we have now secured in a way in advance – that Spinoza identifies God with *Natura naturans* and that this means 'generative action' as per *Ethics* I P29S, 4 Pref (Savan 1994: 4). The participation of the modes in eternity by way of qualitative transformation in duration is a sempiternity, as Savan defines it:

> The universe is an infinite individual. Like any mode, its existence does not follow necessarily from its essence. It endures. Since there is no individual mode external to it that could produce it or destroy it, it must endure always without beginning or end. Its duration must be everlasting, perpetual, or sempiternal. Yet Spinoza called the universe an infinite and eternal mode (E IP21, 22, & Ep 64). (Savan 1994: 7)

Sempiternal comes from *semper*, meaning eternal duration. Savan's goal is 'to show that it is Spinoza's new conception of eternity that enables him to distinguish the eternity of God, incompatible with sempiternity, and the eternity of the infinite and sempiternal universe' (7).

Nature is eternal and durational:

> The identity of essence and existence ... is simply the identity of the unlimited causal power of nature with the infinite variety of its actual and intelligible effects. Eternity is infinite actual existence, *natura naturata*, conceived as the necessary display of an infinitely originative activity, *natura naturans*. There is a divergence here between what is in fact the case – the identity of nature's power with nature's actuality – and the conceived distinction of antecedent from consequent. Eternity is a way of conceiving the real unity of nature, dividing that unity conceptually into two – active cause and necessary effect. (Savan 1994: 21)

Savan defines Spinoza's new concept of eternity in three stages: '(1) plenary existence itself, (2) rendered intelligible to intellect as a limitless variety of singular entities, (3) each of them freely necessary, specifying and fixing through its unique singularity just what nature's causal power is' (1994: 25).

Conclusion

The association of time with communism is consistent through much of Negri's work. In *Marx Beyond Marx* he identifies communism with '*the negation of all* measure' (1991a: 33). Hardt and Negri in *Empire* propose the following definition of time:

> The new phenomenology of the multitude reveals labor as the fundamental creative activity that through cooperation goes beyond any obstacle imposed on it and constantly re-creates the world. The activity of the multitude constitutes time beyond measure. Time might thus be defined as the immeasurability of the movement between a before and an after, an immanent process of constitution. (Hardt and Negri 2000: 402)

And in the Spinoza book, Negri is clear and unequivocal concerning the future-oriented character of Spinozism:

> The anomaly of Spinoza's thought with respect to his times is made ...
> a savage anomaly: savage because it is articulated in the density and the multiplicity of affirmations that rise up out of the unlimited affability of the infinite ... When the paradox of the world and the open tension contained in it between the positive infinity and the infinity of determinations is developed in activity and is recognized in the constitutive process, the pleasure of the world begins to become central, and the anomaly is made savage: savage because it is connected to the inexhaustible multiplicity of being, to its blossomings, which are as vast as they are agitated in flux. (Negri 1991b: 222)

There is no concern for the subordination or impotence of the modes on Negri's view. He then goes on to link Spinozism to the philosophy of the future:

> The Spinozian problematic of spatial being, as spatial constitution, with spatial production, coming to an end, is a proposal for the metaphysics of time. Not of time as becoming, as the most recent Modern philosophy would have it: because the Spinozian perspective excludes every object of becoming outside of the determination of the constitution. Rather, it is a proposal of metaphysics of time as constitution, the time that extends beyond the actuality of being, the being that constructs and selects its future. A philosophy of the future. (Negri 1991b: 199)

For Negri, Spinoza does a better job than Nietzsche for the future, and perhaps Spinoza may also do better than Nietzsche and Bergson on time, duration and eternity. Doing better in thinking time, duration and eternity by way of the imaginative-selection-and-construction-of-new-being:

> the inscription of power in being opens being toward the future. The essential tension wants existence. The cumulative process that constructs the world wants a further time, a future. The composition of the subject acquits the past only to make it tend toward the future. Being is temporal tension. If difference forms the future, then here the future ontologically founds difference . . . A continuous transition toward always greater perfection. Being produces itself . . . Being is greater tension toward the future as its present density grows to a higher level. The future is not a procession of acts but a dislocation worked by the infinite mass of intensive being: a linear, spatial displacement. Time is being. Time is the being of the totality . . . Being that is dislocated from one point to the next in space, in its infinity, in its totality, accomplishes a passage in the order of perfection, that is, in its construction. Not in relation to any other, but only in relation to itself. Therefore, it is liberation, emancipation, transition. Time is ontology. Constitution internal to production, and also internal to freedom. (Negri 1991b: 228)

For Negri, Spinoza plays a more crucial role than even the thinker of immanence and univocity in Deleuze. Negri's Spinoza is the philosopher of the future and of the radical democratic communist constitution of future times, by putting immanence and univocity within a constructive, constitutive, dynamic totality, or growing universe. Repetition and difference, tension, extension and intensification are its basic patterns of operation.

What times are to come? Better: what times will subjects be able to enjoy? Let us return to the time-image. The time-image expresses a new collective experience and constitution of time, and as such, a transformation of subjectivity (by a new human-machine assemblage). This transformation is a liberation: subjectivity expresses itself more and more in pure time. The coincidence of actual and virtual image in the time-image forms its self-reference. The cinematic time-image allows us to live more in the future. The future works on us more by way of the time-image. We are more and more creatures of time.

Notes

1. Class struggle, and hence much of the form of history, is in part a contest over apparatuses of thought, including fluency and literacy in various languages and machines of expression and dissemination; we develop a brief example of

such technological time intervention (activism, militancy) by way of looking at Deleuze's time-image below. The time-image is false in the sense of being a fabulation, and yet it is real and furthermore a transformation of the experience and sense of time.

2. Negri's sense of revolutionary communism, which he and I believe is true to Marx's, is defined precisely – in one of its modes – as the collective constitution of time by the liberated multitudes (see below).

3. Negri echoes McTaggart (1927), including by way of a third option, time C, though the character of this third fundamentally differs, in that McTaggart argues time away as an illusion whereas time C for Negri is the liberation of time (see below).

4. Real subsumption of labour by capital in the contemporary biopolitical global socius forms on the assumption and real development of the commodification of the micro and macro biospheres and the proletarianisation or exploitative coerced necessary laborisation of living, or, in simpler terms, making all things sellable and all activity work.

5. 'In real subsumption *time divides itself in reality*: on the one side, time of living labour, on the other time of dead labour' (Negri 2003: 62).

6. Compare: 'The time of constituent power, a time characterized by a formidable capacity of acceleration – the time of the event and of the generalization of singularity – has to be closed, treated, reduced in juridical categories, and restrained in the administrative routine' (Negri 1999: 2).

7. '[C]onstituent power always refers to the future. Constituent power has always a singular relationship to time. . . . [C]onstituent power is . . . an absolute will determining its own temporality. . . . Power becomes an immanent dimension of history, an actual temporal horizon. . . . [C]onstituent power . . . also represents an extraordinary acceleration of time. History becomes concentrated in a present that develops impetuously, and its possibilities condense into a very strong nucleus of immediate production' (Negri 1999: 11).

8. Note on libidinal economy. Lyotard (1993), which begins '[o]pen the so-called body . . .' (1).

9. I've discussed critically Deleuze's temporal ontology of event counter-actualisation, surfaces and depths, speeds and slownesses in my 'To Follow a Snail' (Trnka 2001).

10. Stumbling blocks for Spinoza reception are many, to begin with the paradox that a book titled *Ethics* supposedly shows the impossibility of ethics or morality; more immediately pertinent are the common criticisms that Spinoza annihilates time and is oversaturated with God/Nature.

11. '*Repetition is a condition of action before it is a concept of reflection*. We produce something new only on condition that we repeat – once in the mode which constitutes the past, and once more in the present of metamorphosis. Moreover, what is produced, the absolutely new itself, is in turn nothing but repetition: the third repetition, this time by excess, the repetition of the future as eternal return. . . . The "once and for all" of the order is there only for the "every time" of the final esoteric circle. The form of time is there only for the revelation of the formless in the eternal return. The extreme formality is there only for an excessive formlessness . . . [T]he ground has been superseded by a groundlessness, a universal ungrounding, which turns upon itself and causes only the yet-to-come to return' (Deleuze 1994: 90–1).

12. And by extension, provides an answer to the residual non-human phenomenology common to Deleuze and Negri.

13. Compare David Savan on the positive difference of modal expression: 'to exist is something positive, affirmative. No entity is a mere cipher, without ponder-

able force of its own, divisible without remainder, into the forces acting upon it' (1994: 6). Savan maps time as measure, duration and eternity onto McTaggart's A, B and C series, which Negri (2003) appears to play with or, rather, deterritorialise in his A, B, W and Y series.

14. Hallett is clear on expressionism in Spinoza: 'The "creation" which is accepted by Spinoza is thus not an action or set of actions initiated in time through which what was previously non-existent came into being. God is not the *causa transiens* of the world but its *causa immanens*, and creation is the infinite self-manifestation of a being whose essence is to express himself. Creation is eternal. And the distinction in the Real between that which is created and that which is incarnate is the same as that within an "expression" between the expression of the expressed, and the expressed expression' (1930: 209).

References

Alexander, S. (1939), 'Spinoza and Time', in *Philosophical and Literary Pieces*, London: Macmillan.

Deleuze, G. (1985), *Cinema 2: L'Image-Temps*, Paris: Les Éditions de Minuit.

Deleuze, G. (1989), *Cinema 2: The Time-Image*, trans. Hugh Tomlinson and Robert Galeta, Minneapolis: University of Minnesota Press.

Deleuze, G. (1990), *The Logic of Sense*, trans. Mark Lester with Charles Stivale, New York: Columbia University Press.

Deleuze, G. (1992), *Expressionism in Philosophy: Spinoza*, trans. Martin Joughin, New York: Zone Books.

Deleuze, G. (1994), *Difference and Repetition*, trans. Paul Patton, New York: Columbia University Press.

Deleuze, G. and F. Guattari (1987), *A Thousand Plateaus: Capitalism and Schizophrenia II*, trans. Brian Massumi, Minneapolis: University of Minnesota Press.

Hallett, H. F. (1930), *Aeternitas: A Spinozistic Study*, Oxford: Clarendon Press.

Hardt, M. and A. Negri (2000), *Empire*, Cambridge, MA: Harvard University Press.

Hunter, G., ed. (1994), *Spinoza: The Enduring Questions*, Toronto: University of Toronto Press.

Lyotard, J-F. (1993), *Libidinal Economy*, trans. Iain Hamilton Grant, Bloomington: Indiana University Press.

McTaggart, J. (1927), *The Nature of Existence, Volume II*, Cambridge: Cambridge University Press.

Massumi, B. (1987), 'Foreword' to Gilles Deleuze and Félix Guattari, *A Thousand Plateaus: Capitalism and Schizophrenia II*, Minneapolis: University of Minnesota Press.

Negri, A. (1991a), *Marx Beyond Marx: Lessons on the* Grundrisse, trans. Harry Cleaver, Michael Ryan and Maurizio Viano, New York: Autonomedia/Pluto.

Negri, A. (1991b), *The Savage Anomaly: The Power of Spinoza's Metaphysics and Politics*, trans. Michael Hardt, Minneapolis: University of Minnesota Press.

Negri, A. (1999), *Insurgencies: Constituent Power and the Modern State*, Minneapolis: University of Minnesota Press.

Negri, A. (2003), *Time for Revolution*, trans. Matteo Mandarini, New York: Continuum.

Negri, A. and M. Hardt (2000), *Empire*, Cambridge, MA: Harvard University Press.

Piercey, R. (1996), 'The Spinoza-Intoxicated Man: Deleuze on Expression', *Man and World*, 29: 269–81.

Savan, D. (1994), 'Spinoza on Duration, Time, and Eternity', in Graeme Hunter, ed., *Spinoza: The Enduring Questions*, Toronto: University of Toronto Press.

Spinoza, B. (1982), *The Ethics and Selected Letters*, trans. Samuel Shirley, Indianapolis: Hackett.

Trifonova, T. (2004), 'A Nonhuman Eye: Deleuze on Cinema', *Substance*, 33 (2): 134–52.

Trnka, P. (1997), 'Women, Animals, and the Unknown: Hume's Philosophy of Nature', *The Journal of the British Society for Phenomenology*, 28 (3): 255–72.

Trnka, P. (2001), 'To Follow a Snail: Experimental Empiricism and the Ethic of Minor Literature', *Angelaki*, 6 (3): 45–62.

PART III

EXPRESSIONS OF TIME

Chapter 8

Kill Metaphor: Kafka's Becoming-Animal and the Deterritorialisation of Language as a Rejection of *Stasis*

Charlene Elsby

Introduction to Metaphor: The Death of the Literary Work

To assign a metaphorical meaning to a work of literature is a matter of arrogance. One has the gall to read a literary work of art and then declare that the author did not mean what they have written, as it was written.[1] Rather, one declares, the author meant something else entirely. Of course, authors have written metaphorical works and done so meticulously, in order to make some point that they felt might be better expressed in symbol rather than literally. The metaphor is intended to add something to the work – to express something that either can't be expressed or is less effectively expressed literally. We're all familiar with metaphorical works that, if written without the metaphor, would be reduced to triviality. The metaphor works to draw out a thesis over the course of hundreds of pages that enforce the thesis by providing a narrative – and narrative appeals to us.

Kafka does not write such metaphors. Gregor Samsa is not metaphorically a bug in the *Metamorphosis*; he's very much a vermin, and *the fact* that he is so isn't a metaphor either.[2] Kafka does not *use* language to accomplish some task external to the text and only accomplished through a procedural encounter with it. This mechanical concept of the function of literature is dead. The ontology of the work of art as a living thing, as described by the early phenomenologist Roman Ingarden, supports the becoming-animal of the work of art for Deleuze and Guattari (to be discussed in the final section of this paper). The death of the work of art results from our rendering it ontologically static and axiologically neutral – something that no longer speaks to us, because it is no longer open to alteration through the living symbolic relation between text and interpretation. To quote Daniel W. Smith, 'A philosophical concept is not a metaphor but a metamorphosis' (2019: 61).[3]

Part of the fault rests in our concept of reference – that is, the concept of reference as a relation between two discrete entities, a word and a thing, one of which symbolises the other. (This definition, which I in no way endorse, renders all language symbolic, and only emboldens the sophists.[4]) Pervasive not only in the interpretation of literature but also in its creation is this insidious habit of always having present to mind some significance outside of the work itself – this tendency to not only produce or consume text but also to kill it, to assign it a meaning outside of the text itself, to set the text aside in favour of this meaning, and then proceed without it, the text becoming incidental to the external significance, the stripping of all that is concrete from the story in favour of some abstraction, which the history of western philosophy tells us is superior to all concretions, the concrete being something of which we must rid ourselves in order to access the idea of the text in the pure realm of ideas, the eternal forms. Assigning metaphor to a text is practising for death. The process fixes the text amongst the known, rendering it static. *The pigs are capitalists → capitalism is bad → the pigs are only there to make a point, to act as a tool, a means or a metaphor, and altogether incidental to the grander idea concerning the ideal political system.*[5]

But since Nietzsche, the redemption of the body in philosophy has become central to both Deleuzian and phenomenological thought. And according to phenomenological conceptions of literature, the body of the work is its materiality, the graphic elements of the text and their phonetic formations, prior to and undergirding the stratum of ideal meaning units by which we assign static meanings to terms. By refusing to render Kafka's text symbolic, these philosophers allow the body of the work to stay alive. It is *anima* and animal. 'Becoming-animal', for Deleuze, is not a metaphor; he is using the term in accordance with its definition.

The human concept of literature, on the other hand, is its death. It's the rationalisation of what is specifically expressed in a non-rational form (the literary work of art), to its detriment. While I'm sure it's not what Kafka meant when he said that his literary works were failures, if only all literary works could be such failures.[6]

By failure here, I mean the existential dichotomy of attempting to overcome the subjective in favour of the objective and always being forced back into the subjective.[7] (It is worthwhile to note that Deleuze was not a fan of the idea that there existed any kind of pure cogito that does or does not persist. All 'subjective' means here is 'perspectival', in the sense of a zero point of orientation unique to an individual human.) I conceive of the literary work of art as active within the realm of particulars, contrary to the attempts at objective forms of writing, in which no viewpoint is immediately evident, which aim at universality. Gregor Samsa is trapped in an evolving subjectivity and a particular form of subjectivity, and his world is concrete. The attempt to apply to the text of *The Metamorphosis* some universal, objective claim, which the author intended to express through the medium of the concrete, will fail. And we should be clear that such an attempt is in fact an attempt at murder.

What remains to be shown is how this state of affairs came to be – the progression of relevant ideas in the history of philosophy that have led to Deleuze and Guattari's resurrection of the literary work, with Kafka as their Lazarus. To quote Réda Bensmaïa's Foreword to Deleuze's and Guattari's text on Kafka:

> Thus, the art (modern art in this sense) that Kafka tried to introduce is effectively no longer an art that proposes to 'express' (a meaning), to 'represent' (a thing, a being), or to 'imitate' (a nature). It is rather a method (of writing) – of picking up, even of stealing: of 'double stealing' as Deleuze sometimes says, which is both 'stealing' and 'stealing away' – that consists in propelling the most diverse contents on the basis of (nonsignifying) ruptures and intertwinings of the most heterogeneous orders of signs and powers. (Bensmaïa 1986: xvii).

The spots of indeterminacy in Kafka's work are what make it effective, and they contribute to its long life as well.

Platonic Forms: Significance, Eternality and Death

Plato's denigration of artists at the end of the *Republic* as merchants of simulacra is certainly ironic, expressed, as it is, in the form of a drama, such that any philosophical claims of Plato's are presented from within the situated viewpoint of a character. The idea in Plato's passage is that artists, by representing reality, present only imitations of imitations.[8] Whereas material reality is an imitation of the ideal realm of the forms, its representation in art is a secondary imitation, of that which is already an imitation – e.g., a bed stripped of its wood and presented instead in paint is worse even than a wooden bed, which is an instantiation of the form of bed, the only object in this triptych worthy of Plato's philosophy. As with Deleuze's concept of the simulacrum, there is an element of malice in the artist's representation. (The simulacra are not only 'not real' but actually 'counterfeit' (Deleuze 2004: 75)). In the *Republic* (597e–598c), Plato writes:

We're agreed about imitators, then. Now, tell me this about a painter. Do you think he tries in each case to imitate the thing itself in nature or the works of craftsmen?

The works of craftsmen.

As they are or as they appear? You must be clear about that. How do you mean?

Like this. If you look at a bed from the side or the front or from anywhere else is it a different bed each time? Or does it only appear different, without being at all different?

And is that also the case with other things?

That's the way it is – it appears different without being so.

Then consider this very point: What does painting do in each case? Does it imitate that which is as it is, or does it imitate that which appears as it appears? Is it an imitation of appearances or of truth?

Of appearances. (Plato 1997b: 1202)

Recognising that material objects appear having fulfilled and unfulfilled aspects (a distinction later formalised by Husserl),[9] Plato's Socrates aims to prove to Glaucon that because a painter cannot paint an entire object but only one of its many appearances, the painted object is ontologically even worse than the material object it represents.[10] It's not clear that Plato meant to denigrate artists at all,[11] but even if he did, there's a notable disanalogy between the visual artist and the literary artist, the latter of whom uses words not to refer to particular material entities (such is the work of the documentarian) but to ideal entities – the ideal meanings of terms which, together, form linguistic structures that represent an abstract, fictional realm, and by the definition of literature, *not* the realm of material objects.

Of course, this passage seems especially relevant because the redemption of literature I'm proclaiming is accomplished with the deterritorialisation of language (the diminishment of the priority of formalised meanings) that Deleuze and Guattari claim Kafka achieves;[12] but I bring it up to highlight the ontology of representations that Plato describes not only here but also in the *Phaedo* – where philosophy, the purge according to which ideas are wrested from material instantiations, is conceived of as the practice of death.

It's enough to notice that all of Plato's arguments presented in the *Phaedo* have easily diagnosed logical errors to conclude that he did not mean for them to be taken as authority. But if that weren't enough, Plato takes care to have his characters point out to the reader that all the arguments presented in favour of the soul's immortality in the *Phaedo* are problematic. At this point, Socrates assures his interlocutors that just because these arguments are bad ones, does not mean that all arguments are bad, and proceeds on a path to soothe his listeners' fear of death through another method (storytelling). It is not beyond the possible inferences one might make to argue that if every argument Plato has Socrates present in favour of the soul's immortality is in fact a bad argument, then perhaps he did not mean to argue toward the conclusion of those arguments at all.[13]

And that conclusion is immediately repugnant, for the conclusion to be drawn from the ideas that the soul is immortal and that after death it reunites with the forms with which it claims an affinity is that *death is good*. This counter-intuitive conclusion is indeed what Socrates aims to prove – in a dialogue in which he has been sentenced to death, *as a penalty*.

The aim of philosophy in the *Phaedo* is the pursuit of theoretical knowledge, and this knowledge is precisely of universals. The philosopher, by pursuing this sort of knowledge, escapes from the lesser world of material instantiations (defined by their particularity) toward a realm of pure form. While our world is characterised by particulars, subject to temporality, the crux of the affinity argument for the soul's immortality is to characterise immortality as significantly similar to a form's eternality – devoid of material, it carries on.[14]

But what of a negative timelessness?

It is possible, within the variables given in Plato's dialogue, that we are meant to notice the disanalogy between the soul's immortality and a form's eternality. For one, the soul's immortality is meant to commence when time comes to an end. This is a distinct state of affairs in comparison to the form's eternality, as the forms were never subject to time. Plato takes as an assumption that a soul exists in time while it is instantiated and even has the capacity to be affected by things in the temporal realm, characteristics which are not shared with the forms. If we are meant to infer this distinction, it is reasonable to assume that death is *not good*, that death is *bad*, and that in contradistinction to eternality, a negative timelessness is also possible, and this is death.

We are motivated to keep the literary work of art alive only if death is negative, if death is conceived not as eternality but as *stasis* – if we value the anima and lament its destruction. A reversal of Plato, or perhaps an argument in support of a secret Platonic argument in favour of the lifeworld, Deleuze and Guattari's concept of Kafka's literature as animal reignites an axiology where particularity, situatedness and motion are favourable to stasis, universality and death. Perhaps the universal is problematic after all.

The Universal as Symbolised in Language, the Referent of Terms and the Abstraction of Human Reason: The Problem of Language as Stasis

According to Aristotle's *Metaphysics*, theoretical knowledge is superior to practical knowledge, while the difference between Aristotle's and Plato's concepts of the source of theoretical knowledge differs. For Plato, in the *Phaedo* and elsewhere, theoretical knowledge (of the forms, existing separately from their material instantiations) is in the soul prior to birth, and the process we call learning is actually recollection. 'Summoners' in the material realm remind the soul of their more perfect counterparts amongst the forms, and we come to recollect those forms as we simultaneously recognise the defects of the summoner. We look at two unequal things and recognise, through them, the universal form of equality they fail to instantiate.

For Aristotle, on the contrary, the universal is abstracted from particulars. The active intellect becomes the efficient cause of our being able to think in universal terms, as the particular forms of perception are universalised. Those universal thoughts are symbolised in spoken sounds, and spoken sounds are symbolised in written language (*De Interpretatione*). The referents of language are *fixed*, but also they aren't. A word comes to symbolise something by convention, and Aristotle recognises that these conventions are not the same for all people at all times. There are not only universal but particular terms, referring to individuals in the perceived universe. There is a disconnect between the referent of 'George' and the referent of 'human' such that we can't make the general claim that 'all word meanings are universal'.

And universality is the problem, because this is the aspect of language according to which we attempt to render it static, eternal – God-like, universal. The concepts become all confused, because, according to Aristotle, God is the form of forms, that which is universal, and the universalisation of particularities by the active intellect is how humanity attempts to mimic the divine – first in thought and then in language.

We purify temporal objects of their temporality and fix them as the referents of equally fixed terms, like 'essence', where both the word and what it refers to are putatively atemporal. Meanwhile the philosophy of language often leaves behind the cases where this is obviously not the case, such as 'George'. 'George' is uninteresting, to those who seek universal theoretical knowledge, because the term and its referent will both die. Some will even attempt to render George a universal, a universal having only one instance, but a universal nonetheless, just to escape his particularity.

These cases in fact open up an extremely interesting version of linguistic reference as a sort of tenuous fixation. Conceived of as such, we could avoid the death of language (and consequently, literary works) by allowing their continuity in flux. But the term 'tenuous fixation' is not even enough, for Deleuze, as it's an attempt to describe something novel by applying old terminology, resulting in contradiction. (For the tenuousness of the fixation renders it unfixed, recognising that what is tenuous is really not fixed at all.) Rather, the attempt to affix a term to a referent in such a way as to kill them both has brought tension to the history of the philosophy of language and metaphysics as well. But most interestingly, the demise of the fixed nature of the relation of signifier and signified occurs in Husserl's grappling with Aristotle in his analyses of linguistic signification, in Ingarden's adaptation of Husserl's phenomenology to his analysis of the literary work of art, and finally in Merleau-Ponty's concept of expression, ultimately leading to the collapse of the signifier and what is signified, which finally lays the groundwork for Deleuze's murder of the metaphor.

The Phenomenologists: Meanings and Signs

In the *Logical Investigations*, Husserl touches on problems related to the syncategorematica; that is, words not included amongst those encompassed by Aristotle's ten categories in the *Categories* (a work of linguistics, logic and metaphysics). Elucidating how there exist words that Aristotle dismissed as insignificant (not meaning anything), Husserl argues to the contrary that the terms are indeed significant, though their significance is dependent. This line of thinking begins phenomenology's collapse of the signification relation, still very much present in Husserl, expanding our concept of communication beyond the notion that it's mainly constituted by the utterance of referring terms, and redeeming our concept of 'meaning' as something language *does* rather than something that it *has*. Deleuze's eventual elimination of distance between the text and its meaning (the death of metaphor and signification more generally) begins with the recognition that not all terms signify, or only signify in some reduced sense.

In order to conceive of how the syncategorematica 'mean', we need first to make a distinction between 'meaning' as a verb and 'meaning' as a noun. 'Meaning' defined in the sense of a noun lends itself to a representational theory of language, as does the Aristotelian usage of 'signification' in his analyses of language. A word is 'significant' if there is something definite to which the term refers, or which the term represents. There are names, which are significant sounds, and verbs, which are significant sounds with the addition of time. Sometimes we translate the terms as 'subject' and 'predicate', the former being the referring terms, and the latter being referring terms with the addition of time. To have a linguistic construct capable of being true or false, we need to specify both a subject and predicate; whether the subject and predicate are related in the same way as the things to which they refer are related will determine if the statement is true or false.

The subjects and predicates are the categorical words, i.e., the words included under the general ten categories of Aristotle's *Categories*. We can therefore take Aristotle's list of categories as a comprehensive list of significant words. The definition of 'signification', I argue, is actually independent signification. Aristotle is careful to distinguish between terms that signify separately and those that don't. In a lot of cases, the same syllables are significant in separation versus those that are not; the difference is located in their linguistic context, i.e., whether they are presented as parts of another word or not. If, for example, we look at the term 'pirate-boat', a single term translated from ἐπακτροκέλης (which Aristotle examines in *De Interpretatione* 2), the terms 'pirate' and 'boat' take on a dependent meaning, in relation to one another, which they would not have were they encountered in separation. And the combined meaning is not a combination of the referents of the terms encountered in separation. The relation between 'pirate' and 'boat' in 'pirate-boat' is not a boat-pirate hybrid, and it cannot be conceived of as any conjunction of 'boat' and 'pirate'. Rather, the complex term 'pirate-boat' has a referent that exists as a unity, and is itself not a combination of pirates and boats. In short, the term cannot be decomposed into separate parts that retain significance in separation, just as its referent is not decomposable into separate objects (i.e., a boat and a pirate). Rather, the terms 'pirate' and 'boat' are dependently significant within the term 'pirate-boat'. They mean though they have no meaning. Together, they constitute what Husserl calls in the Fourth Investigation a 'complete' expression. He specifies that with respect to the distinction between categorematic and syncategorematic expressions, 'It can at least be described by holding the former to be capable of serving as complete expressions, finished locutions by themselves, whereas the latter cannot' (Husserl 2001: 58).

The dependently significant terms as described by Aristotle best exemplify what Husserl is indicating when he conceives of how it is that words mean, rather than how they have a meaning. The intimating function of expressions is their capacity to point toward something, 'meaning' in the sense of an act, while the 'content' of the expression is something else; it's a meaning in the sense of a noun. As Husserl describes in the First Investigation:

> all expressions in communicative speech function as indications. They serve the hearer as signs of the 'thoughts' of the speaker, i.e. of his sense-giving inner experiences, as well as of the other inner experiences which are part of his communicative intention. This function of verbal expressions we shall call their intimating function. The content of such intimation consists in the inner experiences intimated. (Husserl 2001: 189)

In the case of independently significant expressions, the content of the expression is pointed toward by the intimating function of the expression. But in the case of syncategorematic terms, the intimating function becomes internal to the expression, specifying the way in which the terms should be conceived of as related, rather than indicating any additional content. They mean but do not have a meaning. 'And' does not signify a separately existing relation, the third thing in the expression 'this and that', where 'this', 'that' and 'and' specify three separate entities, one of which is representative of a separately existing relationship of conjunction. The 'and' is non-referential, or non-independently significant. It intimates but does not have a content. It is there in order to determine the way in which the conception of 'this' and 'that' are to be concretised in relation to one another. 'And' is incomplete without two things to conjoin.

The distinction between significant and insignificant terms, dependently and independently significant words, is less prominently featured in Roman Ingarden's *The Literary Work of Art* as compared to his analysis of the cognition of the literary work of art in *The Cognition of the Literary Work of Art*. But he recognises that some phrases are meant to convey atemporality while others are not. There is a continuing tension in the work of Ingarden regarding the 'ideal meaning units' that constitute the second stratum of a literary work of art.

That tension is precisely the ideality of the meaning units. Ingarden conceives of the literary work of art as ontologically describable through four strata:

(1) The material
(2) The ideal meaning units
(3) Schematised aspects
(4) Represented objectivities

The base material of the literary work of art is its physical existence, which includes not only the paper or material through which the text survives, but also the marks on the page making up the letters that we perceive as symbols. The ideal meaning units are the units of meaning that these materialities invoke in us, which provide the conduit through which we come to conceive the world of the book, its characters, happenings and circumstances. The ideal meaning units are linguistic constructions of varying complexity, and the fact that they are of varying complexity means that some meaning units are less obviously 'ideal' than others, where 'ideal' means their temporality has been abstracted away.

For individual referential terms, 'ideal' may be applicable, as discussed above, when we are discussing abstract notions like 'time', 'space', 'unity' and other such concepts whose referents, we assume, don't die. Nevertheless, we recognise immediately that the concepts to which these words refer do and have changed over the course of humanity's dealings with them. The problem is more evident when Ingarden discusses more complex meaning units – phrases and sentences. While 'the blue frog' may be conceived (by some) as a phrase constituted of three independent (or dependent) meanings, the phrase taken as a complex, as a combination, appears not nearly as necessary, inevitable or worthy of universality as any term in particular. Sentences, likewise, come and go. The more complex a linguistic meaning unit becomes, the less it seems able to claim ideality. And finally, Ingarden allows that the literary work of art, as a whole, is capable of life and death. It is a thing that comes into being and which may eventually die, as every copy is destroyed and every human memory of it erased. Now it seems almost absurd that anything eternal should ever have constituted it.

Which leads us to two possible conclusions: either a book is not constituted of words, or those words are not ideal meaning units. The latter conclusion seems more reasonable. What Deleuze ultimately aims to achieve is the internalisation of the forms of language into its materiality. Like an Aristotelian rejection of ideal Platonic forms that asserts the 'hereness' of the *eidos* in the material entity, so Deleuze's concept of sense reintegrates meaning and phonetic material by eliminating ideality from meaning, along with separability (contrary to a representational model of language, the meaning of language isn't separate from language, but exists as an embodied *eidos* which, for Aristotle, is any *eidos*).[15] Smith correctly characterises Aristotelian hylomorphism in his *Essays on Deleuze*:

Matter is never a simple or homogeneous substance capable of receiving forms, but is made up of intensive and energetic traits that not only make that operation possible but continuously alter it (clay is more or less porous, wood is more or less resistant); and forms are never fixed molds, but are determined by the singularities of the material that impose implicit processes of deformation and transformation (iron melts at high temperatures; marble and wood split along their veins and fibers). (Smith 2012: 100)

In brief, matter and form aren't two separate things in some kind of combat; they're aspects and causes of a more primary unity (the thing), separable only by abstraction.

Finally, in Merleau-Ponty, an analysis of language arises that allows for its conception outside of pure reference. Relying heavily on Husserl and, in particular, on the concept of the intimating function of expressions, Merleau-Ponty's concepts of speech and expression allow for a living language better representative of the lifeworld in which it subsists.

Materiality, meaning, thought and language are all reconceived in Merleau-Ponty, destroyer of dichotomies. The most obvious dichotomy destruction in *Phenomenology of Perception* is that between the subject and object, and it is not surprising that this dichotomy should also dissolve in a linguistic context. 'Representation', which Husserl defines at least a dozen times in *The Logical Investigations*, is sidelined as nowhere near the primary function of expression.[16] Merleau-Ponty points out that it is in fact not the case that a meaning is first conceived by a human subject, converted to linguistic form, and then related to other nearby subjects. Rather, expression itself generates meaning. It *is* meaning, where meaning is conceived of in the sense of an act (as it is sometimes for Husserl – see above) and not as the dead correlate of a word.[17]

Words mean in the same way that I do. And this is why the novels of Kafka continue to mean after his death. It is simply wrong to think that the book is nothing more than the recorded thoughts of a dead man. It is a living thing that continues to mean in his absence, a sort of quasi-subject with things to say, fully capable of meaning those things on its own. It's our concept of meaning that needs revision. Meaning is not reference.

Deleuze and Guattari on Becoming-Animal and the Death of Metaphor

I have argued that Deleuze and Guattari's concept of 'becoming-animal' applies to the death of metaphor in the sense that language, in becoming-animal, rejects the fixed referent of language and thus saves the literary work from *stasis*. This is evident in the Kafka book, where Deleuze and Guattari write:

> To become animal is to participate in movement, to stake out the path of escape in all its positivity, to cross a threshold, to reach a continuum of intensities that are valuable only in themselves, to find a world of pure intensities where all forms come undone, as do all the significations, signifiers, and signifieds, to the benefit of an unformed matter of de-territorialized flux, of nonsignifying signs. Kafka's animals never refer to a mythology or to archetypes but correspond solely to new levels, zones of liberated intensities where contents free themselves from their forms as well as from their expressions, from the signifier that formalized them. (Deleuze and Guattari 1986: 13)

In a less abstract sense (by which I mean, turning to examine some particular 'becoming-animal' rather than the universal 'becoming-animal' and its definition), Kafka's texts embody the rejection of what is human in favour of the animal. The formalisation toward which humanity tends, as is well known, may tend toward evil. When Arendt calls evil 'banal', she indicates the technical proficiency with which human actors enact the finite and concrete actions through which great evils are accomplished. While Deleuze and Guattari call such diabolical powers 'inhumane', they are in fact quite human. Here 'inhumane' does not exactly refer to the human tendency to abstract, to rationalise, to engage at the level of the universal with no concern for the particular; it means to suffer at the hands of someone who doesn't *also* take into account the particular – evils enacted at a systemic level, from which it is easy to imagine that no particular human suffers, though it is completely wrong to think so. All through western philosophy the concept of humanity has been tied up in the dichotomy of the universal and particular, the infinite and finite, the mundane and the divine, the 'rational animal' wherein 'rationality' and 'animality' are taken as contraries. Becoming-animal, while we have associated animality with particularity, is less a subsumption to a universal than it is a rejection – individuality, as opposed to particularity (a unique one rather than a one of many.)

To the inhumanness of the 'diabolical powers' there is the answer of a becoming-animal: to become a beetle, to become a dog, to become an ape, 'head over heels and away', rather than lowering one's head and remaining a bureaucrat, inspector, judge or judged. All children build or feel these sorts of escapes, these acts of becoming-animal (Deleuze and Guattari 1986: 12–13).

The escape of which Deleuze and Guattari speak is accomplished at the linguistic level in Kafka's texts, especially so when forms are abolished from linguistic expressions. The animal is that which has no voice, where 'voice' is (since Aristotle) the enunciation of sounds that *mean something* (have form). Becoming-animal is the escape from humanity by escaping the concept of human as *logos anthropos*, translated not as 'rational animal' but as 'speaking animal' (though it is assumed that rationality and speech go together, because both constitute the imposition of form on material):

> The sound or the word that traverses this new deterritorialization no longer belongs to a language of sense, even though it derives from it, nor is it an organized music or song, even though it might appear to be. We noted Gregor's warbling and the ways it blurred words, the whistling of the mouse, the cough of the ape, the pianist who doesn't play, the singer who doesn't sing and gives birth to her song out of her nonsinging, the musical dogs who are musicians in the very depths of their bodies since they don't emit any music. Everywhere, organized music is traversed by a line of abolition – just as a language of sense is traversed by a line of escape – in order to liberate a living and expressive material that speaks for itself and has no need of being put into a form. (Deleuze and Guattari 1986: 21)

That is to say, if expression is properly located at the material stratum of language, then there's no need to fix it by rendering it formal and thus static. But to recognise that such an expression is possible is not to exclude other expressions. *For there are formal expressions.* It is the unique place of the philosopher to recognise both; and whereas the Platonic discipline always tends toward becoming god (in the elimination of finitude by a tendency toward universality in the forms), the contrary motion is to become animal. As Nietzsche described: 'To live alone, you need to be either an animal or a god – says Aristotle. But he left out the third case: you can be both – a *philosopher* . . .' (2005: 156).

Conclusion

In *Kafka: Toward A Minor Literature*, Deleuze and Guattari assert that the magic of Kafka's literary works is nothing less than a deterritorialisation of language and a becoming-animal of the literary work (where these terms are almost synonymous). The becoming-animal of the literary work applies specifically to Kafka, whose human characters tend to become literally animal (e.g., Gregor Samsa's metamorphosis); while such transformations have been interpreted as symbolic, Deleuze and Guattari reject their symbolic nature on the basis that it would be internally contradictory to interpret a rejection of stasis as something static. Kafka's books, stories and letters shalt not be frozen in time. (Signification is a territorialisation, a rendering-static or detemporalisation of a relation between what is significant and what is signified – but there is no relation of significance if there are not, in fact, two things.)

There is nothing outside the text to which the becoming-animal refers. Rather, becoming-animal should be interpreted metaphysically. Becoming-animal is the rejection of the human application of formal thinking to the literary work – the taking of something temporal and rendering it static. Becoming-animal, rather, *animates*, i.e., resists the death of language through the application of formal signification relations. Deleuze and Guattari believe Kafka evades this formalisation of language. Rejecting any but a nominal distinction between the writer, the text and some imaginary external referents, Deleuze and Guattari kill the metaphor – the artificial application of stasis to something which is itself not being but becoming – and thereby assert the capacity of the literary work to *move*, to exist in the realm of the informal (where in the realm of the formal, stasis reigns).

Whereas the animal is the rejection of the human, and the human is the tendency toward formalisation, becoming-animal is the assertion (contra Aristotle) of an unformed matter which is not prime matter (the only unformed matter of which Aristotle conceived). And in response to the Aristotelian concern, 'Aren't the animals still too formed, too significative, too territorialized?' (Deleuze and Guattari 1986: 15), Deleuze and Guattari's text asserts a *relative* disinformation of the literary works of Kafka, where form represents an atemporal aspect and materiality a temporal one. The literary work resists its detemporalisation through signification, retaining its *anima*. That is to say, becoming-animal is a deterritorialisation and an assertion of the unformed, insignificative and dynamic nature of the literary work, which necessitates the existence of an unformed matter that is *as* capable of independent existence as the uninstantiated form. The movement from stasis (detemporalisation) to becoming-animal (becoming animate) is necessarily discontinuous – a motion from immobility to mobility, which necessitates a recursive definition of motion and a negation of the definition of time as something abstracted from motion (lest we be saddled with recursive times as well).

Notes

1. A despotic regime of significance, if you will, comparable to the malicious use of semiotics by authoritarian psychoanalysts that Deleuze and Guattari discuss

in *A Thousand Plateaus*: 'Psychoanalysis is a definite case of a mixed semiotic: a despotic regime of significance and interpretation, with irradiation of the face, but also an authoritarian regime of subjectification and prophetism, with a turning away of the face (the positioning of the psychoanalyst behind the patient suddenly assumes its full significance). Recent efforts to explain that a "signifier represents the subject for another signifier" are typically syncretic: a linear proceeding of subjectivity along with a circular development of the signifier and interpretation. Two absolutely different regimes of signs in a mix. But the worst, most underhanded of powers are founded on it' (Deleuze and Guattari 1987: 125).

2. Another instance where Kafka has been accused of using metaphors is the end of *The Trial*, when K. is killed: 'But the hands of one of the men were placed on K'.s throat, whilst the other plunged the knife into his heart and turned it round twice. As his sight faded, K. saw the two men leaning cheek to cheek close to his face as they observed the final verdict. "Like a dog!" he said. It seemed as if his shame would live on after him' (Kafka 2009: 165). The editor claims in a footnote that Kafka uses references to dogs to symbolise the degradation of the human. But there's nothing metaphorical about K'.s treatment. He *is* being treated how a dog might be treated. As Deleuze and Guattari write, 'What Kafka immediately anguishes or rejoices in is not the father or the superego or some sort of signifier but the American technocratic apparatus or the Russian bureaucracy or the machinery of Fascism' (Deleuze and Guattari 1986: 12).

3. I'm sure this is a reference to this statement in the Kafka book: 'Kafka deliberately kills all metaphor, all symbolism, all signification, no less than all designation. Metamorphosis is the contrary of metaphor. There is no longer any proper sense or figurative sense, but only a distribution of states that is part of the range of the word. The thing and other things are no longer anything but intensities overrun by deterritorialized sound or words that are following their line of escape' (Deleuze and Guattari 1986: 22).

4. For a newer, better concept of language's descriptive capacity, see Robbe-Grillet: 'Description once served to situate the chief contours of a setting, then to cast light on some of its particularly revealing elements; it no longer mentions anything except insignificant objects, or objects which it is concerned to make so. It once claimed to reproduce a pre-existing reality; it now asserts its creative function' (1965: 147).

5. Fun fact: at his death, Deleuze was working on a book project tentatively titled *The Grandeur of Marx*.

6. See the translator's introduction: 'For Scarpetta, Kafka's "failure" (the term is his) comes from its reduction of a whole career to a single philosophic force – from its desire to "present texts as 'examples' (if not as 'symptoms') instead of analyzing the process they engage in"' (Deleuze and Guattari 1986: xxiii, referring to Scarpetta 1975: 49).

7. Deleuze and Guattari on the relation of subjectivity and significance are very fun: 'There is no signifiance that does not harbor the seeds of subjectivity; there is no subjectification that does not drag with it remnants of signifier. If the signifier bounces above all off a wall, if subjectivity spins above all toward a hole, then we must say that the wall of the signifier already includes holes and the black hole of subjectivity already carries scraps of wall' (Deleuze and Guattari 1987: 182). In the Kafka book, becoming-animal is the antidote to suspect subjectivities: 'In contrast to the letters, the becoming-animal lets nothing remain of the duality of a subject of enunciation and a subject of the statement; rather, it constitutes a single process, a unique method that replaces subjectivity' (Deleuze and Guattari 1986: 36).

8. Compare Deleuze and Guattari's genetic concept of language: 'The act of becoming is a capturing, a possession, a plus-value, but never a reproduction or an imitation' (1986: 14).

9. Husserl recognises the impossibility of ever perceiving a spatiotemporal object in its entirety and designates the sides of it which are apparent to us at any given time as 'fulfilled', while those that are not apparent are 'unfulfilled'. Unfulfilled aspects of any concrete entity may later be fulfilled and contribute to an overall noema. He says in *Ideas*: 'No perception of the physical thing is definitively closed; there is always room for new perceptions, for determining more precisely the indeterminatenesses, for fulfilling the unfulfilled. With every progression the determinational content of the physical thing-noema, which continually belongs to the same physical thing-X, is enriched. It is an eidetic insight that *each* perception and multiplicity of perceptions is capable of being amplified; the process is thus an endless one; accordingly, no intuitive seizing upon the physical thing-essence can be so complete that a further perception cannot noematically contribute something new to it' (Husserl 1985: 358).

10. Deleuze and Guattari reference the statisticity of an image as memory early in the Kafka book, in a discussion of Kafka's use of images of people with bent heads: 'The memory is a family portrait or a vacation photo showing men with bent heads, women with their necks circled by a ribbon. The memory blocks desire, makes mere carbon copies of it, fixes it within strata, cuts it off from all its connections. But what, then, can we hope for? It's an impasse' (1986: 4). In the diagram that follows, Deleuze and Guattari ascribe territoriality to the image, on account of its being a blocked, oppressed or oppressing, or neutralised desire. (Desire, as we know, is the catalyst of all motion.) It's useful to compare territoriality and deterritorialisation in Deleuze and Guattari to the limited and unlimited in Pythagorean philosophy. Plato's philosophy of forms is a philosophy of the limited – a marking off of coherent concepts from the maelstrom of all that is. In the Pythagorean list of dichotomies from Aristotle's *Metaphysics* 986a22, the limited has something in common with the odd, the one, the right, the masculine, rest, the straight, light, good and the square, while the unlimited would have something in common with the even, many, left, feminine, motion, the crooked, darkness, evil and the oblong.

11. A more cautious interpretation would be that Plato meant to eliminate bad artists, the ones who produced simulacra: 'The *Republic* does not attack art or poetry as such; it attempts to eliminate art that is simulacral or phantastic, and not iconic or mimetic' (Smith, 2012: 15).

12. According to Smith, Deleuze interprets Nietzsche as aiming at the inversion of Platonism. In Deleuzian terms, this means specifically that the 'inversion of Platonism . . . implies an affirmation of the being of simulacra as such. The simulacrum must then be given its own concept and be defined in affirmative terms' (Smith 2012: 12). I've no doubt this is what Nietzsche was doing; the question is whether Plato meant any of what he wrote on the subject – i.e., if there is indeed such a Plato to invert. Deleuze writes in *Difference and Repetition*: 'The whole of Platonism, by contrast, is dominated by the idea of drawing a distinction between "the thing itself" and the simulacra . . . Overturning Platonism, then, means denying the primacy of original over copy, of model over image; glorifying the reign of simulacra and reflections' (2004: 80).

13. For in-depth analyses of each of these arguments in turn, see Dorter 1982.

14. Socrates' affinity argument starts at 78b in the *Phaedo*. Socrates gets Cebes to agree that there is nothing left to say against the conclusion that 'the soul is most like the divine, deathless, intelligible, uniform, indissoluble, always the same as itself, whereas the body is most like that which is human, mortal, mul-

tiform, unintelligible, soluble and never consistently the same' (Plato 1997a: 70).

15. Of course, Deleuze would never say it in those words, and this is not Aristotle's concept of language. I'm identifying an Aristotelian hylomorphism in Deleuze's concept of sense. As Smith phrases it: 'The genesis of language must be found at the relation between the intensive depth (noise) and the extensive surface (sense)' (2019: 59). I'd say, the genesis of language is the relation between an unformed matter (sound) and the imposition of some organisation (form) that renders it sensical and which primarily defines *what it is* (form as essence). That is, language is expression more than it is phonemes.

16. Cf. Chapter 4 of Investigation 2 in Husserl's *Logical Investigations* (Husserl 2001).

17. Deleuze picks up the concept of a living language as *genesis* in *The Logic of Sense*, which Smith elucidates in a fashion reminiscent of Merleau-Ponty: 'This is the function of the surface organisation of sense: it separates sounds from the body and begins to turn them into the elements of speech. The creation of sense (out of non-signifying elements) is what allows the sounds coming out of one's mouth to participate fully in a shared linguistic world. But the converse is also true. If a child comes to a language it cannot yet grasp as a language, but only as a familial hum of voices, perhaps conversely it can grasp what adults no longer grasp in their own language, namely the differential relations between the formative elements of language' (2019: 53). That is to say, in the language of Merleau-Ponty's phenomenology, that linguistic formations are habits that have achieved automaticity – when people talk, we are directly aware of their meaning, and do not (but might, if we choose) focus on the sounds which act as media for meaning. We can confirm this experientially by noticing that when we attempt to recall a conversation, we are more likely to remember what was expressed rather than the individual words or actual sounds. In the Kafka book, Deleuze and Guattari conceive of the production of a minor literature as immediately operating within the realm of expression, rather than the expression of a pre-existing content (the non-minor literatures that have come before). If there's a metaphor in Kafka, it's tacked on to the text later, masquerading as the 'content' of yore. 'A major, or established, literature follows a vector that goes from content to expression. Since content is presented in a given form of the content, one must find, discover, or see the form of expression that goes with it. That which conceptualizes well expresses itself. But a minor, or revolutionary, literature begins by expressing itself and doesn't conceptualize until afterward ("I do not see the word at all, I invent it"). Expression must break forms, encourage ruptures and new sproutings' (Deleuze and Guattari 1986: 28).

References

Bensmaïa, R. (1986), 'The Kafka Effect', in Gilles Deleuze and Félix Guattari, *Kafka: Toward a Minor Literature*, trans. Dana Polan, Minneapolis: University of Minnesota Press.

Deleuze, G. (2004), *Difference and Repetition*, trans. Paul Patton, New York: Bloomsbury.

Deleuze, G. and F. Guattari (1986), *Kafka: Toward a Minor Literature*, trans. Dana Polan, Minneapolis: University of Minnesota Press.

Deleuze, G. and F. Guattari (1987), *A Thousand Plateaus: Capitalism and Schizophrenia II*, trans. Brian Massumi, Minneapolis: University of Minnesota Press.

Dorter, K. (1982), *Plato's* Phaedo: *An Interpretation*, Toronto: University of Toronto Press.

Husserl, E. (1985), *Ideas*, trans. F. Kersten, The Hague: Martinus Nijhoff.

Husserl, E. (2001), *Logical Investigations*, Vol. II, trans. J. N. Findlay, New York: Routledge.

Ingarden, R. (1974), *The Cognition of the Literary Work of Art*, Evanston: Northwestern University Press.

Ingarden, R. (1979), *The Literary Work of Art*, Evanston: Northwestern University Press.

Kafka, F. (2009), *The Trial*, trans. Mike Mitchell, Oxford: Oxford University Press.

Merleau-Ponty, M. (2012), *The Phenomenology of Perception*, trans. Donald A. Landes, Abingdon: Routledge.

Nietzsche, F. (2005), *Twilight of the Idols*, in *The Antichrist, Ecce Homo, Twilight of the Idols and Other Writings*, ed. Aaron Ridley and Judith Norman, trans. Judith Norman, Cambridge: Cambridge University Press.

Plato (1997a), *Phaedo*, trans. G. M. A. Grube, in *Complete Works*, ed. John Cooper, Indianapolis: Hackett.

Plato (1997b) *Republic*, trans. G. M. A. Grube and C. D. C. Reeve, in *Complete Works*, ed. John Cooper, Indianapolis: Hackett.

Robbe-Grillet, A. (1965), 'Time and Description in Fiction Today', in *For a New Novel: Essays in Fiction*, trans. Richard Howard, New York: Grove Press.

Scarpetta, G. (1975), 'Review of *Kafka*, by Deleuze and Guattari', *Tel Quel*, 63: 48–9.

Smith, D. W. (2012), *Essays on Deleuze*, Edinburgh: Edinburgh University Press.

Smith, D. W. (2019), 'Sense and Literality: Why There Are No Metaphors in Deleuze's Philosophy', in Deleuze and Guattari's Philosophy of Freedom: Freedom's Refrains, ed. Dorothea Olkowski and Eftichis Pirovolakis, London: Routledge, pp. 44–67.

Chapter 9

Memories of Cinema

Robert W. Luzecky

Deleuze's concept of temporality undergoes radical revision with his elaborations of time's expressions in cinema. In *Cinema 1: The Movement-Image* and *Cinema 2: The Time-Image*, Deleuze elucidates aspects of Bergson's thought to present a concept of time that is no longer tethered to the movements of entities. Deleuze – in what is perhaps one of the oddest definitions in the history of western philosophy – characterises cinema as attempting to move beyond the representation of the movements of existents to give viewers a 'direct presentation of time' (1997b: 38). In the present chapter, I elucidate Deleuze's tantalising suggestion that cinema, the art form that has moving images as one of its ontic bases, involves a direct representation of a sort of temporality that is conceptually discrete from the movement of existent entities. I further suggest that filmic expressions of time reveal it to be a singularity that enjoys the attribute of radical indeterminacy. Deleuze further suggests that time – as it is presented in film – obtains as that ongoing continuum of variation.

My argument progresses through four stages: (1) I will critically assess the suggestion of various commentators that the *Cinema* texts offer a fraught addition to Deleuze's philosophy of time; (2) I suggest that Deleuze's innovative reading of Bergson's concept of duration is key to understanding how time is expressed in cinema; (3) I observe – through reference to Alain Robbe-Grillet's theory of artistic descriptions – that a direct image of time enjoys nascent expression in the form of 'pure optical and acoustic situations' (i.e., moments of profound change in any of the diegetic elements of a film story); (4) finally – through reference to Deleuze's nuanced reading of Bergson's ontology of virtual and actual modes of existence – I suggest that time gains direct cinematic expression in the peculiar 'crystal-images' that proliferate in post-Second World War cinema. I observe that time's expression in cinema involves a diminishment of the relative importance of the relation of temporal succession, a prioritisation of time's involvement with fundamental ontological change, and a specification of the strictly simultaneous emergence of past and present. Further, I suggest that this temporality forms a continuum of variation without end. Taken together, these yield the claim that the direct presentation of time in cinema involves characterising temporality as a singularity that is intrinsic to the cinematic mode of artistic expression. Perhaps the most magical of all art forms, cinema continues to delight us in no small measure due to its capacity to express a little morsel of time as pure, unceasing variation.

Deleuze's Phenomenology of Cinema?

The nuanced nature of Deleuze's identification of cinema as a presentation of time that is somehow removed from the movements of photographically represented objectivities (i.e., all of the characters, elements of setting, material entities, etc.) has produced some critical befuddlement, in the sense that analyses of Deleuze's claims on the nature of cinema and its expression of temporality tend to be divided. Commentators seem oddly flummoxed when it comes to Deleuze's analyses of film. This consternation is evidenced variously as hesitancy in addressing the substantive philosophical claims about the nature of temporality elaborated in *Cinema 2*, mischaracterisation of the relative importance of Deleuze's re-evaluation of time through reference to cinema, and a strange ambivalence evident in competing identifications of what Deleuze is up to with his striking analyses of film.

In an otherwise superlative elaboration of Deleuze's philosophy of time, James Williams suggests that though the *Cinema* texts stand as remarkable contributions to the philosophy of film, one should be wary of approaching the texts as though they develop a substantive contribution to Deleuze's thought on the nature of temporality. Williams identifies three reasons for being wary of both *Cinema 1* and *Cinema 2*: (1) he observes an apparent ambiguity in Deleuze's use of the term 'image' (2011: 160); (2) he suggests that the analyses of all the artists, works of art and the ontological concepts expressed by these tend to be inadequate, in the sense that these are 'descriptive and restricted' (160) in comparison to more lengthy treatments offered in other of Deleuze's works – particularly *The Logic of Sense* and *Francis Bacon: The Logic of Sensation*, though one also might mention *Coldness and Cruelty*, *Proust and Signs*, as well as *Kafka: Toward a Minor Literature*; (3) he claims that the mode of exposition and the development of substantive claims tends to be rather disjointed in comparison to that evidenced in other texts.[1] Here, I should point out that Williams's reasons for his hesitancy to elaborate on – let alone endorse – the conceptualisations of time developed in the *Cinema* texts are sketchy. Deleuze's use of the term 'image', as I argue (through particular reference to the 'crystalline image of time') in the penultimate section of this chapter, is consistent with that of Bergson. In the absence of a clearly stated set of criteria and means of evaluating the merits of one mode of philosophical exegesis relative to another – neither of which Williams gives – one must reject second and third putative reasons for wariness as akin to an ill-defined axiological complaint.

Though András Bálint Kovács characterises Deleuze's as 'by far the deepest and most developed theory of modern cinema [that] has been formulated', he also observes that it 'does not fit in with any previous theoretical frameworks' (2007: 40–1). Paul Schrader, on the other hand, starkly identifies Deleuze's elucidation of the nature and function of cinema as 'the phenomenology of perception through time' (2018: 3).[2] Vivian Sobchack echoes Schrader's sentiment with her suggestion that Deleuze's philosophy of film parallels phenomenology in the sense that Deleuze's key claims about the nature of cinematic movement and image seem to correlate with insights in Merleau-Ponty's later work (1992: 31). Julien Guillemet suggests pretty much the exact opposite with his stark claim that 'Deleuze's relation to phenomenology appears as a strict refusal of the traditional phenomenological model' (2010: 94). As is the case with most stringent interpretive claims, this reading is dubious, in the sense that Deleuze's relation with phenomenology in the *Cinema* texts tends to be decidedly more nuanced than partisan readings would care to admit. David Rodowick observes that Deleuze tends to characterise phenomenology as an 'ambiguous ally' to the Deleuzian conceptualisation of cinema (1997: 214). Deleuze's nuanced critique of the suggestion that cinematic expression involves aspects that are akin to substantive claims of various phenomenologists (primarily Husserl, Sartre and Merleau-Ponty) involves two observations: (1) it seems that phenomenologists tend to disregard cinematic art as something worthy of analysis; (2) Husserlian phenomenology tends to prioritise a mode of (natural) perception of spatiotemporally extended entities, which is ill-fitting with the experience of viewing a film. Each of these invites elaboration.

Deleuze's suggestion that phenomenology has an 'embarrassed attitude' with respect to cinema has some merit, in the sense that there seems to be a paucity phenomenological analysis of cinematic art relative to the analyses of other art forms (Deleuze 1997a: 57). (Here, one cannot help but think of the numerous phenomenological analyses of paintings and literary works by Heidegger, Merleau-Ponty, Gadamer and their followers.) Deleuze's provocative observation that Husserl 'never mentions cinema at all' (56), though technically true, is not quite as scandalous as one might think. Though Husserl doesn't specifically mention the moving images of film (i.e., cinematographic images), this shouldn't come as a terrible shock, if for no other reason than cinematic art was in its infancy when Husserl was writing. The Lumière brothers are credited with presenting the first series of documentary shorts to a paying audience on 28 December 1895 – *L'arrivée d'un train en gare de La Ciotat*, *Déjeuner de Bébé* and *L'arroseur arrosé*. Georges Méliès founded the first film studio and in-house film theatre in 1896. Méliès is also credited with producing and showing the first single-reel narrative film – *Le Voyage dans la Lune* – in 1902.[3] During this period, Husserl was busy starting his philosophical career at the University of Halle before being uprooted to take residence in Göttingen. He published the first edition of the *Logical Investigations* one year before Méliès entertained audiences with the images of magical aliens dancing on the moon. In all likelihood, Husserl was unaware of the evolution of the magic lantern in France when he published his first major phenomenological text. It should also be noted that Husserl does discuss the moving image (albeit briefly) during this time (2005: 66, 584n3, 645, 646). Unfortunately, the situation does not improve much with Sartre, who – though he mentions going to the movies with his mother in *The Words* and briefly elaborates on the nature of slow motion cinema in *The Imaginary* – refrains from offering a systematic analysis of the art form (Sartre 1964: 119; 2004: 130).[4] Deleuze also suggests that cinema suffers from a cursory treatment by Merleau-Ponty (1997a: 57).[5] Perhaps it is worth noting that Roman Ingarden discusses film in a slightly more substantive way than Merleau-Ponty. Unfortunately, Ingarden's brief analyses of film have – until quite recently – been unduly neglected by North American and French phenomenologists (Ingarden 1973, 1989). Deleuze's observation that phenomenologists tend to treat the filmic art form in a manner analogous to how a family might be inclined to treat a bastard cousin is borne out (with some modification) by history.

Deleuze offers a further clue to the fraught relation between phenomenology and cinematic representation with his explicit suggestion that cinema offers an alternative to the model of natural perception offered by Husserlian phenomenology. In a lecture on the topic given during the autumn of 1981, Deleuze starkly notes that 'cinematic perception is not natural perception. Not at all' (Deleuze 1981). The difference between cinematic perception and natural perception involves the ontic bases of perceived objects. Deleuze suggests that natural perception presents objects in motion – e.g., the object of natural perception might be a bird fluttering its wings, pecking at a worm, prancing along a branch. The object of cinematic perception is explicitly the photographic representation of an entity isolated from motion. Deleuze's analytic point is based on the observation that we typically perceive physical entities in motion and cinematic perception only affords us the perception of entities for which motion is a second-order property. The claim is that the smallest building block of our natural perception – the ontologically primary base of naturally perceived moments – is composed of entities enjoying inter-related motions. Writing a few scant years after the birth of cinema in 1895, Henri Bergson observed that cinematic perception involves (as its ontic base) 'snapshots of a passing reality' (1998: 307). Bergson goes on to suggest that cinematic images are frozen in time, in the sense that they are bereft of any movement (i.e., the cinematic image involves a negation of the motion of the naturally perceived object). Though it is the case that, when watching a film, we perceive entities that have the semblance of motion – e.g., the grotesque image of the razorblade slicing an eyeball in Luis Buñuel's *Un Chien Andalou* (1929), or the horrific image of the blood gushing out of the elevator doors in Stanley Kubrick's *The Shining* (1980) – this is the product of the serial organisation and projection of static photographic images. While natural perception involves entities in motion, cinematic perception involves the mere illusion of entities in motion. In this sense, the perceived motion of cinematic entities is an ontologically secondary event; a cinematographic illusion conjures the projection of still images at very specific temporal rates.[6]

In addition to Deleuze's observations about the ontic base of the cinematographic illusion of movement, one may observe a further difference between natural perception and cinematic perception. Deleuze seems to suggest that cinematic perception differs in kind from natural perception. Here, Deleuze's critique is directed as much against André Bazin as it is against Husserl. One of the fundamental observations of Husserlian phenomenology is that 'all consciousness is consciousness of' (Husserl quoted in Deleuze 1997a: 56). Natural perception suggests that objects (in the real world) are presented to consciousness as composites of various schematised aspects. Intentional consciousness then sets about performing the complex task of fulfilling these aspects through reference to transcendent structures of reality, structures of consciousness, and social conditions evidenced in the lifeworld (most

of which are presented in a schematised fashion), in the ongoing creation of real objects of consciousness.[7] Bazin suggests that perception
of cinema seems to involve a similar process with his observation that
the cinematic image reveals the 'natural image of a world'; a flow of
image which is 'uncompromisingly realistic', in the sense that it perfectly
conveys the aspects of 'the natural world' (2005: 14, 27). Bazin's claim
here is that the camera functions as a prosthesis to the human eye, which
assists in the process of perception (presenting aspects of entities in the
empirically sensed world and fomenting their fulfilment by intentional
consciousness) that is fundamentally analogous to that originally specified by Husserl. Deleuze explicitly denies this analogy when he observes
that 'the cinema can, with impunity, bring us close to things or take
us away from them and revolve around them, it suppresses both the
anchoring of the subject and the horizon of the world' (1997a: 57). The
substantive observation here is that the camera does things which the
human eye cannot do, in ways that are liberated from the direction of
the perceiver's intentional consciousness. With these analyses, Deleuze
appears to be making a complex deduction from premises specified by
Walter Benjamin, Dziga Vertov and Robert Bresson. Benjamin makes
the astute observation that the camera 'can bring out those aspects
of the original that are unattainable to the naked eye yet accessible to
the lens, which is adjustable and chooses its angle at will' (2007: 220).
Vertov observes that cinema's 'kino-eye lives and moves in time and
space; it gathers and records impressions in a manner wholly different
from that of the human eye' (1984: 15). Bresson elaborates on the
camera's capacities to record 'what no human eye is capable of catching,
no pencil, brush, pen of pinning down . . . without knowing what it is,
and pins its down with a machine's scrupulous indifference' (1977: 14).
Deleuze observes that Husserlian phenomenology grants a privilege to
the human eye as the means by which to perceive the world. Without
hesitation, Bazin accepts this privilege, only to suggest that the camera
augments it. Benjamin, Vertov and Bresson each fundamentally deny
that the human eye enjoys this privileged status – the movie camera (with
its swoops, long tracking shots, radical close-ups and sweeping panora-
mas) performs functions to which no human eye could dare aspire. All
of these imply that cinematic perception involves an intentionality that is
decidedly not human. The profound capacities of the kino-eye are illustrated in the – nearly sublime – opening sequence of *Berlin: Die Sinfonie
der Großstadt* (1927): the film begins with the image of the languid ebb
of calm waters, only to give way (through an abstract dissolve consisting
of multi-section white planes and a descending circle) to the metallic

arms of a railway crossing; then, there is a rapid cut to a speeding train, which dissolves into a shot of the pistons of an engine.[8] Here we have an atypical conjunction of typical geometric forms (the abstract dissolve), as well as images of nature viewed in unnatural ways; things are viewed from angles that are seemingly unattainable by the human eye – e.g., hovering over the unblemished surface of water, which is not disturbed by the ripple caused by the immersion of a physical body. These are illustrative of a mode of perception of that is quite removed from any that we would identify as directed by human intentionality. These observations of poets, filmmakers and philosophers suggest that cinema affords a mode of perception which is radically distinct from that so rigorously specified in Husserlian phenomenology.

When taken together, these two complex claims – that there is scant substantive discussion of film in the works of Husserl, Sartre and Merleau-Ponty, and that cinema affords a modality of perception that is distinct from (Husserlian) natural perception – imply that there is a conceptual distance between phenomenological accounts of the cinematic art form and that offered by Deleuze. One might add to these a further observation, which obliquely challenges the notion that Deleuze's account of temporal expression in cinema is akin to aspects of Husserlian phenomenology. In an interview with Raymond Bellour, Deleuze starkly observes that 'there is no dualism at all' involved in his account of the nature of cinema (2020: 226). It has been observed that there is a sort of dualism hard baked into Husserl's phenomenology. This suggestion enjoys ample textual support, in the sense that Husserl explicitly claims that there is a methodological dualism involved in his phenomenology. Husserl stipulates – in *Ideas I* – that the *res cogitans* is separated from the world of physical, material, spatiotemporally extended entities 'by a veritable abyss' (1931: 153). Husserl tries to diminish dualism by prescribing the application of the phenomenological method, but by limiting the scope of his phenomenology to epistemology he avoids really contradicting ontological dualism. In *Phenomenology and the Crisis of Philosophy*, Husserl suggests that the function of intentional consciousness is to intertwine with the external (physical and ideal) world through various acts of clarification achieved by intentionality fulfilling the schematised aspects of entities presented through perception – i.e., by becoming conscious of entities.[9] Were this intertwining achieved (i.e., were the process of fulfilment of schematised aspects ever completely actualised), this would diminish any concerns about an abiding dualism. Unfortunately, the success of Husserl's efforts is a matter of dispute. Françoise Dastur observes that Husserl's phenomenology seems to be

plagued by an intractable dualism.[10] Merleau-Ponty echoes this suggestion with his observation that at 'the end of Husserl's life there is an
unthought-of element in his works which is wholly his and yet opens
out on something else' (1964: 160). The existence of this unresolved
something else which consciousness opens toward fulfils the minimal
condition of an unresolved species of dualism at work in Husserlian phenomenology. The fact that Deleuze explicitly suggests that his concept
of cinema is bereft of dualism implies that it might have less in common
with Husserlian phenomenology than one might expect.

The Filmic Duration (of Memory and Change)

Deleuze's suggestion that temporality is afforded a direct presentation
in film involves a Bergsonian concept of temporal duration that is comprehensive of the memorial past (of memory), the lived present and the
creation of the new. The concept of time presented in the *Cinema* texts
is substantively different than that elaborated in other texts like *The
Logic of Sense* – in which the putatively discrete temporal domains of
past, present and future are explicitly characterised as 'readings' of the
various types of (logical, ontological, axiological) relations that obtain
among Aion and Chronos. Further, though Deleuze quite comfortably
elaborates on the ontological primacy of a synthesis among discrete
ontological entities as giving rise to a comprehensive time in *Difference
and Repetition*, in the *Cinema* texts, this language of syntheses has fallen
by the wayside, having been replaced by discussions of tensions among
virtual and actual modes of being as they obtain in the lived present
that is expressed in cinema. Though Deleuze had written on Bergson
prior to the publication of *Difference and Repetition* (both 'Bergson
1859–1941' and 'Bergson's Conception of Difference'[11] are significant
texts which hint at aspects of a robust concept of temporality), it isn't
until *Bergsonism* and the commentaries on Bergson in *Cinema 1* and
Cinema 2 that Deleuze's Bergsonian account of temporality receives
thorough elaboration. In the *Cinema* texts, Deleuze modifies his prior
concepts of temporality to offer an account of duration that involves
an ontologically comprehensive nature and a radical capacity to modify
existents. Deleuze suggests that we experience this sort of duration in the
cinematic art form – which presents the viewing audience with a series
of visible contractions among the photographically represented past
and the present; a 'well defined tension' (Bergson 1946: 217) among the
living present and the memorial past that is expressed in filmic sequences,
series, and framings of photographically represented events. What this

implies about the nature of temporality and of the cinematic expression of time is staggering, if for no other reason than that it involves: (1) a reconceptualisation of temporality that establishes an identity relation – i.e., the identity enjoyed by the elements of a multiplicity – among putatively distinct temporal domains; (2) a diminishment of the claim that temporality is reducible to a succession relation of temporal moments, $t_1, t_2 \ldots t_n$; (3) a suggestion that cinema can represent these.

Bergson seems never to tire of modifying his concept of duration. In a few remarkable pages in the second chapter of *Time and Free Will*, the concept (of duration) is variously characterised as a 'multiplicity' of temporal moments, which (strangely) don't enjoy any correlation with measurable points distributed in physical space – i.e., a multiplicity of 'pure number' (Bergson 2001: 78, 89); the form assumed by the 'succession of our conscious states' in moments of recollection (100); an intensive magnitude (106); a mercurial ontological process which seems to be like Merleau-Ponty's concept of the flesh, in the narrow sense that it is primary to substance (111). In *Matter and Memory*, the over-determined concept undergoes further revision. Here, duration is characterised as the continuous flow of mental-states through which psycho-social entities 'insensibly' pass in the 'really lived' experience of a continuity that strangely conditions experience, without revealing itself in its entirety; the dynamic 'tension' that obtains among various putatively discrete mental states (Bergson 1991: 186). This characterisation in particular becomes slightly more fraught when taken in conjunction with Bergson's careful observation that any supposed division among mental states is 'artificial', in the sense that these are comprehended as interrelated aspects of a unified – non-divisible, non-reducible – lived experience (186). The situation doesn't get much better when we come to *Creative Evolution*. Here, Bergson characterises duration variously as the flow of unceasing change (1998: 1–3); as a flux of putatively discrete mental states merging into one another (3); and as the past (characterised as an oddly active and expanding process) which 'gnaws into the future and which swells as it advances' (4). Taken together, this dizzying array of sometimes competing definitions suggest an over-determined concept that threatens to lose any sense of unity.

The plurality of aspects associated with the concept of duration seems to have led to some confusion about the nature of the concept. Rebecca Hill starkly observes that Bergson's duration may be identified as a dualistic relation that obtains among tendencies (i.e., proto-entities, transcendental conditions, disparate forces, poorly identified urges, etc., that are involved in multiple processes of transformation). Hill seems to undermine her initial identification when she suggests that these tendencies are sexed, in the sense that they are inherently expressive of masculine or feminine characteristics (2012: 92). Though it is the case that since Bergson explicitly characterises durations as involving pre-individuated tendencies (as opposed to clearly defined quantifiable states), it seems odd to identify any particular sexedness – which would be an individuated trait – as an attribute of these. Bergson explicitly notes that the complex concept of duration tends to resist identification as a metaphysical simple (i.e., a state, or an entity, something reducible to one aspect) in numerous places. Perhaps the clearest identification of the involvement of tendencies and duration is found in *Creative Evolution*, in a remarkable passage where Bergson characterises duration as a complex relation of pre-individuated tendencies (1998: 12–13). Deleuze suggests that tendency and duration enjoy an ontological identity, in the sense that both involve pure difference: 'Duration or tendency is the difference of self with itself; and what differs from itself is, in an *unmediated* way, the unity of substance and subject' (2002: 38). In a lecture on Leibniz, Deleuze further identifies duration as a process of differentiation that bears a striking conceptual similarity with *conatus*, in the sense that these involve ontogenetic forces.[12] These two observations – that duration is similar to a tendency and that it is akin to a pre-individuated force (i.e., *conatus*) – are sufficient to demonstrate a confusion involved in the suggestion that duration involves individuated traits. Hill attempts to support her argument by pointing to a 'hierarchical sexuation' implicit in Bergson's use of metaphor in elaborating on the nature of duration. This is unfortunate for at least two reasons. Hill does very little to clarify what a 'sexuated' hierarchy would look like. Confronted with such a linguistic monstrosity, in the absence of any clear definiens, one is just as apt to produce an accurate identification of Bergsonian duration as one is to conjure a profound ontological confusion. It might also be observed that a dualistic relation among any of existents or tendencies would tend to be expressed as parallelism – i.e., an ontological relation ill-fitting the sort of formation implied by reference to any sort of hierarchy, regardless of the identity of its *relata*. Perhaps it should also be observed that Bergson tends to characterise duration in non-hierarchical terms – i.e., as a qualitative multiplicity; an ontological process akin to an organic unity; a psychological 'flux' – all of which tend to be analytically, logically and ontologically discrete to the type of arrangement associated with any form of hierarchy.

Arguing from more stable conceptual ground, Jean Hyppolite suggests that Bergsonian duration is identical to memory, in the sense that it involves an interrelation of non-discrete moments that are temporally prior to the present.[13] Leonard Lawlor echoes this view when he summarily characterises Bergson's concept of duration as akin to memory, albeit in senses that involve subtle modifications of all of its nature, the objects of recollection, and the purposiveness implied by various acts of recollecting (2003: 80). Indeed, in *Creative Evolution*, Bergson explicitly identifies memory and duration when he observes that 'duration is the continuous progress of the past which gnaws into the future and which swells as it advances' (1998: 4). Bergson's choices of metaphor and verb tense suggest a conceptualisation of memory as a process that is substantively different from the concept of memory as a mental repository of prior experience – i.e., a 'mind palace', a mental labyrinth that is accessed through the repetition of a mnemonic device (the calming rhythms of 'the thread of a tune' that guides one to a 'shelter' which contains the memories of one's childhood (Deleuze and Guattari 1987: 310)) – that is typically used in filmic attempts to visualise memory. (This concept of memory as a repository has been referenced so often that it has become a filmic trope. Recent filmic examples include: the 'mental map' used by Sherlock Holmes in the television episode *The Hounds of Baskerville* (2012); the mesmerising sequence in Ridley Scott's *Blade Runner* (1992), in which Deckard uses the sepia-coloured photographs on his piano to unlock the memories of his childhood – memories which resist washing away into oblivion 'like tears in the rain'; the hellish industrial furnace where K retreats to the memories of childhood in Denis Villeneuve's *Blade Runner 2049* (2017).) The primary difference between Bergson's concept of duration and the type of memory illustrated in these filmic representations is that though memory palaces tend to be illustrated as domains of relative stasis, duration is dynamic. In *Matter and Memory*, Bergson elucidates memory's activity of 'gnawing' into the future through reference to the mental activity of 'recording' occurrences in the temporal present, for the purpose of forming habits (which might become involved in shaping a psycho-social entity's behaviours at a future moment) (1991: 83). The dynamic aspect of memory is further illustrated by Bergson's careful observation that habit (i.e., all of what is remembered; the constantly expanding content of memory) participates in the formation of moral obligation (1935: 29). Bergson further elaborates on the aims of memory (i.e., its functional goal or end) when he notes that each of the moments of our lives 'is a kind of creation' (1998: 7). When taken in conjunction with the stipulation that each temporal moment of existence involves both the content of memory and the ongoing organisation of this content, Bergson's observation yields the implication that memory is involved in the dynamic creation of the utterly unique. No longer identified as merely the repository of now past, slowly fading moments, memory, Bergson suggests, is identical to duration, in the sense that all of its nature, processes and purpose are involved with the creation of something without ontological correlate or precedent.

Deleuze clarifies the role of duration in the production of difference with his elucidation of Bergson's 'third thesis' (of movement and change) in *Cinema 1*. Though there is no explicit mention of the identity relation among duration and memory in these densely argued passages, one might forgive this apparent oversight, if for no other reason than the identity of these had already been stipulated in *Bergsonism*.[14] Deleuze formulates Bergson's third thesis as the complex claim that 'not only is the instant an immobile section of movement, but movement is a mobile section of duration, that is of the Whole, or of a whole' (1997a: 8). Bergson explicitly notes – in *Creative Evolution* – that a movement of entities in space involves a transformation of that space.[15] Bergson's complex ontological argument involves: (1) the stipulation of a distinction among the processes of transformation and translation; (2) positing an uncontentious distinction in kind – i.e., a categorical distinction – among qualities and quantities; (3) the observation that the process of translation involves quantitative change – i.e., it is a translation of quantitative values; (4) the inference that transformation involves the modification of particular qualities; (5) the observation of the corollary that movements in space involve qualitative changes; and finally, (6) the assertion that a transformation of a particular quality implies a qualitative change to the generality that comprehends the particular. Taken together, these yield the profound claim that the displacement of spatiotemporally extended entities implies a fundamental change to the nature of space itself. In this sense, the domain (or medium) that comprehends movements of particulars is revealed to be ontologically correlated with a modification of the qualities of any particular. These are the sorts of ontological transformations that have been illustrated to such terrifying effect in both horror literature and film. Robert Wise's *The Haunting* (1963) – which is an adaptation of Shirley Jackson's *The Haunting of Hill House* (1959) – chronicles the anguish of Eleanora as she resides in a gothic mansion that alters all of its physical dimensions, lighting and interior temperature in response to her memories of childhood trauma. A similar sort of physical change to space brought about by qualitative change is also illustrated in the fiery end of the Overlook Hotel in Steven King's novel (1977), though the hotel remains standing at the end Stanley Kubrick's *The Shining* – a film that is vastly superior to King's derivative novel, because it explicitly correlates the physical changes of the hotel to the mental states of Jack, Wendy and Danny, as well as the memorial history of the Colorado Rocky Mountains, i.e., the qualitative elements of various domains. Thomas Allen Nelson elaborates on how, in Kubrick's film, changes to the hotel's spatiality are directly correlated with – i.e., responses to, expressions of, doublings of – the characters' internal states (2000: 202–8). One cannot help but think of the spatiotemporal discontinuities evident in some of the film's most memorable scenes: the elevator of blood that erupts when Jack, Wendy or Danny feel rage or terror; the appearance of the bloated corpse of a nude crone that greets Jack's aberrant sexual desires in room 237; the ominous appearance of an ancient scrapbook next to Jack's typewriter as he struggles to recall the plot of his horribly repetitive manuscript; the disquieting appearance of the twin girls (the Grady twins) who promise to play with Danny 'forever and ever'; the shifting patterns on both the hallway carpet and the Native American murals in the Colorado Lounge; the population and de-population of the Gold Room; the alteration in lighting of the hotel bar when Jack gets a glass of bourbon; the shifting spatial dimensions of the hedge maze; the strange appearance of a room full of skeletons as Wendy is confronted with memories of Jack's abuse of her and Danny; the deeply disturbing appearance of an entity dressed as a bear performing fellatio on a man in 1920s formal attire as Wendy witnesses a temporally prior event in the hotel (the 1921 New Year's Eve party). All of these spatiotemporal modifications (modifications to the hotel and its surrounding area) are reflective of qualitative variations of various character's mental states. Each of them expresses a spatiotemporal translation of particulars (a quantitative translation). All involve a fundamental qualitative transformation of the whole. These moments of horror have been adduced to aptly illustrate the ontological modification suggested by Bergson's third thesis on the nature of space in relation to qualitative alteration.

Deleuze suggests that filmic duration does something more profound than merely present photographic examples of differentiation through photographic and aural means. In 'Bergson's Conception of Difference', he explicitly identifies duration as the internally differentiated process that involves the capacity to 'englobe' (i.e., ontologically comprehend) ontologically distinct entities (2002: 39). This suggests that the particular filmic species of duration has the capacity to comprehend modifications within entities which are ontologically discrete from filmed persons, settings and other photographically represented states of affairs. The

implication here is that filmic duration involves the capacity to affect –
qualitatively modify – the audience. Roland Barthes echoes this suggestion when he observes that some films involve qualitative modifications
that will 'bruise' the viewer. The claim is that some images, as well
as sequences of images (due to their preternatural powers to foment
change), will modify the bodily experience of those who behold their
spectacle – this is more than the work of a mere example.[16]

Cinema's seemingly magical capacities to modify the physical states of
those who behold its spectacle hint at a complex analogy between duration and Walter Benjamin's concept of an aura. Rodowick observes that
Benjamin's historical reflections on the development of photographic art
suggests a similarity among what Benjamin characterises as the photographic aura and the filmic duration (1997: 8). Though Miriam Bratu
Hansen cautiously observes that Benjamin's identification of the concept
of aura is notoriously difficult to isolate, in the sense that Benjamin
seems to subtly modify the term throughout his 'Little History of
Photography', *On Hashish* and the *Arcades Project*, one might observe
that the concept seems to involve two discrete aspects. The strength
of the analogy between duration and aura is demonstrated by shared
aspects.[17] Benjamin's first elucidation of the nature of an aura is the
consequence of his experimentations with hashish (on 5 March 1930).
Here, Benjamin cautiously observes that, though it is distinct in kind
from the 'spruced-up magical rays' that populate the fantastic visions of
spiritualists, a 'genuine aura' enjoys a similarity with 'an ornamental halo
[*Umzirkung*], in which the object or being is enclosed' (2006b: 58). The
suggestion here is that an aura is a sort of energy field that has the capacity to comprehend existents. The ontologically comprehensive nature of
an aura is akin to duration's capacity to 'englobe' entities. In this sense,
comprehensiveness is an aspect that is common to Bergsonian duration
and Benjamin's concept of an aura. Elaborating on the sublime nature of
Eugène Atget's surrealist photographs of Paris, Benjamin explicitly characterises their aura as involving a 'strange weave of space and time: the
unique appearance or semblance of distance, no matter how close it may
be' (2005: 518). Here, one may identify a parallel aspect in duration's
involvement with memory's ability to qualitatively modify spatiotemporally extended existents and the nature of their circumstances – i.e.,
all of psycho-social entities and their circumstances, the content of the
lived experience of humans, and their environment, however broadly
construed. Remarking on the sort of auras that accompany represented
photographic objectivities, Benjamin suggests that photographic auras
have the capacity to involve themselves in an intentional relation with

the memories of those who behold them – i.e., to 'look back' into the minds and prior lived experiences of those who get transfixed by their unblinking gaze.[18] This observation echoes the suggestion that duration modifies the qualitative aspects of the thought content of people who participate in cinematic duration (through the concrete act of viewing a film).

Nascent Forms of Time's Direct Expression

Deleuze – in some of the most beautiful passages of *Cinema 2* – suggests that filmic art enjoys the power to modify the qualitative experience of viewers, because it has the capacity to present direct images of time. Perhaps the most enigmatic of the concepts Deleuze develops in the *Cinema* texts, the direct time-image is as mercurial as it is essential to understanding the complex nature of temporality in film. Deleuze starkly identifies the direct time-image as presenting a 'little time in its pure state', only to clarify that this pure state is 'the unchanging form in which the change is produced' (1997b: 17). The suggestion here is that time is the general form of variation that comprehends and is expressed in any particular change. Deleuze further observes that this form of time is a nascent aspect of filmic motion pictures that has only recently enjoyed a greater tendency to filmic realisation with the advancement of cinematic art. He writes that direct time-images involves a 'Proustian dimension where people and things occupy a place in time which is incommensurable with the one they have in space' (37). The claim here seems to be that the direct time-image involves aspects of memory, in various senses of the term (i.e., the psychological memories of individuated psycho-social existents, as well as the non-individuated – ontological – memory that comprehends the entirety of the past of all existents). Deleuze illustrates the development of this peculiar concept of time through reference to Robbe-Grillet's critical remarks about the role of mimesis in artistic representation, as well as the natures of the (oddly named) pure optical and sound situations.

One might observe that the concept of a direct presentation of any-thing in film seems flummoxing, if for no other reason than that the entities of a film are explicitly visually accessible entities presented as ele-ments of a filmic universe. It might further be observed that the entirety of the filmic universe (i.e., all its constituent elements) are represented by photographic means in service of a director's purposes (which usually amounts to presenting a narrative, but may also involve explorations of the artistic possibilities afforded cinema as an artistic medium).[19]

One could suggest that cinematically represented objects seem to be distinguishable from objects which enjoy direct presentations. It would seem that recognition of the validity of either a metaphysical distinction between original and copy, or an aesthetic distinction between an object and its representation (by artistic means), would suffice to adduce a critique of the notion that anything is presented directly in filmic art. These would be perhaps even more substantive when they involve something that has non-physical aspects – i.e., any of a species of relation; an 'ideal' entity; a spiritual existent; a process involving non-physical entities; a continuum of abstract terms or relations; in short, many of the sorts of existents we tend to associate or identify with temporality. One could wonder how the immaterial form of time, or any of its (also immaterial) constituent elements, could enjoy direct presentation by cinema.

Deleuze addresses these concerns through reference to Robbe-Grillet's theory of artistic description. The solution here is complex, in the sense that Deleuze invites the reader to have more than a passing understanding of all of Plato's and Aristotle's aesthetics – because a hybrid of these functions as the unspecified target of Robbe-Grillet's critique – as well as the mathematics involved with architectural singularities (which Robbe-Grillet references, but neglects to develop) (Deleuze 1997b: 44–5). Deleuze marshals these to suggest that temporality enjoys direct presentation in film as a type of intrinsic singularity that expresses a sort of variation that is non-mimetic. He stipulates that there is a difference in kind among representations and expressions, in the sense that each is a different kind of aspect of cinematic art. Perhaps one of the most magical qualities of cinema is that it has the capacity to represent entities and processes that enjoy existence in a mode of reality external to that of the filmic universe, as well as the ability to express entities and processes wholly intrinsic to its mode of presentation (i.e., existents that enjoy no correlation with anything outside the film; a spectacle that is entirely new, in the sense that it does not represent anything in the real world). Though each may be an aspect of the same entity, this does not imply that either is reducible to the other. Time enjoys direct presentation in film because film expresses a change relative to the states of affairs in the film. In his essay 'Time and Description in Fiction Today', Robbe-Grillet offers an account of descriptions that diminishes the Ancients' suggestion that art tends to be mimetic (i.e., reducible to the representation of objects, objectivities or processes). Robbe-Grillet cautiously observes that, though it might have been the case that filmic and literary narratives seem to involve duplication (producing a copy or representation) of the real world, in contemporary films and literature the mimetic function seems to enjoy only a diminished role, in the sense that it has been supplanted by a creative function.[20] One might balk at this suggestion, with the observation that mimesis has been taken to be a crucial aspect of art since Plato's observation – in the *Republic*, 604e–605a – that it is the artist's job to produce 'multicolored imitations' of various tangible and intangible aspects of reality (1997: 1209). It might further be noted that Plato's entire condemnation of bad artists presupposes the validity of the metaphysical claim that there exists a true reality (which good art putatively represents).[21] Robbe-Grillet modifies this characterisation of the function of art by radicalising the artist's creative capacities. Though it must be noted that theories of imitation do involve aspects of artistic creation, in the sense that they tend to identify the artist as creating an adequate description of a reality that is extrinsic to the work of art's reality, this is characterised as a secondary, dependent process. Robbe-Grillet radicalises this creativity when he suggests that the work of art is akin to an architectural 'point' of invention (i.e., a singular point, a singularity, a point of inflection) (1965: 148). Bernard Cache carefully observes that architecture involves two analytically discrete kinds of singularities, extrinsic singularities and 'points of inflection' (or intrinsic singularities). An extrinsic singularity is a hypothetical point with which the tangent of the physical curve, were it conceived as an ideal curve, would be perpendicular (it is the point of a hypothetical y-axis which is involved in the specification of one part of the curve's coordinates). An intrinsic singularity is identified as a point along the curve that 'designates a pure event of curvature' (Cache 1995: 16). Intrinsic singularities are actualised (or at least illustrated) by the ogives that are so often instantiated in the architecture of medieval European churches. Architectural works, it might also be observed, are a particular species of the general class of artwork. Here, it seems that Robbe-Grillet is stipulating that the property of a particular – in this case, the property of having intrinsic singularities as elements of the particular's formal ontological content – may be generalised as the property of a class. Given that the property of a class may gain expression in any particular species or member that is comprehended by the class, this yields the substantive observation that films and novels (because they are also works of art) involve intrinsic singularities. Robbe-Grillet further observes that intrinsic singularities tend to gain artistic expression as diegetic moments of radical upheaval, profound correction, or bifurcation into non-compossible series of events. Robbe-Grillet explicitly notes that his conceptualisation of artistic description is distinct from the mimetic relation through direct reference to temporality when he observes that

the types of temporal changes expressed in films need not correlate with
the temporality evidenced by the quantitative measurement of physical
(as opposed to artistically presented) clocks and calendars (1965: 151).

It should be observed that Robbe-Grillet's suggestion implies a
subtle reformulation of Aristotle's observation that art tends to involve
moments of great dramatic reversal. In *Poetics*, Aristotle suggests that
lyric poems tend to represent reality adequately, in the sense that they
involve περιπέτεια (reversals). Robbe-Grillet seems to suggest that these
moments of great reversal in the lives, fates and fortunes of the characters evidence a rupture from the mimetic order, in the sense that none
of these needs to be representative of any circumstance in the world.
These profound shifts involve an element of temporality, in the senses
that they occur within time, evidence a temporal duration and express a
moment in temporal continuum. This suggests that a direct expression
of time involves the illustration of these sorts of changes, characterised
as any of the properties (or attributes) of the relation that obtains among
entities in the artwork; thus it is discrete from the sorts of modification
that obtain as a property of the mimetic relation that might or might not
obtain between these and entities in the physical world. Stated again,
the direct expression of temporally saturated change is immanent to the
relation among fictive *relata*, which is different in kind and content from
the sort of changes that are involved (as attributes, immanent conditions
or emergent properties) in the relation that obtains among artistically
presented objects and their correlates in the universe populated by physical entities and psycho-social entities with physical attributes.

Deleuze observes that analogous disjunctions may be found in pure
optical and acoustic situations, which are constituted by 'opsigns' and
'sonsigns'. In *Cinema 1*, he explains that these situations (and their
correlated signs) are filmic precursors to the direct presentation of time
(1997a: 210). Properly speaking, both opsigns and sonsigns are indica-
tive of a breakdown of the sensory-motor order (i.e., the sequence of
shots, montage) that tends to be identified with realist cinema. Each of
these discrete types of sign – though they may be, and often are, present
in the same shot, sequence or film – indicates a disjunction among any
of the photographically expressed entities relative to one another, as
well as any of the narrative, implied character arc, or thematic content
attributed to a film or its aspects. In these senses, opsigns and sonsigns
are intrinsic singularities that stand apart from (i.e., enjoy a disjunctive
relation with) other aspects of the film.[22] Deleuze elucidates the natures
of these peculiar moments of filmic upheaval when he observes that
these sorts of purely optical and acoustic situations force any of the

characters or spectators of the film to encounter 'something intolerable and unbearable … a matter of something too powerful, or too
unjust, but sometimes also too beautiful, and which henceforth outstrips
our sensory-motor capacities' (1997b: 18). Deleuze further observes
that a character immersed in such situations behaves as though they
don't know how to respond to their circumstance, as though they are
wandering through a terrain that – for whatever reason or confluence
of causes – has diminished their capacities to navigate its labyrinthine
contours.[23] Though Deleuze suggests that opsigns and sonsigns emerged
with striking prominence in Italian Neo-realist films, it would be a
mistake to associate them only with the films of a particular historical
period. These signs are evident in films from as diverse a set of direc-
tors as Roberto Rossellini, Michelangelo Antonioni, Andrei Tarkovsky
and Wim Wenders. To think of a clear expression of a purely optical
and acoustic situation, one need only recall, for example, the profound
alienation (from her dead son, her overly judgemental mother, her
utterly oblivious husband, and the seductive charms of socio-economic
privilege) evidenced on Ingrid Bergman's face as she wanders through
the monolithic factory in *Europe '51* (Rossellini 1952); or Harry Dean
Stanton's desperate wandering through the nameless – and seemingly
limitless – desert during the mesmerising opening sequence of *Paris,
Texas* (Wenders 1984); or the strange industrial wasteland surrounding the petrol-chemical plant which causes an existential crisis for
Monica Viti's character in *Red Desert* (Antonioni 1964); or Alexander
Kaidanovsky's wandering though the strange wasteland after an accidental alien visitation in Tarkovsky's masterpiece *Stalker* (1979). Taken
together, these filmic expressions illustrate something more significant
than the mere psychological or physical displacement of a character; the
travails of each can be adduced as evidence of a comprehensive alienation. It is a profound indeterminacy that is reflected in these cinematic
moments of profound upheaval. Here, the claim is that the pure optical
and sound situation presents a filmic representation of the crisis of
indeterminacy; its purity is a perfection of a world without answer – a
perpetual vagueness without temporal cessation; a comprehensive lost-
ness in which characters are separated from the world of which they are
putative inhabitants.

A Direct Presentation of Temporality: Crystals of Time

If the pure optical and acoustic situations presented in film offer a
disquieting glimpse into the nature of time characterised as a singularity

– a moment of change – then film's various hyalosigns (a linguistic play on the Attic Greek ὕαλος) further develop the claim that time's direct expression in film amounts to a direct expression of variation. Deleuze carefully elaborates time's direct expression through identification of the natures of time and its relation to filmic expressions of change through reference to filmic 'crystal-images'. It is important to note that crystal-images are unities of analytically discrete processes. The ontological implication here is that the time crystal (which is a representation of the nature of time itself) is constituted by a series of mutually implicated processes: (1) the continual exchange among the couple of the virtual and the actual; (2) the relation among 'the limpid and the opaque'; and (3) the generative relation of 'seed and the environment' (Deleuze 1997b: 71). Deleuze further identifies a close conceptual proximity among the exchange of virtual and actual, and the relation of limpid and opaque, in the sense that the terms seem to enjoy transposability: virtuality is akin to opacity; that which is actual (in film) tends to enjoy visibility (71). It will be further observed that these imply a diminishment of the relevance of temporal succession to the nature of time. The third process – involving seed and environment – suggests a temporal continuum of ceaseless variation. Each invites elucidation.

Deleuze elaborates on the nature of each of these processes through reference to Bergson and Proust. The suggestion that film has the capacity to express time directly is hinted at by Bergson in *Matter and Memory* and 'Memory of the Present and False Recognition' (Bergson 1991, 2012). In *Matter and Memory* he explicitly characterises the act of recollection as akin to the mechanism of a camera focusing on a vaguely determined intentional object.[24] The metaphoric allusion to filmic (or perhaps, theatrical) art is continued with Bergson's observation that the process of recollection tends to yield the psychological sensation of neurotic depersonalisation – i.e., the disquieting feeling that one is standing apart from oneself, a participant in the life of another, as though they were merely an actor, a sentient simulacra reciting the lines and performing the actions associated with someone else's lived experience.[25] Bergson further alludes to a relation between film and the virtual when he observes that the recollected past appears to consciousness as the changing image reflected in 'a moving-mirror' (2012: 165). In addition, he observes that the recollected content of the past gradually appears to one as the ill-defined content of dream-states, deliriums and hallucinations – i.e., as though 'they were phantoms superadded to solid perceptions and conceptions of our waking life, will-o-wisps which hover above it' (154). Perhaps it is worth observing that the visual image of mirrors as well as the content of their optical reflections have been used throughout the history of cinema to fulfil the diegetic function of revealing something essential about the nature of particular characters. In some of the most profound uses of this visual metaphor of the mirror, these revelations involve a character coming to terms with their past. In film, it tends to be the case that when there is a mirror present, someone is undergoing a profound modification. The presence of mirrors in the history of western cinema is evidenced by their prevalence in the films of Orson Welles, Robert Clouse, Martin Scorsese and Wim Wenders. Here, one cannot help but think of Rita Hayward's riveting elaboration of her past as she stumbles blindly through a hall of mirrors in *The Lady from Shanghai* (Welles 1947); Bruce Lee's recollection that 'the enemy is only images and illusions' as he battles infinitely recurring images of a phantasmal foe in *Enter the Dragon* (Clouse 1973); Robert De Niro's psychotic self-examination in *Taxi Driver* (Scorsese 1976); or Harry Dean Stanton's heart-breaking elaboration of his past to his ex-wife through a two-way mirror in the penultimate sequence of *Paris, Texas*. In each, there is a visual linkage among the mirror, hallucination and moments of profound modification of at least one character. Though it might be observed that these instances of mirrors in film prioritise visual expressions of change, it should be pointed out that both Bergson and Deleuze explicitly stipulate that change is an aspect of temporality. When coupled with the observation that the filmic representation of mirrors tends to be concomitant with change in some sense of the term (as a modification of a character's sense of self, a variation of the identities or motives of other characters, or a change to other elements of the filmic universe), this implies an involvement of aspects of temporality, and (thus) is a cinematic representation of time. Bergson's textual allusions to mirrors and the mercurial elements of the past expressed in their reflected contents, when coupled with the plurality of filmic representations of mirrors, suggest a conceptual foundation for Deleuze's elaboration of the nature of time through reference to filmic expression.

Ronald Bogue observes that Deleuze identifies filmic sequences involving mirrors as the most basic expression of virtual and actual exchange involved in crystal-images (2003: 121). Deleuze explicitly notes that crystal-images afford a direct presentation of time. What does it mean to suggest that time may be the sort of metaphysical entity that may be presented directly? Deleuze contends that crystal-images express two claims about the nature of temporality (which he formulates negatively): (1) that temporal ordering is 'not made up of succession' (1997b: 274); (2) that time is non-reducible to an isolated temporal instant (i.e., a static

200 Robert W. Luzecky

moment isolated from a temporal continuum or temporal flow). The suggestion that it would be inaccurate to artificially isolate the object presented as a temporally extended element of a duration is uncontentious on ontological grounds – parts are non-identical to wholes. Deleuze's claim that crystal-images diminish the importance of linear temporal succession $(t_1, t_2 \ldots t_n)$ invites explanation. The claim is that temporality is non-reducible to succession. It is important to point out that Deleuze is *not* denying that linear temporal ordering appears to obtain in film (as it does in the non-filmic world). In this sense, Deleuze's distinction is analogous to Aristotle's identification – in *Physics IV*, 219b2–219b9[26] – that time may be characterised as something other than either what is measured (i.e., the motion of existents) or the linear succession of numbers that one uses when one measures the motion of existents. Deleuze modifies Aristotle's distinction to suggest that the measure of the movement of existents is ontologically secondary to the form of temporality. Deleuze's claim here is that linear temporal succession is ontologically dependent on a more fundamental ontological relation. It is this fundamental relation that is directly expressed by the crystal-image. Deleuze is suggesting that there is an ontological process more fundamental to temporality than the succession of temporal moments; though there still may be the succession of scenes in a film (just as the succession of minutes, hours and years seem to obtain as adequate measures of the moments of the durations enjoyed by the real entities that may or may not be represented in film), there is some ontological process primary to these. It is this process that is presented in the crystal-image; the direct-image of time is a filmic representation of the ontologically primary process of time.

Deleuze's elaboration of the direct presentation of time through filmic hyalosigns is a Bergsonian film philosophy that Bergson never got around to writing. This philosophical lineage is evidenced by Deleuze's observation that crystal-images illustrate an ontologically primary 'indivisible unity of an actual image and "its" virtual image' (1997b: 79). Each of these terms and the relation between them cries out for clarification. Bergson elucidates the complex nature of the relation through reference to the metaphor of an object and its reflection in a mirror.[27] Bergson makes two stipulations about the natures of the *relata*: the objects reflected by the mirror enjoy an actual mode of existence; the reflected images are virtual. These two modes of being may be distinguished from one another by their respective properties (or predicates). Bergson explicitly identifies materiality and (by implication) material causal efficacy as the relevant predicates. The claim is that both causal efficacy and materiality may be predicated of actual objects. Virtual entities enjoy none of the capacities to be influenced by entities that characterise physical material existence; virtual entities are immaterial and neutral with respect to material causation. In contradistinction, an entity is actual if it is causally relevant in a material circumstance. If one were to characterise materiality and causal efficacy as ontological conditions which must be met for an object to enjoy actuality, then one must observe that virtual entities do not obtain as actual, because they fail to fulfil these. Bergson positively identifies the virtual as the ontological domain which most closely resembles 'the plane of a dream' (2012: 165) (i.e., the domain populated by phantasmal entities that – for all their apparent reality – lack the capacity to affect actualised entities). The specification that virtual entities enjoy the predication of immateriality seems to invite a comparison of virtual entities to either of any of the species of abstract entities (i.e., *abstracta*) or possibilities. Virtual entities are none of these. Citing Proust's formulation, Deleuze insists that virtuality is 'real without being actual, ideal without being abstract' (1991: 96; Proust 1982: 902). He observes that the possible may be conceptualised as that which subsists in opposition to the real, in the sense that what is possible is not yet realised: the possible does not obtain as something realised, in the sense that it obtains as either that which is ontologically prior to that which is realised or that which is a potential result of a deduction that has not yet been made. The suggestion here is that possibility enjoys a modality that is categorically distinct from that enjoyed by real entities – i.e., 'the possible has no reality' (Deleuze 1991: 96). Deleuze further specifies that the virtual may be identified as a species of ideality, in the sense that it enjoys the property of immateriality – a property that tends to be associated with ideal objects. Here, it is essential to note that the property of immateriality does not imply indeterminacy. The quality of immateriality implies only that an entity is not subject to quantitative determination. If Ingarden has demonstrated anything, it is that immaterial entities – like reflections in mirrors, literary characters, photographically represented objectivities – are subject to rigorous qualitative determination. A viewer of *Cool Hand Luke* (Rosenberg 1967) knows the exact nature of the protagonist, right down to how many hard-boiled eggs he can eat. Because virtual entities may be qualitatively determined, they enjoy none of the ontological ambiguity that tends to be associated with abstract entities. It is perhaps worth noting that the metaphysical conditions implied by the distinction between virtuality and actuality are adequate, in the sense that were they denied, the result would be an existential terror of the kind evoked by certain horror movies. Here one cannot help but think of the virtual image clawing its way out of a television screen in David Cronenberg's *Videodrome* (1983), or the terrifying moments of monsters materialising out of reflective surfaces in the trilogy of Japanese *Ring* films (Nakata 1998, 1999; Tsuruta 2000). The terror elicited by these scenes of the virtual being actualised as material is sufficient to demonstrate the metaphysical truth of the complex distinction between the virtual and actual.

The crystal-image involves a relation of the virtual memory and the actual present. The tension of these is the content of time's direct expression in cinema. Bergson suggests that the past emerges as a moment of temporal bifurcation, a relation among the virtual and actual that yields a division of the instant into 'two jets exactly symmetrical, one of which falls back toward the past, whilst the other springs forward to the future' (2012: 160). Deleuze explicitly characterises this relation as the simultaneous creation of two discrete temporal modalities (the memorial past and the fleeting present).[28] The staggering implication is that the past does not follow after the lived present – one's memory of an object obtains simultaneously with one's perception of the object. Proust beautifully illustrates this through reference to the lingering scent of madeleines:

> But let a noise or scent, once heard or once smelt, be heard or smelt again in the present and at the same time in the past, real without being actual, ideal without being abstract, and immediately the permanent and habitually concealed essence of things is liberated and our true self which seemed – perhaps for long years seemed – to be dead but was not altogether dead, is awakened and reanimated as it receives the celestial nourishment that is brought to it. A minute freed from the order of time has re-created in us, to feel it, the man freed from the order of time. And one can understand that this man should have confidence in his joy, even if the simple taste of a madeleine does not seem logically to contain within it the reasons for this joy, one can understand the word 'death' should have no meaning for him; situated outside time, why should he fear the future?
>
> But this species of optical illusion, which placed beside me a moment of the past that was incompatible with the present, could not last for long. The images presented to us by the voluntary memory can, it is true, be prolonged at will, for the voluntary memory requires no more exertion on our part than the turning over of the pages in a picture book. (Proust 1982: 906)

Perhaps what is most remarkable about this eloquent elaboration of the function of a time-crystal is that it seems to involve a denial of the hypothesis that a dependency relation obtains among the present and the past; the past does not subsist from the present; the two (characterised as any of past and present, virtual and actual, perceived object and content of recollection) emerge in immanent relation to one another as ontological correlates, each designating a discrete temporal modality. Perceptual moments of quantifiably existent entities are co-created as virtual entities that obtain as existing qualities. Further, Deleuze carefully notes that a crystalline-image never reaches a state of completion – it never obtains as 'altogether dead' – in the sense that its process of producing the virtual and actual never ceases. That is, the crystal involves an 'indiscernible exchange [that] is always renewed and reproduced' (1997b: 274). The suggestion here is that time is continually regained in the ongoing process of generating the past and the present simultaneously. This is a regeneration of discrete modes of time, in which each enjoys a temporal difference from what was immediately prior as well as an ontological difference from the other. In this sense, the attribute of finitude cannot be predicated of time. Though the relation among the virtual and the actual is stabilised in the form of a relation, this stability does not imply any temporal, logical or ontological cessation. In the most general sense, one cannot predicate an end to time – i.e., temporality is an ongoing relation, a continuum of differentiation. Taken together, these elucidations reveal that the direct-image of time involves four non-competing aspects: (1) the fundamental indeterminacy of a singularity; (2) virtuality and actuality, which enjoy a categorical distinction (as is demonstrated by their non-reducible properties); (3) a simultaneous creation of the past and present, each of which is characterised as a non-reducible (non-subsistent, relatively autonomous) way of time's being; (4) its expression as an ongoing stable relation (i.e., a continuum) that is akin to the process of a seed involved in a germination, in the sense that it produces difference, in multiple senses.

Concluding Remarks: The Time of Cinema

Perhaps there has been no greater change in the visual arts than the tectonic shift of the camera recording the movements of the workers leaving the Lumière brothers' factory. No more were we condemned to simply viewing the arrested movements of entities in repose. No more was all visual art a still life. No more was the realism of art forced to capture entities arrested in time. The birth of cinema changed everything for those who were able to apprehend entities expressing themselves as singular moments of time.

In his *Cinema* texts, Deleuze suggests that the changes heralded by cinema involved a change to our conceptions of time. Film reveals temporality to be a singularity. The cinema is a temporal art form, in the sense that it conveys the actions of entities over a temporal duration, and these effect qualitative changes in the lives of the audience for an extended duration of moments in time. Deleuze observes that some of cinema's most sublime moments – the pure optical and acoustic situations – suggest a deeper involvement with temporality and cinema. In these, the viewer is treated to a glimpse of time's radical indeterminacy. When a character looks into a mirror or catches a reflection of themselves in the window of a passing streetcar, this reveals a further aspect of the nature of temporal change. With the proliferation of crystal-images, cinema reveals time to be something other than the mere succession of temporal instants. The image in the mirror illustrates an exchange of the virtual and the actual – an occurrence that is ontologically primary to a succession of existents. Further, it is observed that this relation of virtual and actual involves the strictly simultaneous and continual creation of past and present as correlated modalities of time.

Notes

1. Referring to Deleuze's *Essays Critical and Clinical* and *The Logic of Sense*, Williams observes that in these 'concepts and artwork grow inwards and explode outwards together, in a style with more rhythm, texture, complexity of pace, and linguistic invention' than is evident in either of Deleuze's books on *Cinema* (2011: 161).
2. With his suggestion that Deleuze seems to bear an affinity to various phenomenologists and explicitly phenomenological claims, Schrader is hardly a voice in the wilderness. Particularly interesting recent studies advancing similar theses include Somers-Hall 2019; Wambacq 2017; Lampert 2015; Bryant 2008; and Shores 2014. It should be pointed out that most of these tend to focus on Deleuze's early work – primarily *Difference and Repetition* – while leaving aside Deleuze's critiques of Husserl (and the Husserlian concept of 'natural perception') in *The Logic of Sense*, *Cinema 1: The-Movement Image*, and *Cinema 2: The Time-Image*. François Zourabichvili suggests that when one takes Deleuze's characterisation of 'becoming' – particularly, the various cinematic becomings that are evidenced by the changes in the way films are made, as well as the ways cinematic narrative style has altered with the French New Wave – Deleuze's conceptual distance 'from phenomenology and its heirs' becomes apparent (Zourabichvili 2012: 173).
3. Cook offers a lovely, condensed history of the art form, including its genesis from the zoetrope (2016: 7–14).
4. Perhaps due to their brevity, Sartre's observations have generated scant critical analysis. Dana Polan is one of the few to have elaborated on Sartre's 'occasional' thought on cinema (Polan 1987).

5. Here, Deleuze mentions Merleau-Ponty's remarks in *Phenomenology of Perception* (Merleau-Ponty 1962: 68). Wambaq notes that Merleau-Ponty also makes passing reference to cinema in a few other texts (2017: 233 n.3).

6. Typically, the illusion of perceived motion is achieved by projecting still images at a rate of rate of twenty-four frames per second. Settling on this frame rate was the result of a fraught history of technological evolution that spanned almost two-thirds of the nineteenth century: beginning with the invention of Plateau's Phenakistoscope (1832), progressing through Horner's Zoetrope (1832), Muybridge's Zoopraxiscope (1879) and Edison's Kinetograph (1891), to finally be perfected with the Lumière brothers' Cinématographe (1895).

7. Spiegelberg observes that Husserlian intentional directedness at an object involves four discrete characteristics: (1) objectivation; (2) identification; (3) connection; (4) constitution. The intentional act of fulfilling schematised aspects occurs in the intuitive fulfilment of an entity which appears as an incomplete – not yet fully determined – form. This tends to be associated with the intentional process of connection (Spiegelberg 1971: 108–11). Mitscherling presents an excellent elaboration of the complex process of fulfilling schematised aspects that are presented in literary works of art. The model presented here is analogous to the process of natural perception. Mitscherling writes: 'When consciousness attends to (or "intends") a particular object, it is usually the case that only some of the "aspects" of that object are presented immediately to consciousness, and these aspects are said to be either fulfilled or unfulfilled. For example, when we look to a table from above, the table presents us with the aspect of "table-top" and "table-bottom", and the former is fulfilled while the latter remains unfulfilled. When we look at the table from beneath, the former (table-top) aspect is unfulfilled, and the latter (table-bottom) is fulfilled. A similar situation obtains in the case of the literary work of art, but here the reader is often forced to fulfil for herself many of those aspects that are presented by the author as unfulfilled, and she does so with regard to those aspects that are presented more fully, i.e., as fulfilled. The latter provide the reader with a direction to follow in her intentional activity of fulfilling these unfulfilled aspects, which are said to have been presented as "schematised". This intentional activity of the fulfilment of schematised aspects is a central component of the general activity of "concretisation". As no character, for example, can ever be exhaustively presented by an author – no character, that is to say, can ever be portrayed as fully and completely determined – the manner in which this concretisation is to proceed can only be schematically determined by the literary work through its stratum of these schematised aspects' (Mitscherling 2010: 143–4, n.10).

8. Deleuze elaborates on Walter Ruttmann's masterful sequence during a lecture on the movement-image (Deleuze 1982).

9. Husserl writes: 'to the extent, however, that every-consciousness is "consciousness-of", the essential study of consciousness also includes that of consciousness-meaning and consciousness-objectivity as such. To study any kind of objectivity whatever according to its general essence (a study that can pursue interests far removed from those of knowledge theory and the investigation of consciousness) means to concern oneself with objectivity's modes of givenness and to exhaust its essential content with the process of "clarification" proper to it' (1965: 90–1).

10. Dastur writes: 'because, even if transcendental phenomenology remains dualistic in spite of Husserl's efforts toward monism, its purpose is not to assert dualism dogmatically, but rather to demonstrate, in line with the phenomenological way of thinking, that unity can only be given pretheoretically (*vortheoretisch*): the awakening of thought splits this unity irrevocably into pieces. That

is why, for Husserl, dualism never ceases to be a problem – a problem which pointed to itself as the most thought deserving' (1983: 65).

11. In Deleuze 2002: 22–32 and 32–52.

12. Deleuze observes: 'In other words, if I want to speak in more scholarly terms, mathematical or physical terms borrowed from Leibniz's terminology, movement in the process of occurring implies a differential, a differential of movement. The unity of movement in the process of occurring is, in the first place, the differential of movement, that is, the difference between the movement that has just occurred and the one that's occurring, or between the one that is occurring and the one that is going to occur. We can call this differential effort (or urge); in Latin, we will call it *conatus*, that is, effort, or urge, or admit that Bergson is not far off when he calls it tendency' (Deleuze 1987).

13. Hyppolite observes: 'This [Bergsonian] duration – which is pure succession, the extension of the past into the present, and therefore already memory – is not a series of distinct terms outside of one another, nor a coexistence of past with present' (2003: 112).

14. Here Deleuze observes: 'Pure duration offers us a succession that is purely internal, without exteriority; space, an exteriority, without succession (in effect, that is the memory of the past; the recollection of what has happened in space would already imply a mind that endures)' (1991: 37).

15. Bergson writes: 'The wholly superficial displacements of masses and molecules studied in physics and chemistry would become by relation to that inner vital movement (which is transformation and not translation) what the position of a moving object is to the movement of that object in space' (1998: 37).

16. Barthes characterises this capacity as the *punctum* of an image. Barthes elaborates: 'it is this element which rises from the scene, shoots out of it like an arrow, and pierces me. A Latin word exists to designate this wound, this prick; this mark made by a pointed instrument . . . *punctum*; for *punctum* is also: sting, speck, cut, little hole – and also a cast of the dice. A photograph's *punctum* is that accident which pricks me (but also bruises me, is poignant to me)' (1981: 26–7).

17. Hansen highlights the fraught nature of a hermeneutic investigation of the nature of Benjamin's concept when she observes: 'Anything but a clearly delimited, stable concept, aura describes a cluster of meanings and relations that appear in Benjamin's writings in various configurations and not always under its own name; it is this conceptual fluidity that allows aura to become such a productive nodal point in Benjamin's thinking' (2008: 339).

18. Benjamin elaborates on the disquieting experience one might have when viewing the haunting gazes of subjects in Daguerreotype images of the late nineteenth and early twentieth centuries – i.e., the sorts of images that would have most certainly been familiar to Bergson when he was conceptualising the nature of duration and the effect of the 'cinematographic illusion'. Benjamin writes: 'Experience of the aura thus arises from the fact that a response characteristic of human relationships is transposed to the relationship between humans and inanimate or natural objects. The person we look at, or who feels he is being looked at, looks at us in turn. To experience the aura of an object we look at means to invest it with the ability to look back at us' (2006a: 338).

19. Avant-garde films tend to be at the vanguard of these explorations of the possibilities of filmic representation. Though rarely enjoying critical or commercial success, these films – which are often rich in symbolic meaning and dream sequences that confound the passive viewer – truly show the way for future cinematic artists. Maya Deren's and Alexander Hammid's *Meshes in the Afternoon* (1941) is a wonderful example.

20. Robbe-Grillet writes: 'Description once served to situate the chief contours of a setting, then to cast light on some of its particularly revealing elements; it no longer mentions anything except insignificant objects, or objects which it is concerned to make so. It once claimed to reproduce a pre-existing reality; it now asserts its creative function' (1965: 144–7).

21. It would be difficult to overstate either the longevity or importance of Plato's identification of art as mimetic. Charles Sanders Peirce offers only a slight modification of Plato's suggestion with his observation that visual art tends to represent 'iconic signs' of the real (1982: 53–4). John Hyman develops the epistemological aspects of Plato's claim by insisting that one can only understand the truth of a painting – i.e., understand its sense – through reference to the immaterial or material objects that it represents (2009: 495–8). This is not to say that Robbe-Grillet is a voice in the wilderness. Echoing John Ruskin, E. H. Gombrich observes that visual art tends to involve a creation of the 'innocence of the eye' (1960: 296). One implication of Gombrich's suggestion is that such innocence might not pre-exist the viewer's participation with the work of art. This further suggests that art is non-mimetic, in the sense that it cannot resemble (or copy) that which does not exist.

22. Deleuze continually modifies his concept of singularity. It seems each of the books following *The Logic of Sense* – in which Deleuze first uses the term – witnesses a further evolution of the nuanced nature of singularities. Though Manuel DeLanda suggests that singularities may be characterised as 'spaciotemporal dynamisms' and 'passive selves', these attempts at definition seem inadequate, in the sense that both of these are profoundly opaque, and perhaps even involve definitional aspects that would confound any assertion of identity (2002: 206–7). Steven Shaviro observes that Deleuze tends to identify singularities as 'acategorical' entities, in the sense 'that they cannot be categorized in any terms broader than their own . . . they cannot be fitted into a hierarchy of species and genera, of the particular and the general: just as they cannot be derived as instances of any larger, more overarching and predetermining structure' (2012: 89, n.11). Daniel W. Smith traces Deleuze's concept of singularities to a modification of Albert Lautman's suggestion – in his *Essay on the Notions of Structure and Existence in Mathematics* – that points on a geometric curve may be distinguished from one another in terms of whether or not they are involved in a change of direction in the curve: ordinary points do not radically alter the direction of the curve; singular points (or singularities) are moments on the curve at which the trajectory of the curve alters (2012: 302). Smith further observes that Deleuze generalises the variability implied in Lautman's strictly mathematical definition, to suggest qualitative and affective components. It should be noted that not all of these need be temporal, in the sense that some have suggested that mathematical entities enjoy an a-temporal existence. Taken together, these suggest that a singularity may by rigorously characterised as any of a temporal or non-temporal moment of variation or difference (i.e., change). It is conceivable that such moments could be visually or aurally represented in film. This is plainly the case in films involving profound crisis, if it is granted that these are not – and perhaps never aspired to be – copies, imitations or duplications of a world marked by the striking appearance of continuity, banality or putative normalcy, all of which might be characteristics of a circumstance bereft of profound variation. It might be further observed that all of these apparent traits of normalcy could obtain as representations in film – the typical, even quotidian, has often been the subject matter of some of the more fascinating films of the last hundred years of cinema; e.g., the films of Antonioni, but this would not negate (or otherwise diminish) the possibility of singularities

being present in these, as long as one acknowledges that the seemingly banal may involve understated crises, which are – for all their subtlety – just as profound as those expressed in the most bombastic Hollywood blockbuster.

23. Deleuze elaborates: 'These are pure optical and sound situations, in which the character does not know how to respond, abandoned spaces in which he ceases to experience and act so that he enters into flight, goes on a trip, comes and goes, vaguely indifferent to what happens to him, undecided as to what must be done' (1997b: 272).

24. Bergson writes: 'Whenever we are trying to recover a recollection, to call up some period of our history, we become conscious of an act *sui generis* by which we detach ourselves from the present in order to replace ourselves, first, in the past – a work of adjustment, something like the framing of a camera' (1991: 133–4).

25. Bergson writes: 'The more he analyses his experience, the more he will split into two personages, one of which moves about on the stage while the other sits and looks. On the one hand, he knows that he continues to be what he was, a self who thinks and acts comfortably to what the situation requires, a self-inserted into real life, and adapting itself to it by a free effort of the will; this is what his perception of the present assures him. But the memory of this present, which is equally there, makes him believe that he is repeating what has been said already, seeing again what has been seen already, and so transforms him into an actor reciting his part' (2012: 169).

26. It is important to observe the limited scope of this analogy. The conceptual differences between Deleuze's and Aristotle's respective philosophies of time are substantive, as are the differences in their metaphysics. Daniel W. Smith (2001) elaborates on the differences between Deleuze's and Aristotle's metaphysics.

27. Bergson writes: 'The memory seems to be the perception of what the object in the mirror is to the object in front of it. The object can be touched as well as seen; acts upon us as well as we on it; it is pregnant with possible actions; it is actual. The image is virtual, and though it resembles the object, it is incapable of doing what the object does' (2012: 165).

28. Deleuze observes: 'What constitutes the crystal-image is the most fundamental operation of time: since past is constituted not after the present that it was but at the same time, it has to split itself in two at each moment as present and past, which differ from each other in nature, or, what amounts to the same thing, it has to split the present in two heterogeneous directions, one of which is launched toward the future while the other falls into the past' (1997b: 81).

References

Barthes, R. (1981), *Camera Lucida: Reflections on Photography*, trans. Richard Howard, New York: Hill and Wang.

Bazin, A. (2005), *What is Cinema? 1*, trans. Hugh Gray, Berkeley: University of California Press.

Benjamin, W. (2005), 'Little History of Photography', in *Selected Writings 2, 1931–1934*, trans. Rodney Livingstone, ed. Michael W. Jennings, Howard Eiland and Gary Smith, Cambridge, MA: Belknap Press.

Benjamin, W. (2006a), 'On Some Motifs in Baudelaire', in *Selected Writings 4, 1938–1940*, trans. Rodney Livingstone, ed. Michael W. Jennings, Howard Eiland and Gary Smith, Cambridge, MA: Belknap Press.

Benjamin, W. (2006b), 'Protocols of Drug Experiments (1–12)', in *On Hashish*, trans. Howard Eiland, Cambridge, MA: Belknap Press.

Benjamin, W. (2007), 'The Work of Art in the Age of Mechanical Reproduction', in *Illuminations*, trans. Harry Zohn, New York: Schocken.

Bergson, H. (1935), *Two Sources of Morality and Religion*, trans. R. Ashley Audra, Cloudesley Brereton and W. Horsfall Carter, Notre Dame: Notre Dame University Press.

Bergson, H. (1946), *The Creative Mind*, trans. Mabelle L. Andison, New York: The Philosophical Library.

Bergson, H. (1991), *Matter and Memory*, trans. Nancy Margaret Paul and W. Scott Palmer, New York: Zone.

Bergson, H. (1998), *Creative Evolution*, trans. Arthur Mitchell, Mineola: Dover.

Bergson, H. (2001), *Time and Free Will: An Essay on the Immediate Data of Consciousness*, trans. F. L Pogson, Mineola: Dover.

Bergson, H. (2012), 'Memory of the Present and False Recognition', trans. H. Wildon Carr, in *Mind-Energy, Lectures and Essays*, London: Forgotten Books, pp. 134–85.

Bogue, R. (2003), *Deleuze on Cinema*, New York and London: Routledge.

Bresson, R. (1997), *Notes on Cinematography*, trans. Jonathan Griffin, New York: Urizen Books.

Bryant, L. R. (2008), *Difference and Givenness: Deleuze's Transcendental Empiricism and the Ontology of Difference*, Evanston: Northwestern University Press.

Cache, B. (1995), *Earth Moves: The Furnishing of Territories*, trans. Anne Boyman, ed. Michael Sparks, Cambridge, MA: MIT Press.

Cook, D. A. (2016), *A History of Narrative Cinema*, London and New York: W. W. Norton.

Dastur, F. (1983), 'Husserl and the Problem of Dualism', in *Analecta Husserliana XVI: Soul and Body in Husserlian Phenomenology*, ed. Anna-Teresa Tymienieka, Dordrecht: D. Reidel.

DeLanda, M. (2002), *Intensive Science and Virtual Philosophy*, London: Continuum.

Deleuze, G. (1981), 'Lecture 1, 10 November 1981', *Seminar on Cinema: The Movement-Image*, transcription: *La voix de Deleuze*, Fanny Douarche and Lise Renaux; transcription augmented, Charles J. Stivale, trans. Charles J. Stivale, at <https://deleuze.cla.purdue.edu/seminars/cinema-movement-image/lecture-01>.

Deleuze, G. (1982), 'Lecture 7, 19 January 1982', *Seminar on Cinema: The Movement- Image*, transcribed by Céline Romagnoli, Pierre Gribling and Binak Kalludra, at <https://deleuze.cla.purdue.edu/seminars/cinema-movement-image/lecture-07>.

Deleuze, G. (1987), 'Lecture 16, 5 May 1987: The Theory of Substance in Aristotle, Descartes and Leibniz', trans. Charles J. Stivale, at <https://deleuze.cla.purdue.edu/seminars/leibniz-and-baroque/lecture-16>.

Deleuze, G. (1990), *The Logic of Sense*, trans. Mark Lester with Charles Stivale, New York: Columbia University Press.

Deleuze, G. (1991), *Bergsonism*, trans. Hugh Tomlinson and Barbara Habberjam, New York: Zone.

Deleuze, G. (1994), *Difference and Repetition*, trans. Paul Patton, New York: Columbia University Press.

Deleuze, G. (1997a), *Cinema 1: The Movement-Image*, trans. Hugh Tomlinson and Barbara Habberjam, Minneapolis: University of Minnesota Press.

Deleuze, G. (1997b), *Cinema 2: The Time-Image*, trans. Hugh Tomlinson and Robert Galeta, Minneapolis: University of Minnesota Press.

Deleuze, G. (2002), *Desert Islands and Other Texts: 1953–1974*, trans. Michael Taormina, ed. David Lapoujade, South Pasadena: Semiotext(e).

Deleuze, G. (2020), 'Interview on *Anti-Oedipus* with Raymond Bellour', in *Letters and Other Texts*, trans. Ames Hodges, ed. David Lapoujade, South Pasadena: Semiotext(e), pp. 195–240.

Deleuze, G. and F. Guattari (1987), *A Thousand Plateaus: Capitalism and Schizophrenia II*, trans. Brian Massumi, Minneapolis: University of Minnesota Press.

Gombrich, E. H. (1960), *Art and Illusion: A Study in the Psychology of Pictorial Representation*, London: Phaidon.

Guillemet, J. (2010), '"The 'New Wave" of French Phenomenology and Cinema: New Concepts for the Cinematic Experience', *New Review of Film and Television Studies*, 8 (1): 94–114.

Hansen, M. B. (2008), 'Benjamin's Aura', *Critical Inquiry*, 34: 336–75.

Hill, R. (2012), *The Interval: Relation and Becoming in Irigaray, Aristotle, and Bergson*, New York: Fordham University Press.

Husserl, E. (1931), *Ideas*, trans. W. R. Boyce Gibson, London: Allen and Unwin.

Husserl, E. (1965), *Phenomenology and the Crisis of Philosophy*, trans. Quentin Lauer, New York: Harper and Row.

Husserl, E. (2005), *Collected Works XI: Phantasy, Image, Consciousness, and Memory (1898–1925)*, trans. John B. Brough, ed. Rudolf Bernet, Dordrecht: Springer.

Hyman, J. (2009), 'Realism', in *A Companion to Aesthetics*, ed. Stephen Davies et al., Chichester: Wiley-Blackwell.

Hyppolite, J. (2003), 'Various Aspects of Memory in Bergson', trans. Athena V. Colman, Appendix II in Leonard Lawlor, *The Challenge of Bergson: Phenomenology, Ontology, Ethics*, London: Continuum, pp. 112–27.

Ingarden, R. (1973), *The Literary Work of Art*, trans. George G. Grabowicz, Evanston: Northwestern University Press.

Ingarden, R. (1989), *Ontology of the Work of Art: The Musical Work, the Picture, the Architectural Work, the Film*, trans. Raymond Meyer, Athens: Ohio University Press.

Jackson, S. (1959), *The Haunting of Hill House*, New York: Penguin.

King, S. (1977), *The Shining*, New York: Doubleday.

Kovács, A. B. (2007), *Screening Modernism: European Art Cinema, 1950–1980*, Chicago: University of Chicago Press.

Lampert, J. (2015), 'Deleuze's "Power of Decision", Kant's = X and Husserl's Noema', in *At the Edges of Thought: Deleuze and Post-Kantian Philosophy*, ed. Craig Lundy and Daniela Voss, Edinburgh: Edinburgh University Press, pp. 272–92.

Lawlor, L. (2003), *The Challenge of Bergson: Phenomenology, Ontology, Ethics*, London: Continuum.

Merleau-Ponty, M. (1962), *Phenomenology of Perception*, trans. Colin Smith, New York: Routledge.

Merleau-Ponty, M. (1964), *Signs*, trans. R. C. McQeary, Evanston: Northwestern University Press.

Mitscherling, J. (2010), *Aesthetic Genesis: The Origin of Consciousness in the Intentional Being of Nature*, Toronto: University of America Press.

Nelson, T. A. (2000), *Kubrick: Inside A Film Artist's Maze*, Bloomington: Indiana University Press.

Peirce, C. S. (1982), *The Writings of Charles S. Peirce: A Chronological Edition 2*, ed. M. Fisch, C. Kloesel, E. Moore and N. Houser, Bloomington: Indiana University Press.

Plato (1997), *Republic*, trans. G. M. A. Grube and C. D. C. Reeve, in *Complete Works*, ed. John. M. Cooper, Indianapolis: Hackett.

Polan, D. (1987), 'Sartre and Cinema', *Post-script*, 7 (1): 66–88.

Proust, M. (1982), *Remembrance of Things Past 3: Time Regained*, trans. C. K. Moncreiff, Terence Kilmartin and Andreas Mayor, New York: Vintage, 1982.

Robbe-Grillet, A. (1965), 'Time and Description in Fiction Today', in *For a New Novel: Essays in Fiction*, trans. Richard Howard, New York: Grove Press.

Rodowick, D. (1997), *Gilles Deleuze's Time Machine*, Durham, NC: Duke University Press.

Sartre, J-P. (1964), *The Words*, trans. Bernard Frechtman, New York: George Braziller.

Sartre, J-P. (2004), *The Imaginary*, trans. Jonathan Webber, ed. Arlette Elkaïm-Sartre, London and New York: Routledge.

Schrader, P. (2018), *Transcendental Style in Film: Ozu, Bresson, and Dreyer*, Oakland: University of California Press.

Shaviro, S. (2012), *Without Criteria: Kant, Whitehead, Deleuze, and Aesthetics*, Cambridge, MA: MIT Press.

Shores, C. (2014), 'In the Still of the Moment: Deleuze's Phenomena of Motionless Time', *Deleuze Studies*, 8 (2): 199–229.

Smith, D. W. (2001), 'The Doctrine of Univocity: Deleuze's Ontology of Immanence', in *Deleuze and Religion*, ed. Mary Bryden, London: Routledge.

Smith, D. W. (2012), *Essays on Deleuze*, Edinburgh: Edinburgh University Press.

Sobchack, V. (1992), *The Address of the Eye: A Phenomenology of Film Experience*, Princeton: Princeton University Press.

Somers-Hall, H. (2019), 'Merleau-Ponty and the Phenomenology of Difference: Difference and Repetition, Chapter One', *Deleuze and Guattari Studies* 13 (3): 401–15.

Spiegelberg, H. (1971), *The Phenomenological Movement: A Historical Introduction I*, The Hague: Martinus Nihoff.

Vertov, D. (1984), *Kino-Eye: The Writings of Dziga Vertov*, trans. Kevin O'Brien, ed. Annette Michelson, Berkeley: University of California Press.

Wambacq, J. (2017), *Thinking Between Deleuze and Merleau-Ponty*, Athens: University of Ohio Press.

Williams, J. (2011), *Gilles Deleuze's Philosophy of Time: A Critical Introduction and Guide*, Edinburgh: Edinburgh University Press.

Zourabichvili, F. (2012), *Deleuze: A Philosophy of the Event together with The Vocabulary of Deleuze*, trans. Kieran Aarons, ed. Gregg Lambert and Daniel W. Smith, Edinburgh: Edinburgh University Press.

Films

Michelangelo Antonioni (dir.), *Red Desert*, Rizolli, 1964.

Luis Buñuel (dir.), *Un Chien Andalou*, Les Grands Films, 1929.

Robert Clouse (dir.), *Enter the Dragon*, Warner Brothers and Concord Productions Inc., 1973.

David Cronenberg (dir.), *Videodrome*, Universal, 1983.

Maya Deren and Alexander Hammid (dir.), *Meshes of the Afternoon*, 1943.

Stanley Kubrick (dir.), *The Shining*, The Producer Circle Company, 1980.

Paul McGuigan (dir.), *The Hounds of Baskerville*, BBC, 8 January 2012.

Hideo Nakata (dir.), *Ring*, Ringu/Rasen Production Committee, 1998.

Hideo Nakata (dir.), *Ring 2*, Asmik Ace Entertainment, 1999.

Stuart Rosenberg (dir.), *Cool Hand Luke*, Jalem Productions, 1967.

Roberto Rossellini (dir.), *Europe ' 51*, Roberto Rossellini, Carlo Ponti, Dino De Laurentiis, 1952.

Walter Ruttmann (dir.), *Berlin: Die Sinfonie der Großstadt*, Fox Europa, 1927

Martin Scorsese (dir.), *Taxi Driver*, Bill/Phillips Productions and Italo/Judeo Productions, 1976.

Norio Tsuruta (dir.), *Ring 0: Birthday*, Ring 0 Production Group, 2000.
Orson Welles (dir.), *The Lady from Shanghai*, Mercury Productions, 1947.
Wim Wenders (dir.), *Paris, Texas*, Road Movies, Filmproduktion GmbH, Argos Films S.A., 1984.
Robert Wise (dir.), *The Haunting*, Argyle Enterprises, 1963.
Denis Villeneuve (dir.), *Blade Runner 2049*, Columbia Pictures: 2017.

Chapter 10

Time, Truth and the Power of the False

Vernon W. Cisney

In his parabolic masterpiece, *Thus Spoke Zarathustra*, Friedrich Nietzsche famously writes, 'Of three metamorphoses of the spirit I tell you: how the spirit becomes a camel; and the camel, a lion; and the lion, finally, a child' (1966: 25). Nietzsche traces a progression – of a people or of an individual – through the laborious and toilsome bearing of a culture's 'truths' and values, to the sacred no-saying of leonine adolescence whereby those truths are cast off, and finally to a renewed power of innocence and forgetfulness – akin to the affirmation and openness of childhood – that enables genuine creation. The child knows no shame or inhibitions, longs for and believes in the impossible, and forms playful assemblages with anyone (human or non-human, real or imaginary) willing and able to do so. Each day she creates her world anew, while the man of the so-called 'real world' fritters his life away resentfully paying obeisance to his ideological and corporate masters. In a surprising proximity to Nietzsche's philosophical nemesis, we might say that to enter the kingdom, one must become a child.[1] Truth itself, Nietzsche also famously (some might say 'infamously') claims, is a 'movable host of metaphors, metonymies, and anthropomorphisms . . . illusions which we have forgotten are illusions' (1979: 84). Unlike most of the philosophical tradition before him, Nietzsche calls into question the very value of *truth* itself and of the drive that sets truth upon its pedestal in the clouds, sacrificing everything upon its altar: 'The will to truth is in need of a critique' (1998: 110). In its place, Nietzsche provocatively emphasises the process of truth-*creation*, which, he argues throughout the body of his work, is a kind of artistry.

Given the pride of place that Nietzsche occupies in the thinking of Gilles Deleuze, it is hardly surprising that when Deleuze approaches the question of *truth*, and in particular in relation to creation, as in his expansive, two-volume taxonomy of the cinema, his discussion is framed by Nietzsche's critiques and reformulations of truth. In place of Nietzsche's camel, lion and child, Deleuze recasts the chain of the 'truthful man', 'the forger' and 'the artist'. This arc is traced in response to the problem of the relation between *time* and *truth*; and it is the forger and their relation to the artist with which this chapter is primarily concerned.

In his work, *Gilles Deleuze's Philosophy of Time*, James Williams marginalises the importance of the *Cinema* books for an understanding of Deleuze's philosophy of time. Dedicating a mere six pages to the volumes, he refers diminutively to the *Cinema* project as the 'most extensive application of Deleuze's philosophy of time' (Williams 2011: 159). Treating them as 'application' suggests a structural or methodological form or stasis at the heart of Deleuze's understanding of time, one that Deleuze then merely casts, unchanged, over his taxonomical history of cinema. This would explain why Williams defends his criticisms as 'an explanation of why the film works add little and in fact might take away from [Deleuze's] philosophy of time in its most consistent and extensive form' (161). Leaving aside the oddness in saying that the *Cinema* volumes constitute a mere 'application' of Deleuze's thoughts on time (while simultaneously marking the various ways in which those books depart from the temporal concepts of *Difference and Repetition* and *The Logic of Sense*), more pernicious, perhaps, is the suggestion that there could be 'a' philosophy of time in Deleuze's work, a once-and-for-all understanding that might be simply applied in various other contexts. This is particularly unusual given that Williams himself rightly argues throughout the book that time in Deleuze is a 'multiplicity of processes, where times are dimensions of one another according to asymmetrical syntheses' (164). If time itself is multiple – such that we should more accurately speak of 'times' – it makes little sense to argue that Deleuze's treatments of time constitute 'a' singular philosophy that can be simply applied in other contexts.[2]

The point of this piece, however, is not to lob criticisms at Williams's book, which is impressive in many respects, but rather to take as my point of departure the rejection of Williams's own reason for neglecting a treatment of the *Cinema* books.[3] Contrary to his view, it seems to me that the books put into play the very elaboration of an adaptive temporal multiplicity that Williams's book highlights – *times* that change with the times. Through his own creative conceptual taxonomy, Deleuze temporalises the very concept of truth, tracing the history of the concepts of the cinema, and the ways in which these concepts think their own history as well as the history of their present (and perhaps, their future):

A theory of cinema is not 'about' cinema, but about the concepts that cinema gives rise to and which are themselves related to other concepts corresponding to other practices, the practice of concepts in general having no privilege over others. It is at the level of the interference of many practices that things happen, beings, images, concepts, all the kinds of events. (Deleuze 1989: 280)

One of the most perplexing among the many innovative concepts in the *Cinema* volumes is the 'power of the false which replaces and supersedes the form of the true' (Deleuze 1989: 131). This 'power of the false', introduced as early in Deleuze's work as 1962's *Nietzsche and Philosophy* (1983: 96, 185), is immediately connected to what, in the *Cinema* volumes, Deleuze characterises as *truth*: 'What the artist is, is *creator of truth*, because truth is not to be achieved, formed, or reproduced; it has to be created. There is no other truth than the creation of the New' (1989: 146–7).

Overlooking for the moment the apparent tension in the fact that Deleuze valorises the false as the supersession of the form of the *true*, while also celebrating the *creation of truth*, there is an even more dangerous obstacle afoot. For the notions that truth is in any way subject to the force of time, such that it must be created, or that there is a *power* – a *positive* power, no less – inherent to the *false*, these notions are antithetical not only to banal, common-sense understandings (as when parents, for instance, attempt to impress upon their children the obvious superiority of truth to falsehood), but, more importantly, to the philosophical tradition's understandings of truth and falsehood. Speaking broadly, we can say that truth is traditionally characterised in terms that are static, atemporal and *positive* (in senses that are at once ontological, epistemic and moral), while falsehood has been predominantly characterised as an absence, a lack of truth or of reality. Thus, the task of this paper will be to explore the connections between the *power of the false* and the *creation of truth*. To do so, we must look at the reasons for which Deleuze argues that 'time has always put the notion of truth into crisis' (1989: 130). We will characterise this crisis of truth in both Platonic and Aristotelian senses. We will then look at the notion of incompossibility that Deleuze adopts from Leibniz, whereby he offers a forking of incompossibilities as the basic 'form' of time, as a strategy for responding to the notion of truth that is put into crisis – this is the sense of the 'power of the false' that we will explore. Finally, we will see that this power of the false, as Deleuze conceives it, makes possible the creation of truth, in the form of 'minor art' that conduces to the invention of a people.

Time and the Crisis of Truth

Throughout the history of philosophy, there has *always* been an antagonistic relation between truth and time, in that time – its passage and the fluctuations that it entails – is precisely what the philosophical conception of truth attempts to repress or overcome. This antagonism is first put on explicit display in the fifth century BCE, between the 'becoming' of Heraclitus and the 'being' of Parmenides. Heraclitus had posited the world as 'an everliving fire, being kindled in measures and put out in measures' (DK22B30),[4] an intensive chaosmos in which one cannot step twice into the same river, as there is no stasis, either to the self who steps or to the river itself. Despite the pre-eminence of becoming, however, Heraclitus also holds that underlying and structuring the flow of this everliving fire is the λογος (*logos* – reason, word, argument, language, account, rational principle, etc.), the principle that, in human beings, reflects a tiny ember of the divine: 'It is wise to hearken, not to me, but to the Word [*logos*], and to confess that all things are one' (DK22B50). Against this Heraclitean doctrine of flux and just a few decades later, Parmenides posits the 'steadfast heart of persuasive truth' (DK28B1.29), that what is '*is*, and that it *cannot not be*' (DK28B2.3). Truth is changeless, synonymous with *being* itself, and neither comes to be nor passes away, and while the natural world may give every *appearance* of constant becoming, this is not where the philosopher's truth is discovered; rather, truth is found in the knowledge of whatever there may be that is impervious to time and change.

With his theory of forms, Plato provides the ontology and epistemology to reconcile the Heraclitean and Parmenidean views, with his thumb firmly on the scale for Parmenides. In echo of Parmenides' claim that wisdom pertains only to that which is not subject to time and change, Plato writes:

> Indeed, it isn't even reasonable to say that there is such a thing as knowledge, Cratylus, if all things are passing on and none remain. For if that thing itself, knowledge, did not pass on from being knowledge, then knowledge would always remain, and there would *be* such a thing as knowledge. On the other hand, if the very form of knowledge passed on from being knowledge, the instant it passed on into a different form than that of knowledge, there would be no knowledge. And if it were always passing on, there would always be no knowledge. Hence, on this account, no one could know anything and nothing could be known either. But if there is always that which knows and that which is known, if there are such things as the beautiful, the good, and each one of the things that are, it doesn't

appear to me that these things can be at all like flowings or motions, as we were saying just now they were. (Plato, *Cratylus*, 440a-c)

If there is a *form* of knowledge, then the empirical instantiation of knowledge must *participate* in that form. But the form of knowledge, being a *form*, cannot change, and hence the empirical *content* of knowledge – the knowing of the knower – must remain immobile as well. It does so, Plato argues, by concerning itself only with those *things* which, themselves, are not subject to the force of time – the beautiful, the good, the just, etc.; that is, the forms. Indeed, in the *Theaetetus*, where Plato explicitly engages the Heraclitean and Parmenidean views, highlighting exactly what he takes from each, he writes of the Heracliteans:

> We were most anxious to prove that all things are in motion, in order to make that answer come out correct; but what has really emerged is that, if all things are in motion, every answer, on whatever subject, is equally correct, both 'it is thus' and 'it is not thus' – or if you like 'becomes', as we don't want to use any expressions which will bring our friends to a standstill. (Plato, *Theaetetus*, 183a).

Lacking *any* static templates of knowledge, the Heracliteans leave themselves in a situation such that every statement of the form, 'X is y', is no more or less true than the statement 'X is *not* y'. Knowledge, according to Plato, is impossible on such an understanding, and thus the Heraclitean desire for the *logos* is doomed from the off. But of course, as should be obvious, this argument has hidden within it the assumption, outlined above, that knowledge can pertain only to that which is fixed and atemporal (for which Plato offers up his theory of forms). As Francis Cornford writes, 'Plato is determined to make us feel the need of his Forms without mentioning them' (1935: 99). In the *absence* of such static models, Plato argues, our epistemic comportment toward the world is merely one of *opinion*: 'As for those who study the many beautiful things but do not see the beautiful itself and are incapable of following another who leads them to it, who see many just things but not the just itself, and so with everything – these people, we shall say, opine everything but have no knowledge of anything they opine' (Plato, *Republic*, V.479e). The Parmenidean presuppositions in this framework are clear, and Plato's understanding of the antagonistic relation between time and truth would broadly characterise the philosophical tradition for millennia.

Aristotle deepens and formalises this antagonism with his articulation of the problem that would come to be known in more recent scholarship as the 'problem of future contingents',[5] statements of possibility concerning future events. Aristotle writes: 'With regard to what is and what has been it is necessary for the affirmation or the negation to be true or false . . . But with particulars that are going to be it is different' (*De Interpretatione*, Chapter 9). It is either true or false to say that 'It is raining', or that 'It rained yesterday', but the claim, 'It might rain tomorrow', is subject to different considerations, it seems. To say that 'it may rain tomorrow' is akin to saying 'it is possible that it *will* rain tomorrow or it is possible that it will *not* rain tomorrow', which opens us to problems, in that one of these eventualities will not come to pass. Citing Aristotle's famous example of the sea battle, Deleuze frames the problem in the following way: 'If it is *true* that a naval battle *may* take place tomorrow, how are we to avoid one of the true following consequences: either the impossible proceeds from the possible (since, if the battle takes place, it is no longer possible that it may not take place), or the past is not necessarily true (since the battle could have not taken place)' (1989: 130, translation modified). Aristotle endeavours to solve the problem by arguing that propositions regarding future contingents must be understood as *neither* true *nor* false: 'Clearly, therefore, not everything is or happens of necessity: some things happen as chance has it, and of the affirmation and the negation neither is true rather than the other' (*De Interpretatione*, Chapter 9). Once more, the Platonic considerations pertaining to truth, that it is necessary, universal and unchanging, are evident in Aristotle's reflections, however different his question in this instance may be.

The Stoics – in particular, Diodorus Cronus, with his so-called 'Master Argument' – offer a different resolution to the problem of future contingents. Epictetus reports that, for Diodorus, 'of the following propositions, any two imply a contradiction to the third. They are these: "That everything past is necessarily true"; "that an impossibility is not the consequence of a possibility"; and, "that something is a possibility, which neither is nor will be true"' (1944: II.19). Diodorus, Epictetus claims, argues for the truth of the first two propositions, at the exclusion of the third. Contrary to appearances from within our finite situatedness within time, there *are* no future contingents, in other words. Of the two statements – 'The sea battle will take place', and 'the sea battle will not take place' – one is true and the other false, and they are so necessarily, even if *we* are unable to discern their truth or falsity beforehand. However semantically overburdened this whole exercise may appear, it nonetheless demonstrates the complications that arise whenever we bring the concept of *truth* into interaction with the notion of time.

Leibniz's Proposal – Incompossible Worlds

It is seventeenth-century philosopher Gottfried Wilhelm Leibniz who, for Deleuze, proposes the most interesting solution to Aristotle's problem of future contingents, and thereby, to the relation between time and truth. Distinguishing between necessary and contingent truths, Leibniz argues that 'necessary truths depend upon the principle of contradiction' (1989: 28). If we analyse the terms of the proposition, it becomes evident that the predicate is contained within the subject, as in the hackneyed example that 'all bachelors are unmarried men'. It is a necessary truth in that, in light of the very meanings of the terms, it is impossible for it to be false. This is *not* so for *contingent* truths, however, for while it may be *true* to say that 'My car is *blue*', there is nothing analytically contradictory (however false it may be) in the claim that 'my car is *red*'. Nevertheless, even regarding contingent truths, Leibniz claims, it is still the case that 'there is always, underneath, a reason for the truth', that is, there is ultimately an exhaustive explanatory account for *why it is* that I own this particular car, why that car was on the lot that day, and why this particular car happened to have been painted blue. This is so even if the 'reason is understood completely only by God' (28). Simply put, even in the case of contingent truths, the predicate is ultimately contained within the subject. Thus, if the proposition, 'Caesar crossed the Rubicon', is *true*, it is so because the predicate of crossing the Rubicon is contained within the subject of Caesar, even if it was know-able beforehand only by God.

To see how this relates to our account of time and the crisis of truth, we return to the example of the naval battle. The naval battle may or may not take place – Fleet A will go to battle with Fleet B or Fleet A will not go to battle with Fleet B. Put otherwise, the predicate of going to battle with Fleet B may or may not be contained within the subject of Fleet A. But here we notice, if the predicates ('going to battle with B', 'going to battle with A') are contained within the subjects of Fleets A and B independently of each other, they are so only because there must a precisely tuned arrangement obtaining between the subjects – A and B. A cannot go to battle with B without B also going to battle with A, so their respective predicates must complement each other. Each fleet, of course, consists of ships, each of which is guided and operated by individual human beings, and each of these – the human beings, the ships, the fleets – is itself a subject, containing within it all the predicates pertaining to it, which means therefore that each subject in its own way contains perspectives on all the rest, and ultimately, this implication can theoretically be extended throughout the entirety of the cosmos. In his 'Primary Truths', Leibniz writes, '*Every individual substance contains in its perfect notion the entire universe* and everything that exists in it, past, present, and future' (1989: 32).

Therefore, the predicates within any *one* subject could be different only if the predicates in all other subjects were complementarily adjusted. Each individual subject in the cosmos, along with every predicate pertaining thereto, is part of a vast and intricately orchestrated, finely tuned, series. Leibniz then accounts for the notion of *possibility* by claiming that 'There are, in fact, an infinite number of series of possible things. Moreover, one series certainly cannot be contained within another, since each and every one of them is complete' (1989: 29). Each is 'complete' in the sense that each one consists of its plenum of subjects, each of which is finely determined by its predicates, all of which reflect all other predicates within all other subjects in that one individual series (or 'world' in Leibniz's terminology). Possibility, then, is expressed in Leibniz's terminology by way of an infinity of these possible worlds (series) in the mind of God, each of which consists of all possible subjects with their finely harmonised arrangement of predicates, each of which reflects all the others in a unique way. However, while each of these worlds is *possible*, they are each *in-compossible* with all the others – only one of these worlds can be real. The world in which Adam does not sin is incompossible with the world in which he sins. God creates '"sub ratione possibilitatis", as many divergent Adams as there are worlds, each Adam containing the entire world to which he belongs (and to which, also by including it, belong all other compossible monads of such a world)' (Deleuze 1993: 63). In *Cinema 2*, Deleuze writes: 'Leibniz says that the naval battle may or may not take place, but that this is not in the same world: it takes place in one world and does not take place in a different world, and these two worlds are possible, but are not "compossible" with each other' (1989: 130). With this notion, Leibniz attempts to sidestep the two undesirable solutions to the problem of future contingents, as offered by Aristotle and Diodorus. We do not have to say, with Aristotle, that the statement 'The naval battle might take place tomorrow' is neither true nor false. It is true in some possible worlds, false in others. Nor do we have to embrace the fatalism of Diodorus in saying that *one* of the stated possibilities is necessarily false while the other is necessarily true. According to Leibniz, 'it is not the impossible, but only the incompossible that proceeds from the possible; and the past may be true without being necessarily true' (Deleuze 1989: 130).

Time and Possibility in Leibniz

But Leibniz's proposed solution seems to assume an understanding of time and the present such that each 'instant' is completely filled out and determined to its limits by its unique and precise arrangement of predicates (each of which we may imagine as a nexus of all events pertaining to this particular subject) that can give rise to exactly one new arrangement of predicates, *ad infinitum*. In his correspondence with Samuel Clarke, Leibniz claims that 'time is an order of successions' (2000: 14), these successions being understood as precisely determined configurations of *things*, considered at any one particular 'moment', even if those moments are only *theoretically* isolable.[6] There are at least two problems with this characterisation, however: (1) The possibility of an event or an eventuality is *only* possible on account of its existing in one or more of the possible worlds in the mind of God. However, given that God created *this particular* world and *not* one of the infinitely many other possible worlds in God's mind, it is *not* in fact possible that any other eventualities, besides the ones that *do* occur, *could* occur. In our world, Julius Caesar was *not* capable of not crossing the Rubicon, because *this particular Caesar* was the one in *this particular world*, which just so happens to be the really existent world, and this particular, really existent Caesar contained within him, from before creation, the predicate of crossing the Rubicon. Leibniz says, 'I say that whatever happens in conformity with these predeterminations is certain but not necessary, and if one were to do the contrary, he would not be doing something impossible in itself,[7] even though it would be impossible [*ex hypothesi*] for this to happen' (1989: 45). For Caesar to not cross the Rubicon might be possible in the mind of God, but it is entirely impossible in reality, given that God created *this* world and not another. In the final sections of his *Theodicy*, Leibniz stages a dialogue between Theodorus and Pallas, daughter of Jupiter, in which, in a dream state, Pallas reveals to Theodorus the pyramid-shaped 'palace of the fates', replete with 'representations not only of that which happens but also of all that which is possible' (2007: 375). Each hall of the pyramid contains one of these possible worlds. In each, Theodorus is given a glimpse of the life of a particular individual, named Sextus, which he acts out 'as in a stage presentation' (376). Each individual Sextus in each individual hall can no more alter his future than an actor in a play can alter her script. This is also true, obviously, for the really existent Sextus, whose choices, affects and actions are all completely determined prior even to his birth: 'You see that my father did not make Sextus wicked; he was so from all eternity, he was so always and freely. My father only granted him the existence which his wisdom could not refuse to the world where he is included: he made him pass from the region of the possible to that of the actual beings' (377). His nature is written into the larger script of a world designed in its tiniest detail entirely by God, and not subject to change once actualised. As Deleuze writes, while this might enable Leibniz to deal with the problem of future contingents, 'it in no way guarantees the character of so-called voluntary events, or the freedom of whoever wants to engage a naval battle, or of whoever does not want to' (1993: 69). This seems a most limited and unsatisfying notion of possibility, as 'possibility' would seem to suggest an openness of eventualities. On Leibniz's understanding, that openness is foreclosed by God from the moment he brings into existence *this* particular possible world and not some other. The infinite worlds of infinite possibilities obtain *only* in the abstract, only in the mind of God. Thus, while Deleuze finds Leibniz's resolution to be the most interesting, it is also 'the strangest and most convoluted' (1989: 130).

(2) It presents a problematic notion of time as well, insofar as there is no reason to think that there's a smallest isolable 'unit' of time that would be required in order to determine it to its limits and establish the unbreakable links from one arrangement of predicates to the next.[8] Indeed, one of the most significant analyses in Deleuze's 1969 text, *The Logic of Sense*, is the distinction, which Deleuze lifts from the Stoics, between the conceptions of time as 'Chronos', where 'only the present exists in time' (1990: 162), and 'Aion', where 'Instead of a present which absorbs the past and the future, a future and past divide the present at every instant and subdivide it ad infinitum into past and future, in both directions at once' (164). The time of Chronos is not unlike Husserl's concept of the 'living present' (Husserl 1991: 56), the experiential moment, pregnant with retention and protention, past and future. But with the notion of Chronos, we can expand this progressively further, such that surrounding each present one can imagine an even *greater* present (pregnant with past and future), with the greatest present being God's eternally contentful present, as the 'external envelope' of all human moments (Deleuze 1990: 162). As such, the imagistic model of Chronos is the circle, whose radius marks the infinity of God.[9] The model of the Aion, on the other hand, is the straight line, run through by the Instant, ever displaced, forking limitlessly into past and future.

Cronos, the Forking Paths and the Power of the False

We turn, once more, to Nietzsche for our point of entry. In the famous passage from *Zarathustra* titled 'On the Vision and the Riddle', Zarathustra weaves a parable of a conversation between him and the so-called spirit of gravity, the physical and intellectual embodiment of heaviness, sombreness and austerity. Ascending a winding mountain path, the two pause at what we are given to understand is a free-standing doorway, and Zarathustra poses to his antagonistic fellow traveller a problem:

> Two paths meet here; no one has yet followed either to its end. This long lane stretches back for an eternity. And the long lane out there, that is another eternity. They contradict each other, these paths; they offend each other face to face; and it is here at this gateway that they come together. The name of the gateway is inscribed above: 'Moment'. But whoever would follow one of them, on and on, farther and farther – do you believe, dwarf, that these paths contradict each other eternally? (Nietzsche 1966: 157–8)

This passage provides one of the more famous presentations of Nietzsche's concept of eternal return. While many scholars interpret eternal return as a cyclical repetition of every minute detail of cosmic history,[10] Deleuze rightly notes that Zarathustra chastises the dwarf for his response that 'time itself is a circle'. For Deleuze, Nietzsche's brilliance lies in his reflection on the Moment itself as the 'eternal' instant, in which only the past and future inhere, limitlessly colliding and dividing each would-be 'present'. This infinitely subdivided instant allows only the New to return – rather than a revolving ring of identity, a frenzied line of becoming. It is thus not surprising that in *The Logic of Sense*, the concept of eternal return is placed in a synonymic chain that also includes 'the pure form of the Aion' (Deleuze 1990: 180).

Although *Cinema 2* includes no appearances of the word 'Aion', Deleuze's Aionic model of time plays a significant role in the elaboration of the time-image. Here it appears, explicitly but only once, under the moniker of 'Cronos' (still opposed to 'Chronos') (Deleuze 1989: 81). But while it may be tempting to see this importation as a mere 'application' (as Williams would say) of the Aion, it seems, rather, that in bringing this model into *Cinema 2*, Deleuze also complicates it, highlighting an element that is not prevalent in *The Logic of Sense*, namely, the 'virtual'.[11] The notion of the virtual, contrasted with the actual and characterised as '[r]eal without being actual, ideal without being abstract' (Deleuze 1994: 208), plays a central role in 1968's *Difference and Repetition*, but hardly appears at all just one year later in *The Logic of Sense*. There, the primary ontological distinction occupying Deleuze is the contrast of 'bodies with their tensions, physical qualities, actions and passions, and the corresponding "states of affairs"', and 'incorporeal events which would play only on the surface, like a mist over the prairie' (1990: 4–5). But with the translation of the Aion into Cronos in *Cinema 2*, the virtual returns:

> What constitutes the crystal-image is the most fundamental operation of time: since the past is constituted not after the present that it was but at the same time, time has to split itself in two at each moment as present and past, which differ from each other in nature, or, what amounts to the same thing, it has to split the present in two heterogeneous directions, one of which is launched toward the future while the other falls into the past . . . We see in the crystal the perpetual foundation of time, non-chronological time, Cronos and not Chronos. This is the powerful, non-organic Life which grips the world. (Deleuze 1989: 81)[12]

This description of Cronos closely resembles the structure of Aion that we saw in *The Logic of Sense*. However, Deleuze draws from this discussion new implications. Specifically, insofar as what he calls in *The Logic of Sense* the 'Instant' is limitlessly divided into past and future, this means that past and future intensively mirror each other within the infinite divisibility of the instant itself (hence the category of the 'crystal-image' in *Cinema 2*). At the heart of the instant, there is a 'point of indiscernibility' between '"the immediate past which is already no longer and the immediate future which is not yet . . ."', virtualities at play in the frenzied constitution of the present (Deleuze 1989: 81). The past is already reaching into the future, and the future is already giving way to the past, and there *is* no 'present' other than this intensive reciprocal reflection. The present is undone and transformed before it ever *is*. This is the 'power of the false'.

To ascribe a 'power', positive and affirmative, to the false, is to think it on its *own*, apart from the traditional binary of the true and false. Truth, as we have seen, has been conceptualised as timeless, unchanging and positive, synonymous with goodness and with reality itself. The highest form in Plato's metaphysics is the form of the good, the 'reality' of which supersedes even the form of being, and the knowledge of which is essential for all other knowledge (*Republic* VI, 505a–509b), insofar as the 'truth' of each form is its being the perfect ('eminently good') template of each thing in question. The false has always (until Nietzsche) been characterised simply as a *lack* of this truth. For Deleuze, the power of the false 'replaces and supersedes the form of the true' (1989: 131). It is not, in other words, simply an *affirmation* of the *false*, because to assert the false is to operate still under the form of the *true* – 'it is true that it is false'. As Dan Smith says, the false takes on a power when 'it is freed from the model of truth: that is, when *the false is no longer presented as being true*' (2012: 139). Likewise, the power of the false is 'not error or doubt' (Deleuze 1989: 133), both of which are again conceived as deviations from the true. It is the power that *unsettles* the very form of the true, and this *power* is ascribed when the form of the true is challenged by the form of time, 'the pure form of the Aion' (Deleuze 1990: 180). The power of the false is the power of becoming, and it is, therefore, synonymous with the very 'powers of life' itself (Deleuze 1989: 135).

Conceiving time in this Aionic way elicits a shift in our understanding of the notion of possibility, where the *possibilities* of multiple eventualities are in fact the pregnancy of time with multiple *in*-compossibilities; but contrary to Leibniz's possible worlds, these incompossibles coexist, virtually and, in a way, simultaneously, within the real world. Argentinian author Jorge Luis Borges, in his famous 'The Garden of Forking Paths', writes:

> In all fictions, each time a man meets diverse alternatives, he chooses one and eliminates the others; in the work of the virtually impossible-to-disentangle Ts'ui Pen, the character chooses – simultaneously – all of them. *He creates*, thereby, 'several futures', several *times*, which themselves proliferate and fork. That is the explanation for the novel's contradictions. Fang, let us say, has a secret; a stranger knocks at his door; Fang decides to kill him. Naturally, there are various possible outcomes – Fang can kill the intruder, the intruder can kill Fang, they can both live, they can both be killed, and so on. In Ts'ui Pen's novel, *all* the outcomes in fact occur; each is the starting point for further bifurcations. (Borges 1998: 125)

In Deleuze's words, Borges' response to Leibniz is that 'the straight line as force of time, as labyrinth of time, is also the line which forks and keeps on forking, passing through *incompossible presents*, returning to *not-necessarily true pasts*' (1989: 131). Leibniz's band-aid for the crisis of truth is ripped off, revealing the bleeding wound of time itself.

For Deleuze, this realisation reaches the arts in the character of the 'forger', understood through the 'power of the false' which 'poses the simultaneity of incompossible presents, or the coexistence of not-necessarily true pasts' (1989: 131). Classical, 'truthful', narration assumes a logically ordered world where the instants of time connect in the same direct, sequential, linear way that governs Leibniz's notion of 'possible worlds'. Certain events in the narration necessitate certain other events, which ultimately necessitate a specific response from the protagonist, in accordance with what Deleuze calls 'legal connections in space and chronological relations in time' (133). But who is the 'hero' of the truthful narration? Deleuze, once more invoking Nietzsche, identifies the 'truthful man' as this hero (137). For Nietzsche, the truthful man seeks, as we have discussed, the form of the true, in order to measure against it the imperfections of this world: 'he makes life an "error" and this world an "appearance"' (Deleuze 1983: 96). The truthful man of truthful narration is no less nihilistic, no less sanctimonious, and no less resentful. He seeks out the criterion of order and his collection of facts, in order to expose the rot at the core of everyday life. 'The truthful man in the end wants nothing other than to judge life; he holds up a superior value, the good, in the name of which he will be able to judge, he is craving to judge, he sees in life an evil, a fault which is to be atoned for: the moral origin of the notion of truth' (Deleuze 1989: 137).

Falsifying narration, on the contrary, dispenses with the assumptions pertaining to truth. Though Deleuze employs a multitude of literary and cinematic authors as examples,[13] I will focus exclusively and only briefly on Orson Welles, whose work best maps onto the account I've traced in this chapter. From *Citizen Kane* in 1941, throughout the entirety of his work, Welles is interested in questions pertaining to the nature of truth and its relation to falsity, and the character of those persons in pursuit of each. *Citizen Kane* itself concerns a multitude of points of entry into the past of Charles Foster Kane, all in pursuit of the elusive 'Rosebud' (the last word he spoke before he died), which is never discovered and is revealed to the viewer only in the film's conclusion, when it is thrown into the furnace.

In *Touch of Evil* (1958), a car bomb explodes and kills two people near the Mexican-American border, where Miguel Vargas (Charlton Heston) is on his honeymoon with his new bride, Susie (Janet Leigh). Detective Hank Quinlan (Welles) arrives and the investigation begins. Vargas, whose only stake in the affair is that it happened near him and his wife, takes an interest and begins an investigation of his own, ultimately pursuing Quinlan in order to expose what he believes (correctly, we should note) to be Quinlan's corrupt tendency to plant evidence in order to collar his suspects. But while there is no doubt that Quinlan is the villain in this story, and Vargas the hero, Deleuze argues that they are two opposing perspectives on the same nihilistic view. Quinlan sees the world for what it is, but rather than overcoming it through his own adaptation, he gives into it and allows it to break him. But Vargas is no less grotesque for his relentless pursuit of truth. His concerns lie, not so much with the question of justice (for it is very likely that the suspected criminal is indeed culpable), but with exposing the corruption of his nemesis, and to this pursuit he is willing to sacrifice everything, leaving his wife in extreme danger in order to trap his villain. Vargas is the 'truthful man', who has 'strange motives, as if he were hiding another man in him, a revenge' (Deleuze 1989: 137).

Welles's power of the false culminates in his masterpiece, *F for Fake* (1973), which explicitly examines the nature of art, authorship, authenticity and forgery. Inspired by the Clifford Irving book, *Fake*, the film focuses on famous art forger, Elmyr de Hory, who fraudulently sold to museums and galleries over a thousand hand-painted forgeries in the artistic styles of such famous artists as Picasso, Matisse and Renoir. *F for Fake* is narrated by Welles himself, who acts as a host of what is presented in the form of a documentary, which is to say, a cinematic presentation of factual content. Indeed, the film opens with a promise from Welles that everything to come for the next hour will be true. He then addresses the case of Elmyr de Hory, and in particular, the fact that de Hory was so tremendously successful in his career as a forger, leading Welles to speculate on the question of whether perhaps the art critics and dealers who were fooled by his forgeries, and, by extension, the bourgeois world of modern art, are themselves frauds. If the forger is capable of mimicking a style so as to fool the experts, are the 'experts' themselves not the greater frauds? Is the forger not an expert in his own right? The film then concludes with a story about Oja Kodar, Welles's partner at the time. Kodar had purportedly been at the middle of a controversy involving Pablo Picasso and a series of twenty-two Picasso paintings with Kodar as their subject, paintings later revealed to be forgeries, mimicries of Picasso's style painted by Kodar's grandfather. Welles then admits that the entire Kodar segment was a lie, pointing out that the promised hour of truth had long since passed: 'What we professional liars hope to serve is truth; I'm afraid the pompous word for that is "art". Picasso himself said it: "art", he said, "is a lie, a lie that makes us realize the truth"'.

Conclusion: The Creation of Truth

This brings us, at last, to Deleuze's notion of the artist, in particular to her status as a creator of truth, bringing our attention back to the following passage: 'What the artist is, is *creator of truth*, because truth is not to be achieved, formed, or reproduced; it has to be created. There is no other truth than the creation of the New' (1989: 146–7). On its face, there are multiple ways that we might understand this passage. We might interpret it in a shallow relativistic sense, characteristic of all the worst interpretations of 'postmodernism', whatever that term means – that is, we might say that what the passage entails is that there *is* no such thing as truth, and so the only truth is the one that *we*, that is, human beings, assert. This opens us not only to philosophical problems, but more immediately and dangerously, it opens us as well to serious political concerns, because the folks adjudicating in matters of 'the truth' are almost always the ones in positions of power and privilege who use their truth-creating powers in order to hang on to and to expand that power and privilege. Indeed, in the aftermath of the 2016 US presidential election, with the preponderance of 'fake news' and the repeated doubling-down on demonstrably false claims (not the least of which culminated in the storming of the United States Capitol building on 6 January 2021), there were multiple attempts in the public sphere to blame the success of Donald Trump on 'postmodernism', broadly construed as a widespread absence of truth.[14]

But this is *not* what Deleuze's passage says. Deleuze does *not* say that there *is* no truth, but rather, that there is no truth other than the creation of the New. Truth, in other words, is *always* created, even when it is a *truth* of the natural world. If it is *true* that it is raining today, it is because the forces of nature constituted the atmospheric conditions in such a way that rain, in this particular location, resulted; the forces of the natural world created that truth. Truth, in this sense, is *always* created. As we saw with the Aionic structure of time, it is the return of the different, the miraculous production of the New. The artist, Deleuze says, is one who recognises this secret of nature, and who *participates* in that creation of the New. But this creation is no less 'true' or no less 'real' than the creations of nature; its effects, likewise, are no less true. As Anne Sauvagnargues writes, 'Art is real; it produces real effects on the plane of forces and not forms' (2013: 19). And for Deleuze, this artistic power is evident most saliently in what we might call, following Deleuze and Guattari's book on Kafka, *minor art*, the art of the minoritarian: 'What is opposed to fiction is not the real; it is not the truth which is always that of the masters or the colonizers; it is the story-telling function of the poor' (Deleuze 1989: 150). Minor art is, first and foremost, the artistic mode that sees, beyond the world as it *is*, the world as it *can be*. Minor art strives to constitute 'a people' *against* the forces of capital, servitude, oppression, exclusion and domination. It utilises the power of the false in order to give to itself a new truth, a new mythos, a new pantheon, a new history, a new people, a new earth. It rewrites its own story, recognising that its story *is* and can only ever be, one that is created, and one that can always be *re*-created. Where the forces of life are impeded, it charts new channels. 'There is creation, properly speaking, only insofar as we make use of excess in order to invent new forms of life rather than separating life from what it can do' (Deleuze 1983: 185).

Deleuze fully recognises the danger inherent to this power of the false, in that it can easily be co-opted by the forces of domination. As he says, 'The power of the false is delicate, allowing itself to be recaptured by frogs and scorpions' (1989: 147), and, we might add, Cheeto-coloured, would-be dictators. What, then, distinguishes between a *good* use and a *bad* use of this power? The response is embedded in the way that we have framed the entirety of this discussion: an acute sensitivity to the form of time, in the way that Deleuze outlines, engenders a deepening of awareness that the power of life lies in its creativity, in its enabling new expressions of itself and the liberation of new modes of existence. The exercise of the power of the false in order to break down impediments to such liberation will almost always, in Deleuze's sense, be manifestations of 'goodness' or 'generosity' (147). As Janae Sholtz writes, 'A Deleuzian *ethos* is a practice of living that is more adequate to the conditions of living, the genesis of beings, which celebrates the fabulatory artifice of living, but even more so instantiates the aesthetic in the heart of becoming' (2015: 259). But finally, I'm going to turn briefly to the Nigerian author, Chinua Achebe, who explicitly poses the question of the distinction between the 'fictions' that undergird racism, sexism, classism, etc., and the 'fictions' that give birth to a people. His response, I think, is apropos in our reading of Deleuze: 'What distinguishes beneficent fiction from such malignant cousins as racism is that the first never forgets that it is fiction and the other never knows that it is' (Achebe 1988: 148). It is, to bring us back to Nietzsche, an illusion whose illusory status its wielders have either forgotten or, more likely, repressed, an illusion that immediately places under erasure its use of the power of the false, because it *must* so eclipse that power in order to then carry out its atrocities in the name of its truth. So the power of the false *is*, admittedly, delicate, and it is dangerous. And yet, it is important to note, tyrants, fascists and warmongers have been hard at work creating their exploitative truths for millennia; history didn't wait for Nietzsche or Deleuze to talk about the 'creation' of truth before giving birth to humanity's evils. What Deleuze is attempting, I think, is to persuade the minoritarian elements within us all to *reclaim* that power of the false, that has *always* been exploited by the powerful, as he sees within it the only genuinely liberatory possibilities. As Deleuze claims, 'it is the only chance for art or for life' (1989: 147).

Notes

1. See St. Matthew's Gospel, chapter 18, verse 3.
2. It is also worth noting that almost the entirety of Williams's book is dedicated to the three syntheses of time in *Difference and Repetition*. The one chapter *not* dedicated to *Difference and Repetition* is dedicated to *The Logic of Sense*. But even there, Williams ultimately claims, 'I will argue later that the two times [of *The Logic of Sense* – Chronos and Aion] lead to the same six relations as the three syntheses [of *Difference and Repetition*]' (2011: 138).
3. For good measure, neither do I accept John Mullarkey's criticisms of 'Deleuze's essential dualism of the two [movement-images and time-images], born from his non-Bergsonian dissociation of time from movement' (2009: 101), or David Bordwell's characterisation of Deleuze's 'uncritical adherence to historiographic tradition' (1997: 117).
4. All DK references refer to the Diels-Kranz numbering system for Pre-Socratic philosophy.
5. For a thorough account of this problem, see Øhrstrøm and Hasle 2015.
6. Admittedly, this is more my own extrapolation of the implications of Leibniz's understanding of *possible worlds* than it is a direct assertion about the nature of time by Leibniz. In point of fact, Leibniz's own reflections on time are ever evolving and tremendously nuanced, and in many ways, as is well-known, Leibniz's relationalist view of time anticipates much of what would later become the accepted physical understanding of time with Einstein's theories of special and general relativity in the early twentieth century. For instance, in the Leibniz-Clarke correspondence, Leibniz claims that 'instants, considered without the things, are nothing at all and that they consist only in the successive order of things'. See Leibniz 2000: 15. For an excellent account of Leibniz's understanding of time, see Futch 2008. However, for my purposes, even if time is merely a 'well-founded' phenomenon, its 'instants' only isolable theoretically or in the mind of God, if time *is*, as Leibniz says, an 'order of successions', a linear order of precisely tuned cosmic arrangements, each of which is completely determined, the 'instant' is still there, even if only in abstraction.
7. It is not impossible in itself because it does not violate the law of contradiction.
8. There is much that can be said on this score. Broadly speaking, philosophical views on time are typically broken into the two primary camps of absolutism and relationalism. Absolutist views of time hold that time is, like space, something of a container for events to occur in, with the container existing independently of the events. There are ancient versions of temporal absolutism, such as that of Plato, who, in the *Timaeus*, famously characterises time as a 'moving image of eternity' (37d). This conception would be thoroughly theologised in accordance with the doctrines of Christianity in the sixth century CE by Boethius. Isaac Newton also famously argued for an absolute conception of time, and it was Newton's understanding that dominated scientific thinking until Einstein in the early twentieth century. The most famous defenders of relationalist accounts of time are Aristotle and, as we saw above (note 6), Leibniz. Relationalists hold that time cannot be conceived apart from the physical events that it marks or measures. Aristotle, for instance, famously claims that 'time

is number of movement in respect of the before and after, and is continuous since it is an attribute of what is continuous' (*Physics* IV, 220a25–220a26). Aristotle also holds that the 'now' is bounded by both the future and the past, analogous to the way in which a point divides a line. But by the same rationale, time is not 'made up' of 'nows', any more than a line is 'made up' of points, and likewise, 'one "now" cannot be next to another, any more than a point to a point' (*Physics* IV, 218a11–218a21). An interesting outlier in this account is René Descartes, Leibniz's French predecessor. Descartes poses something of a conundrum, in that, in a certain sense, he straddles the divide between absolutism and relationalism. Descartes' writings on time are notoriously complex and difficult, but at various points in his works, he argues some version of the claim that 'a lifespan can be divided into countless parts, each completely independent of the other, so that it does not follow from the fact that I existed a little while ago that I must exist now' (1984: 33). As Newton would later hold (and against Aristotle), Descartes explicitly asserts that time is made up of 'parts' (or 'instants'), each of which is logically and ontologically independent of the others, and it is only as a result of God's continued 'concurrence' with the order of things that time persists at all, such that divine creation and divine preservation are two ways of saying the same thing. In and of itself, there is nothing inherently contradictory about Descartes' understanding of time in this fashion. However, an apparent problem arises when we consider Descartes' views on space and, more specifically, his rejection of physical atomism. In the *Principles of Philosophy*, Descartes writes, 'We also know that it is impossible that there should exist atoms, that is, pieces of matter that are by their very nature indivisible <as some philosophers have imagined>. For if there were any atoms, then no matter how small we imagined them to be, they would necessarily have to be extended; and hence we could in our thought divide each of them into two or more smaller parts, and hence recognize their divisibility. For anything we can divide in our thought must, for that very reason, be known to be divisible' (1985: 231–2). If there are *parts* to space, Descartes argues, those *parts* must be divisible, even if only in our *minds*, which means that they must be *essentially* divisible. Hence even the smallest *parts* would be *further divisible*, and hence there can *be* no 'smallest parts'. Philosophically, it would seem that the very same arguments that lead Descartes to conclude that there is no smallest part of *space* should commensurately lead him to conclude that there is no smallest part of *time*, no isolable instant that is ontologically and logically independent of the rest. Aristotle, as we saw, uses the analogy of the line in order to argue that, just as a line is not *made up* of points, time is not *made up* of nows. And for Descartes, it would seem that, if there must be extension in even the smallest 'part' of space, there must also be duration in the smallest 'part' of time. Perhaps this conundrum arises in Descartes' thinking because he straddles the worlds of antiquity and of modernity. But at the very least, we can say that Descartes' thinking about time, as divisible into isolable instants, helps frame what we might consider to be the common understanding of time, the punctilinear model of time, of the moments of time as points on a line. For an attempt to reconcile these seemingly contradictory approaches to time in Descartes, see Lloyd Waller 2014. For a thorough account of Aristotle's conception of time, see Coope 2005.

9. Indeed, Boethius explicitly compares time to a circle, the centre of which is conceived as the eternal perspective of God: 'Therefore as reasoning is to understanding, as that which becomes is to that which is, as time is to eternity, as the circle is to its centre, so is the moving course of fate to the unmoving simplicity of providence' (Boethius 1973: 363).

10. See Hatab 2005; McNeil 2021; Löwith 1997.
11. See also Deamer, who appears to use the terms 'Aion' and 'Cronos' interchangeably, speaking of 'the migration of the terms Chronos and Aion into Chronos and Cronos' (2009: 172). At the same time, it isn't accurate to say that he completely collapses the two, because any would-be distinctions between Aion and Cronos simply are not the focus of his piece.
12. It is worth noting that Cronos is the Titan Greek equivalent to the Roman Saturn. This is interesting because, already in *The Logic of Sense*, Deleuze writes, 'Saturn grumbles from deep within Zeus' (1990: 164).
13. In literature, Herman Melville, Raymond Roussel, Borges and Alain Robbe-Grillet; and in film, Robbe-Grillet, Alain Resnais and Jean-Luc Godard, among many others.
14. The most prominent representative of this position is likely that of Michiko Kakutani's *The Death of Truth* (2018).

References

Achebe, C. (1998), *Hopes and Impediments: Selected Essays*, New York and Toronto: Anchor Books.

Boethius (1973), *Tractates; The Consolation of Philosophy*, trans. H. F. Stewart, E. K. Rand and S. J. Tester, Loeb Classical Library, vol. 74, Cambridge, MA: Harvard University Press.

Bordwell, D. (1997), *On the History of Film Style*, Cambridge, MA: Harvard University Press.

Borges, J. L. (1998) *Collected Fictions*, trans. Andrew Hurley, New York: Penguin.

Coope, U. (2005), *Time for Aristotle: Physics IV.10–14*, Oxford: Oxford University Press.

Cornford, F. M. (1935), *Plato's Theory of Knowledge*, London: Routledge.

Deamer, D. (2009), 'Cinema, Chronos/Cronos: Becoming an Accomplice to the Impasse of History', in *Deleuze and History*, ed. Jeffrey A. Bell and Claire Colebrook, Edinburgh: Edinburgh University Press, pp. 161–87.

Deleuze, G. (1983), *Nietzsche and Philosophy*, trans. Hugh Tomlinson, Minneapolis: University of Minnesota Press.

Deleuze, G. (1986), *Cinema 1: The Movement-Image*, trans. Hugh Tomlinson and Barbara Habberjam, Minnesota: University of Minnesota Press.

Deleuze, G. (1989), *Cinema 2: The Time-Image*, trans. Hugh Tomlinson and Robert Galeta, Minnesota: University of Minnesota Press.

Deleuze, G. (1990), *The Logic of Sense*, ed. Constantin Boundas, trans. Mark Lester with Charles Stivale, New York: Columbia University Press.

Deleuze, G. (1993), *The Fold: Leibniz and the Baroque*, trans. Tom Conley, Minneapolis: University of Minnesota Press.

Deleuze, G. (1994), *Difference and Repetition*, trans. Paul Patton, New York: Columbia University Press.

Descartes, R. (1984), *The Philosophical Writings of Descartes: Volume II*, trans. J. Cottingham, R. Stoothoff and D. Murdoch, Cambridge: Cambridge University Press.

Descartes, R. (1985), *The Philosophical Writings of Descartes: Volume I*, trans. J. Cottingham, R. Stoothoff and D. Murdoch, Cambridge: Cambridge University Press.

Epictetus (1994), *Discourses*, in *Discourses and Enchiridion*, trans. Thomas Wentworth Higgins, New York: Walter J. Black.

Futch, M. (2008), *Leibniz's Metaphysics of Time and Space*, Berlin: Springer.

Hatab, L. J. *Nietzsche's Life Sentence: Coming to Terms with Eternal Recurrence*, New York: Routledge.

Husserl, E. (1991), *On the Phenomenology of the Consciousness of Internal Time (1893–1917)*, trans. John Barnett Brough, Dordrecht: Kluwer Academic Publishers.

Kakutani, M. (2018), *The Death of Truth: Notes on Falsehood in the Age of Trump*, New York: Tim Duggan Books.

Leibniz, G. W. (1989), *Philosophical Essays*, ed. and trans. Roger Ariew and Daniel Garber, Indianapolis: Hackett.

Leibniz, G. W. (2007), *Theodicy*, ed. Austin Farrer, trans. E. M. Huggard, Charleston: BiblioBazaar.

Leibniz G. W. and S. Clarke (2000), *Correspondence*, ed. Roger Ariew, Indianapolis: Hackett.

Lloyd Waller, R. (2014), *Descartes' Temporal Dualism*, Lanham, MD: Lexington Books.

Löwith, K. (1997), *Nietzsche's Philosophy of the Eternal Recurrence of the Same*, trans. J. Harvey Lomax, Berkeley: University of California Press.

McNeil, B. E. (2021), *Nietzsche and Eternal Recurrence*, Cham: Springer Nature.

Mullarkey, J. (2009), *Philosophy and the Moving Image*, London: Palgrave Macmillan.

Nietzsche, F. (1966), *Thus Spoke Zarathustra*, trans. Walter Kaufmann, New York: Penguin.

Nietzsche, F. (1979), *Philosophy and Truth: Selections from Nietzsche's Notebooks of the Early 1870s*, ed. and trans. Daniel Breazeale, Amherst, NY: Humanity Books.

Nietzsche, F. (1998), *On the Genealogy of Morality*, trans. Maudemarie Clark and Alan J. Swenson, Indianapolis: Hackett.

Øhrstrøm, P. and P. Hasle (2015), 'Future Contingents', *The Stanford Encyclopedia of Philosophy*, ed. Edward N. Zalta, at <https://plato.stanford.edu/archives/win2015/entries/future-contingents/>.

Sauvagnargues, A. (2013), *Deleuze and Art*, trans. Samantha Bankston, London: Bloomsbury.

Sholtz, J. (2015), *The Invention of a People: Heidegger and Deleuze on Art and the Political*, Edinburgh: Edinburgh University Press.

Smith, D. W. (2012), *Essays on Deleuze*, Edinburgh: Edinburgh University Press.

Williams, J. (2011), *Gilles Deleuze's Philosophy of Time: A Critical Introduction and Guide*, Edinburgh: Edinburgh University Press.

Chapter 11

Gilles Deleuze, A Man Out of Time

Charles J. Stivale

> I'd like to tell you, [but] we won't have time; we never have enough time.
> I don't know, I'll never get finished if this continues. (Deleuze)[1]

Of all of Gilles Deleuze's weekly activities, teaching his seminar ranks among the most important given the considerable preparation and energy, both physical and mental, that he devoted to each session.[2] However, a recurring theme revealed by the session recordings is the challenges to class time and duration faced by Deleuze, who was acutely aware of the temporal limitations for a full development of seminar topics. Although Deleuze attempted to maintain focus, and, dare I say, control, in order to complete adequately the segment under consideration according to his demanding standards, time within his seminar teaching was decidedly 'out of joint'.[3] Furthermore, besides such time constraints, Deleuze faced an even greater challenge, one that was self-imposed, in terms both of the conditions in which he taught his seminar and of the methods for encompassing the concepts that he wished to impart to his students. From this perspective, he was 'out of time' not simply due to temporal limitations but, more importantly, due to the difficulty of synchronising his immense grasp of the material with the participants' possibilities for understanding.

I propose to examine the time of Deleuze's seminar in light of these temporal and epistemological disjunctions by considering the obstacles that Deleuze faced and the many tactics that he developed to unfold successive facets of his complex thought, thereby clarifying Deleuze's distinct relationship with the time of the seminar. I argue that, despite the many challenges, his goal was to practise a pedagogy of 'Deleuze-time', a deliberately focused creative unfolding of concepts relying on the participants' active attention and participation. I also consider how space in the seminar rooms was linked to the temporal challenges of these weekly encounters. For while the exchanges between Deleuze and the participants offered openings for potential creation, such encounters were menaced in terms of limitations to actual duration as well as compression of space upon time.

Through access to the seminar recordings and transcripts from 1979 to 1987,[4] I consider the numerous ways in which time and duration played fundamental roles in Deleuze's articulation of his ongoing research within the pedagogical framework. Given this valuable research tool, I choose to be guided in this study by the sessions themselves and the institutional contexts in which they are circumscribed to allow the practices therein to suggest different facets of Deleuze's strategies in relation to time, and especially to remain open to unusual or surprising intersections that emerge from the seminar exchanges. While I acknowledge the many perspectives developed on Deleuze's philosophical conception of time, by Deleuze himself in different contexts as well as in James Williams's masterful introduction to this topic (Williams 2011), I believe that allowing this archive to speak its own lessons, as it were, provides a unique opportunity for understanding Deleuze's teaching more fully.

A Class Out of Space

> Courses are something quite special, they're a cube; it's a space-time, . . . something that stretches out from one week to the next. It's a space and a very, very special temporality. ('P as in Professor')

I first consider the space of the seminar, since the session recordings convince me that the peculiarities of classroom space in the French university system, as well as Deleuze's own requirements, made the 'spatial question' a backdrop to any understanding of temporal issues. Not just a man frequently out of time, Deleuze as an educator was nearly always out of space. Video clips reveal Deleuze's regular teaching location consisting of him seated with students at his elbows, cassette recorders arrayed around him, with room for his notes and texts.[5] Why did this esteemed professor put up with such conditions? The answer is simple: Deleuze chose such cramped quarters rather than accept the available solution, to schedule the seminar within a more spacious university amphitheatre. Deleuze repeatedly opposed this option since, as he put it, 'What I would do would not work there', and because 'we would need a microphone, so if someone wanted to say something, they would have to come to the microphone, which puts everyone off.' Whatever the inconveniences, then, the cramped seminar space allowed direct exchanges with students, creating the 'circus [quality] that amuses me and tends to be more involved (*profond*)' ('P as in Professor').

Besides the difficulties just noted of Deleuze's own making, the seminars' popularity resulted in regular overcrowding, and these space difficulties were but one kind of limitation, or striation, that Deleuze endured while teaching at Vincennes and then at Vincennes/St Denis.[6] Deleuze clearly dreamed of the teaching venue as a site of an ideal smooth space, one unfettered by any limitations whatsoever for possibilities of creative exchange. However, given his work with Félix Guattari on these concepts, Deleuze understood fully that his work unfolded within a State institution inevitably subject to striations, that is, numerous institutional and particularly spatial constraints.[7] Deleuze also recognised that within these smooth–striated spatial distinctions, 'they are mixed together the whole time' (TDS ATP V 1–061179), meaning that the 'smooth' ideal he dreamt of necessarily existed only in striated form. In short, the spatial backdrop emphasised here had unforeseen consequences for the time of the seminar from one year to the next.

Before shifting to temporal aspects, I note another important detail that emerges from comments that Deleuze made following the move to the St Denis location, notably his attempt to find a classroom adequate for his and his students' needs. Among numerous classroom space issues – for example, noises and interruptions from outside the room – one detail, the security bars placed on the classroom windows, was something that alarmed Deleuze constantly.[8] Hence, this distinguished scholar was forced to do his own footwork to find a better location, an effort that seemingly came to fruition during the 17 January 1984 session (in the Cinema III seminar) when Deleuze returns after a mid-session site visit to announce that henceforth the course would meet in a larger room, 'a palace where we will discover happiness' (TDS Cinema III 8–170184).

Of course, any teacher actively seeks to obtain or create the most effective space for teaching and learning, but in Deleuze's case, his requirements meant limitations that he had to accept for several years following his arrival at Vincennes/St Denis. While possibly reflecting some peculiar professorial idiosyncrasies, Deleuze's demands for a more intimate space corresponded to his conception of using the classroom to support the potentially creative ends of his pedagogical ideals.

Inspiration and Echoes

> A course is a kind of *Sprechgesang*, closer to music than to theater. Indeed, there's nothing in principle to stop courses being a bit like a rock concert. (Deleuze 1995: 139)[9]

As in each course, a semester's work begins with the best of intentions, and in Deleuze's case, this 'ideal game' cannot 'be played by either man or God. It can only be thought as nonsense. But precisely for this reason, it is the reality of thought itself and the unconscious of pure thought . . . This game is reserved then for thought and art' (Deleuze 1990/2015: 60/62–3).[10] Ideally, then, an academic year for Deleuze would include twenty-six sessions, but the vagaries of university scheduling (holidays breaks – notably, Christmas and Easter – as well as a semester break in February) and unforeseen interruptions resulted in only two seminars between 1979 and 1987 containing this complete number (Cinema IV and Foucault). Moreover, while each session's length was scheduled for two hours, Deleuze almost invariably extended sessions well into the third hour, thereby retrieving otherwise lost chronological time on the schedule.

It is tempting to search for sessions that correspond as closely as possible to what Deleuze might consider 'ideal'. By this, I follow Deleuze's comments that his prior course preparation would yield the maximum of what he termed 'inspiration' through his partially improvisational, but usually carefully outlined, session framework. For Deleuze maintained that 'a course is something requiring an enormous amount of preparation . . . to reach these moments of inspiration . . . If one hasn't rehearsed enough, there's no inspiration . . . without which the course means nothing . . . And to do so, one sometimes has to . . . get oneself stimulated (*se monter soi-même*) to the point that one is able to speak about something with enthusiasm: that's what rehearsing is' ('P as in Professor'). As Daniel W. Smith has discerned, 'Deleuze's seminar lectures were delivered orally, without a manuscript or lecture notes. At best, Deleuze brought small pieces of paper to the seminars (few of which have survived) with outlines of the conceptual deduction he wanted to undertake in the seminar, and he then delivered the lecture spontaneously';[11] hence the students' initiative to record the lectures on cassette tapes, actively encouraged by Deleuze.

However, the complete audio corpus of the seminars suggests that, much like the continuum between overlapping smooth and striated spaces, the temporal and pedagogical continuum into which Deleuze slid in each session was fragile, with frequent disturbances of the focus required for him to create impulsions of inspiration. The impact of Deleuze's teaching 'always [consisted of] something that was not destined to be understood in its totality. A course is a kind of matter in movement (*matière en mouvement*), ... in which each person, each group, or each student at the limit takes from it what suits him/her' ('P as in Professor'). As he exhorted the participants at the start of the Cinema IV seminar, 'It hardly matters if you don't understand yet; it will come, there's no need to hurry; first you listen, and then you understand much later' (TDS Cinema IV 1–301084). And in fact, following his retirement, Deleuze expressed how much he owed to the audience in the seminars, insisting that this process did not at all resemble 'argument (*discussion*)' – 'philosophy has absolutely nothing to do with arguing about things' – but rather consisted of attempting to understand 'the problem someone's framing and how they're framing it; [thus] all you should ever do is explore it, play around with the terms, add something, relate it to something else, never argue about it. [The seminar] was like an echo chamber, a feedback loop, in which an idea reappeared after going, as it were, through various filters' (Deleuze 1990: 190–1; 1995: 139).[12]

Furthermore, while discussing distinctions between the modes of time's synthesis during the Cinema III seminar (TDS 16–170484), Deleuze emphasises the importance of an 'apprehension of the present', something that one can focalise (*fixer*), but that is also contingent on a wide variability of presents between individuals. He offers the revealing example of what occurs in his seminar:

> I'm here teaching the course, you're there listening; a third case, one of you intervenes. When I arrive here, let's say I have a two-hour long present, but I mean, I have no impression of time passing. I've arrived focalized, and my entire act of consciousness consists in focalizing this kind of time period, a two-hour present, that is, these two hours are present ... This is why the two hours for me ultimately go so fast, whereas for you, they don't move fast enough at all except when this works sufficiently for you to come into my present. At that point, you are living the same time as I do. (TDS Cinema III 16–170484)

The challenge of selecting particular sessions as exemplary certainly faced Claire Parnet and Richard Pinhas, who produced three different seminars as CDs released by Éditions Gallimard – Spinoza 13–170381, Leibniz & the Baroque 10–240287 and selected excerpts from Cinema seminars I and III (1981–82 to 1983–84) – that provide sources for initial commentary on the time of the Deleuzian seminar.[13] Each of the sessions in the Spinoza and Leibniz CDs was prepared by weeks of fairly consistent development of the seminar's 'matter in movement', thus constituting these selected sessions as turning points of sorts for each seminar's development.

However, in each case, we glimpse how the 'ideal game' of a session can go awry through temporal impediments, that is, how Deleuze's nearly one-pointed focus on achieving 'inspiration' (however fleeting) collides with the other key facet of this process, namely, the advantages he hoped to derive from extremely close proximity with seminar participants. For, as he notes in his discussion on apprehending and focalising the present, the participants' apprehension tends to be briefer, less focalised, and a participant who intervenes 'has determined, at least in a confused way, what he/she is going to say, why he/she wants to intervene, the motives for intervening also determining a present, one that is very different for others' (TDS Cinema III 16–170484).

As regards these two presumably exemplary CD seminars, although Deleuze intended the Spinoza session to be the last one so that he could commence the seminar on Painting, different interventions following his 70-minute presentation transform the subsequent 80 minutes into a question-answer session, ultimately preventing Deleuze from returning to the session's main point.[14] In contrast, while the 1987 Leibniz session opens in progress on the BNF recording with a 9-minute presentation by Richard Pinhas (omitted from the CD), Deleuze then reflects nearly without interruption on the topics of individual choice and inclination, and then the successive states as these relate to monads, to the soul's amplitude and clarity, and hence to freedom. In contrast to the previous 'exemplary' CD session, the participants intervene minimally, and yet one indeed grasps Deleuze's deep engagement with those around him, occasionally directing remarks to different students, and clearly gaining energy step by step as he develops these concepts at the centre of the seminar's focus.

Hence, the two sessions selected as sufficiently exemplary for production as CDs by one of France's most prestigious publishers offer distinctly different profiles in terms of Deleuze's interaction with students: one session is seemingly derailed by questions, the other kept steadily on track by minimal overt student interventions. These polar differences raise the implicit question of whether Deleuze was more inspired by remaining open to questioning with the risk of dispersion of different presents, or by the more subtle, implicit engagement of students quietly following his every word and possibly focalising extensively within his present.[15] Still, both sessions constitute significant lessons that are 'interesting' in the threefold Deleuzian sense, at once inspirational in terms of the 'matter in movement', distinctive in terms of the 'feedback loop' linked to the participants, and finally crucial in terms of the session's place within the overall flow of ideas within the seminar. It is the intersection of 'matter in movement', based on Deleuze's prior preparation, and the 'feedback loop' with participants, focalising on Deleuze's present, that we must explore as constitutive of 'Deleuze-time'.

Impediments

> One must settle in at the extreme point of one's knowledge or one's ignorance ... [at] this very border between knowing and non-knowing: it's there that one must settle in to have something to say. ('N as in Neurology', in Deleuze and Parnet 1997)

The conflict between two poles – of the 'ideal game' in Deleuze's seminars, that is, sessions in which 'inspiration' arising from the 'matter in movement' yielded a possible temporal synchronisation of 'presents', on the one hand, and on the other, sessions in which, for many different reasons, this was not the outcome – created a developing tension across the years, from one seminar to the next, especially in terms of the time of the seminar. Deleuze's belief in his approach of seeking 'inspiration' through the seminar's 'echo chamber' collided on occasion with his frustrations regarding classroom practices, and he sought different approaches to assuring student interventions, provided that these might allow him to maintain his focus on the 'matter' at hand.

One notable expression of frustration linked to pedagogical considerations occurred at the start of the second Cinema seminar in autumn 1982. While justifying his decision to continue the same topic as the previous year – since he felt that by going too fast, he had 'let certain things escape' in 1981–82 – Deleuze presents an acerbic judgement of his own teaching activity, observing that 'for ten years, I've been acting like a clown! ... It's a show (*spectacle*), since the proof is right here: ... I speak facing half [an audience] of humans and half tape recorders' (TDS Cinema II 1–021182). Hence, he ponders how to maximise the course's implied goal of a collaboration between listeners and the speaker, that is, how to 'obtain reactions – not objections, which are always painful and intolerable' – that is, assistance from the participants which might result in 'correct[ing] me, to extend things longer'. As he admitted, 'Believe me, this [process of going back over topics] is not meant to speed things up.'

To some extent, this insight reveals his awareness of the tension between temporal limitations and his own need to provide greater clarity, but these and other more tendentious organisational remarks led to a lengthy exchange with the participants, some of whom asserted that, despite Deleuze's explicit request, they in fact had no place truly to speak within this seminar. But Deleuze maintained his insistence: 'Your task consists in speaking either on the basis of your thoughts or of your feelings (*sentiments*), but not your opinion (*avis*). That means saying: yes, in your [topic] there, I get the impression that there's something that doesn't work, that's unbalanced; or else, you tell me: what you're saying has awakened this in me, something I hadn't thought of.'[16]

Let me underscore initially the strategic circumstances of these ongoing seminars: whatever the topic, Deleuze consistently emphasised his own concerted focus within a set of moving problematics as well as the steps of his arguments to which he expected the seminar participants to respond, hence the interchange potentially returning to him in various ways. The feedback loop he sought would constitute an in-between of pedagogy and creation, what he termed an 'encounter' in a strong sense, not with people 'but with things . . . I am "on the lookout" (*aux aguets*) for encounters, wondering if there might be material for an encounter, in a film, in a painting' ('C as in Culture', in Deleuze and Parnet 1997). By projecting Deleuze's active engagement with cultural production onto his classroom interactions, I maintain that he is entirely 'on the lookout' within the flow of the feedback loop for sources of creation through thought. Hence his concerted attempts to find a pedagogical model to enable the 'encounter' within each session to produce the kind of creative research he sought.

To ensure the continued forward movement of such encounters, Deleuze on occasion deliberately halted forward progress, particularly at the start of a session in order to summarise previously acquired points, most importantly after breaks and unscheduled interruptions (for example, demonstrations and strikes). At other times, such reviews arose from Deleuze's severe assessment of the limitations of his own previous performance (for example, in TDS Cinema IV 3–131184), and one might consider much of the 1982–83 Cinema II seminar in this light, as a kind of 'mise en ordre' or clean-up, although clearly Deleuze's purpose there was to 'reculer pour mieux rebondir', to retreat strategically in order better to leap forward.

However, from the perspective of the time of the seminar, numerous impediments arose that enabled or inhibited the creative engagement that Deleuze continually sought. While some of these temporal impediments were external, due to the aforementioned striations of the academic institution as well as national events,[17] others were more mundane, yet no less disruptive.[18] In some cases, Deleuze's own students caused the disturbance, in one session by exiting one by one midway through class with Deleuze responding: 'Aie, aie, aie, aie, aie, aie, aie . . . So, those who want to leave, you just leave, but do so quickly. [*Pause*] . . . No, really, this is too much . . . I can't work in these conditions . . .' (TDS Leibniz & Baroque 12–100387).

The 'ideal game' of the seminar, of course, would consist of Deleuze's uninterrupted and undistracted immersion within the flow of the creative 'matter in movement', an event akin to a purely 'smooth space', hence quite impossible. In contrast, we can now envisage how this hypothetical, concentrated folding of 'matter in movement' and over-lapping of 'presents' (Deleuze's own with the participants') yield constantly to his need to negotiate various aspects of each session. In other words, each session exists along a continuum between the intensity and purpose of 'Deleuze-time', on the one hand, and sources that diminished Deleuze's intensity of focus, on the other. By outlining different types of impediments, we can judge more clearly the extent to which Deleuze manoeuvred around them to develop the creative exchanges he sought.

Mid-session breaks. As noted earlier, the seminar's scheduled two-hour length usually extended well into a third hour. Hence, Deleuze often declared at a session's start that they would break at mid-point so he could visit the main office (closed for lunch before the end of each session). This repeated practice actually served a pedagogical purpose: the time pressure created by the errand, no doubt quite necessary, provided Deleuze with both a pretext and an impetus to focus even more intensely on developing the 'matter in movement' within the concentration of 'Deleuze-time'.

Anticipated questions and interventions. Another step along the continuum of 'Deleuze-time' is Deleuze's use of invited student interventions, assisting Deleuze with particular topics in depth. Privileged interlocutors of long date include Félix Guattari (particularly during sessions in the 1970s and in the Foucault seminar) and Claire Parnet.[19] Moreover, at different times, Deleuze called on certain regular participants, notably Éric Alliez (whose dissertation Deleuze directed), Richard Pinhas and Georges Comtesse.[20]

Anticipated panels. As the Cinema IV seminar commenced, Deleuze announced an epiphany of sorts: instead of the prepared 'exposés' or interventions, Deleuze would designate participants to be interviewed by him on specific topics with which he was less familiar and with which they were already fully informed (TDS Cinema IV 7–181284). This 'solution' resulted subsequently in several sessions with designated 'non-presenters', that is, interviewees who nonetheless did make brief presentations before being questioned by Deleuze and other participants.[21] Unfortunately, whatever its advantages, this 'solution' held inherent problems: as Deleuze discovered, the participating 'interviewees' could not prevent discussion with other participants from throwing the focused direction off track.[22]

Unanticipated student questions. Despite the importance of exchanges with students for Deleuze's teaching practice, such questions were another step on the continuum away from the hypothetical 'ideal'. Often when unmanaged or unforeseen interventions occurred, Deleuze would acknowledge the contribution positively and quickly attempt to turn it into something he could employ within the flow of the ongoing development. Indeed, even with some questions that seemed confrontational, Deleuze succeeded in this folding process.[23] However, Deleuze often was unable to stay within the focused flow, as illustrated by one astounding 'contribution' by a woman student who intervened in a session ostensibly to make a brief presentation, but mainly to express her amorous infatuation with the philosopher. Deleuze treated this somewhat confused student very gently and generously, asking her to leave but inviting her back the next week to present her work on semiotics. He then admitted to the class, 'After all this, I don't recall what I was going to say!' (TDS Cinema IV 18–160485).[24]

The Comtesse phenomenon. As I shift toward the less productive, less focused exchanges, those moving toward Deleuze's decreasing intensity of focus and dissipation of seminar time, it is strange to turn in this context to possibly the most active seminar contributor, Georges Comtesse.[25] As a long-term participant – the earliest comment by him for which we have a record is from 1971 (TDS Anti-Oedipus I 1–171171) – he became a privileged interlocutor, and not only in the sense that the number of his interventions (of greater and lesser length, in over sixty sessions) far exceed those of any other seminar participant. This privilege is evident simply from the Foucault seminar: the only other participants who intervened at any length in the twenty-six sessions besides Comtesse (with three substantial presentations) were the truly privileged interlocutors Félix Guattari, Éric Alliez and one unnamed musicologist.[26] In the best circumstances, the substance of many of Comtesse's questions and interventions allowed Deleuze to fold them into the 'matter in movement' as he then developed quite precise and even longer responses. And however ambivalent Deleuze's reactions to

Comtesse might seem on certain occasions, it was clear that Comtesse truly hoped to contribute to the seminars.

However, whatever his intentions, Comtesse stands alone among all participants in his ability to provoke Deleuze to extreme reactions, and usually less by the substance of the statements than by Comtesse's manner in stating them. The final scene of the 1976 RAI 3 video shows Comtesse standing alone in a crowd of students, challenging Deleuze on particular points, much to Deleuze's and the other students' delight.[27] From this scene, I conclude that Comtesse enjoyed contesting the 'master's' word and, most particularly, maintaining his own forthright resistance among Deleuze's acolytes. The number of sessions in which Deleuze takes issue strongly with Comtesse is remarkably small, no more than five, but they truly stand out both due to Deleuze's vehemence and, more importantly for this discussion, due to the disruptive result for the creative and temporal flow.[28]

Two sessions, both from the Cinema IV seminar and still untranslated, highlight how these interventions disrupted the pedagogical process. In the first case, following a long intervention by Comtesse, Deleuze agreed with the substance of Comtesse's remarks, but objected to Comtesse's formal edicts: 'You have a tendency to present what you're reading ... as, in its very nature, reducing everything else to zero ... Try to understand that when you are speaking, you say some very interesting things, but these things aren't supposed to annul every other discourse.' Deleuze then became only more aggravated by Comtesse's attempted justification, first, due to his failing (in Deleuze's judgement) to provide the actual texts on which his assertions were based, then by his seeming to want to draw Deleuze into endorsing an unacceptable rationale and pretending to base his perspectives on another scholar's works: '[Your statements] may well come from Derrida, but I am certain that Derrida is much more nuanced than you are. But I insist on this: don't come here to tell us "Here's the truth!" You may be able to say this in Derrida's course, I don't know, but not here, not here' (TDS Cinema IV 7–181284).[29]

Three months later, another point of contention arose between them, notably Comtesse's repeated tendency to object at great length that 'there are other aspects' to be considered and that these aspects 'are more profound' than the ones already presented. Again, Comtesse's attempted justifications raised Deleuze's ire: 'I tell you, no, that's your favourite argument ... it's this Stalinist argument that disgusts me. Bah, no, stop! Listen, because suddenly we're getting behind.' In other words, not only did Comtesse's arguments disgust him, but he was wasting the seminar's time. Comtesse then added insult to injury by concluding his argument about a particular film with the arrogant demand, 'Try to grasp that!' (*Essayez d'entendre ça!*). Here, Deleuze summed up matters in no uncertain terms: 'Who do you take yourself for? You dare to finish something by saying "try to grasp that!", try to understand the imponderable depth of what I just said! No, that's just wrong! I can't take it any more! Break time! Five minutes break!' (TDS Cinema IV 16–190385).[30]

These scenes illustrate how the temporal flow and especially its intrusion into 'Deleuze-time' through discussion could throw off any attempt to focus on the 'matter in movement'. The 15 March 1983 session from Cinema II reveals the variability of Deleuze's efforts to remain in the flow of 'Deleuze-time': while the participants' objections that Deleuze judged 'mean' forced him at one point to ask defensively for mercy, his opening discussions with Pascal Auger provided Deleuze with new insights to which he returned productively in subsequent sessions.

Infirmities. Whereas the previous examples reveal significant impediments to the flow of 'matter in movement', some unforeseen difficulties brought any progress to a halt, specifically Deleuze's fatigue, occasional illness, forgetfulness and befuddlement, and in a very few cases, complete breakdown. On the one hand, Deleuze's weariness after four years working on cinema and philosophy resulted in what he describes as 'everything going blank' (TDS Cinema IV 24–280585); on another occasion, a misplaced text stopped the session (TDS Leibniz & Baroque 6–130187). On the other hand, after a five-week break, Deleuze began session five in Cinema I with an abject apology for a scheduling error: 'I no longer have the heart to apologize to all those who turned up for the lesson . . . In short, all that was just a mess, and because of this mess, now I'm going to have to try to make up for lost time' (TDS Cinema I 5–050182).

At other times, rather than take a break, Deleuze simply requested delaying an answer, and in fact, he usefully reverted to this time-saving strategy on occasion, suggesting in one case that 'the question is so far from what I'm involved in right now, I seriously regret having brought it up' (TDS Cinema II 14–150383), and in another case, saying simply that while the question was valid, nonetheless 'you're getting ahead of me' (TDS Spinoza 6–130181). However, the defensive posture adopted in the 15 March 1983 session indicates the rare and unfortunate moment along the continuum I have been tracing, the point at which the experimentation of 'matter in movement' and 'apprehending the present' within 'Deleuze-time' collapses. As we shall see, this defensive posture occurred in circumstances other than solely with Comtesse, and yet curiously, it can also help us to conceptualise Deleuze's ultimate goal within the time of the seminar.

Temporalities and Events

> With these delayed effects in a course . . . there's a kind of retroactive effect [in comprehension]. So . . . that's why I find interruptions so stupid, or even certain questions people can ask. [If] you are asking a question because you're in the midst of not understanding, well, you would be better off waiting. ('P as in Professor')

Perhaps the most poignant example of collapse occurred during session three of the first Leibniz seminar, when Deleuze took a 'tiny question' that then led to a discussion on differential calculus (TDS Leibniz 3–290480). Ironically, a question from Comtesse buffered the initial question sufficiently to allow Deleuze to segue into his main development. Midway through the session, however, the first student's abruptly repeated question inexplicably resulted in what I can only describe as a kind of meltdown: in a rasping voice, Deleuze says, 'Spare me (*Pitié*) . . . My God . . . He broke me since . . . You know, speaking is a fragile thing; speaking is a fragile thing.' Pausing, then whispering to the extremely silent class, Deleuze attempted to continue but finally concedes, 'No, it's . . . I don't know any more.' During the ensuing silence, a student near Deleuze seemed to whisper and ask if there's something he or she could do, to which Deleuze could only answer, 'Ah, no, ah, no, it's what's in my head.'

In some ways, this extreme example along the continuum allows us to join both ends and examine the ongoing tension existing in every seminar and in each session through Deleuze's method for pursuing an ongoing *recherche*, his research, not for 'lost time' in a Proustian way, but rather for dual aspects of the event. In *The Logic of Sense*, Deleuze points to 'the two moments of sense, impassability and genesis, neutrality and productivity', indicating that aspects of the impassability as event 'form a constant without which the event would not have eternal truth and could not be distinguished from its temporal actualizations' (1990/2015: 100/103). In the previous example, Deleuze was 'broken' from his flow, from his tenuous insertion within and expression of 'Deleuze-time', whispering the words I translate as 'speaking is a fragile thing': 'c'est fragile, parler, c'est fragile' (TDS Leibniz 3–290480). Notice the emphasis on the fragility that surrounds the infinitive 'parler'; as Deleuze asserts, 'effects on bodies . . . are not things or facts, but events . . . that subsist or inhere, . . . [that are] verbs, . . . not living presents, but infinitives: the unlimited Aion, the becoming that divides itself infinitely in past and future and always eludes the present' (1990/2015: 4–5/5). This infinitive, 'parler'/to speak, is especially fragile in the seminar, where Deleuze's aim is to insert himself into this fleeting interstice between past-future and present, constantly attempting to create an ongoing balancing act 'to grasp [time] in two complementary though mutually exclusive fashions . . . as the living present in bodies which act and are acted upon [Chronos] . . . [and] as an entity infinitely divisible into past and future [Aion], and into the incorporeal effects which result from bodies, their actions and their passions' (1990/2015: 5/5–6).

This insight corresponds to the ongoing struggle of sense-making along a continuum that constituted Deleuze's experimentation with 'Deleuze-time' in the seminars, aptly described as follows: 'If the battle is not an example of an event among others, but rather the Event in its essence, it is no doubt because it is actualized in diverse manners at once, and because each participant may grasp it at a different level of actualization within its variable present' (1990/2015: 100/103). It is remarkable to glimpse this 'Event in its essence' through so many sessions and across so many seminars and decades, from *The Logic of Sense* into the Cinema seminars, with Deleuze developing this thought from past to future, as Aion, and yet also in actualisations of Chronos.[31] Just as smooth space in relation to striated space is a variable mixture of both, the Aion–Chronos doublet is likewise conjoined yet distinct.

However, rather than considering this a limitation, say, of a pure Aion, we can discern the event of Aion in its ongoing intersection with Chronos. The tension between Aion and Chronos for Deleuze is his *recherche* for the event as it plays out in contrast to variable actualisations within a time that inevitably in the classroom is frequently 'out of joint'. If Deleuze could do little about the striated space of his seminar room (in some ways, by his own choice) as well as the educational regime under which he worked, he attempted to parry these constraints with the philosophical becomings toward Aion (or eternity) consisting of 'this copresence of all the degrees of power of action (*puissance*)' (TDS Cinema III 15–270384).[32] Yet, he was also fully aware that, just as one can never reach an entirely smooth space, such movement toward Aion could only be achieved momentarily, always in moments of extreme fragility, 'matter in movement'. As Deleuze suggested about listeners' reactions within the 'musical conception of a course', a delayed effect is always possible, even preferable, in grasping the 'matter in movement' within its 'variable present' ('P as in Professor').

Moreover, given that 'the battle *hovers over* its own field, being neutral in relation to all of its temporal actualizations . . . it is all the more terrible. Never present but always yet to come and already passed, the battle is graspable only by the will of anonymity which it itself inspires' (Deleuze 1990/2015: 100/103). In light of the many steps along the continuum traced above, I maintain that the extreme, inherent focus and flow toward the 'ideal' end of the continuum – that is, the in-between of pedagogy and creation or 'Deleuze-time' at its extreme – tend toward this neutrality, this hovering over its 'field', in relation to the temporal actualisations within individual sessions. For the sessions where Deleuze is most immersed, tending toward the extreme of 'Deleuze-time', are simply those in which Deleuze is effaced and an anonymity of thought is manifested, however difficult it is for listeners to glimpse this effacement. The immersion into the event constitutes Deleuze's ongoing *recherche* for 'counter-actualization', a tending toward the Event that he described in *The Logic of Sense* as 'the actor's or dancer's simple, flat representation' (1990/2015: 157/161).

This *recherche* becomes clearer precisely when such immersion is impeded through the diverse actualisations traced previously. That is, the impediments themselves, at varying degrees along the continuum, confirm the possibility of the 'ideal' end of the continuum, clarifying why, at certain moments, especially in his different comments, defensive postures and extreme reactions, Deleuze had to take time out, to reset, to regroup in his battle for immersion into the counter-actualisations of 'Deleuze-time' which had been thrown so terribly 'out of joint'. For the impediments that he most firmly rejected were those that he identified unmistakably as 'objections, which are always painful and intolerable' (TDS Cinema II 1–021182), since they reveal the extent to which a listener was not understanding and that waiting would be best: 'what someone doesn't understand, there is the possibility that he'll understand it afterwards' ('P as in Professor').[33]

Hence, given that for Deleuze the essential element in a course was 'to become alert at the right moment to grasp hold of what suits you, what suits you personally' ('P as in Professor'), rather than posing objections, Deleuze argued that the '[students'] task consists in speaking either on the basis of [their] thoughts or of [their] feelings (*sentiments*), but not [their] opinions (*avis*)' (TDS Cinema II 1–021182). Although this distinction might seem self-serving for Deleuze – 'thought' and 'sentiments' corresponding to comments with which Deleuze could agree, 'opinions' or 'objections' being quite the opposite – this perspective at least provides an alternative to the impression that Deleuze's supposed openness to students' views was mitigated, at best. On the contrary, as indicated above, Deleuze was almost always ready to engage with participants' comments, provided that he could either fold them into his development toward counter-actualisation or readily point out more pedagogically where a particular misunderstanding arose. In this light, the exchanges with Comtesse would seem to fluctuate between both extremes, usually with comments that Deleuze could encompass, but also offering certain fixed ideas on occasion that Deleuze recognised as repetitive and, for him, fatiguing objections. As for those moments in which Deleuze needed a break or simply could not cope, these exceptions seem to indicate the intensity of his commitment to the 'ideal' engagement within 'Deleuze-time'.

Feeling/Intellect

> I'm going fast, really fast as you notice, very fast, but I am speaking toward your feeling (*sentiment*), not your intellect (*intelligence*). (TDS Cinema IV 26–120684)

Deleuze insisted moreover that 'a course entails as much emotion as intelligence, and if there is no emotion, then there is nothing in the course, it has no interest' ('P as in Professor'). The distinction Deleuze made between 'objections', on one hand, and speaking on the basis of 'thoughts' or 'feelings', on the other, complemented the important emphasis he placed on emotion. For Deleuze repeatedly urged students above all to embrace a strategy of allowing themselves to *feel* the philosophical concepts and interplay of linkages between them, to grasp hold of what suited them personally, a 'grasping hold' so personal that it need not be on the level of understanding.[34] While discussing Whitehead, Deleuze maintained that 'really, to each his (or her) own – you have no need to know anything at all to understand, or at least to feel. As far as "feeling" goes, according to Whitehead, you can sense and even see this world form itself' (TDS Leibniz & Baroque 12–100387). Beyond these numerous modes of communicating the importance of emotion in the learning process, Deleuze employed the verb 'sentir' (to feel) to state the urgency of what he was saying, his desire for students to sense the progress they were making, however slow or fragile it might have been.

The insistence that Deleuze expressed toward 'feeling' in relation to 'intellect' had its impetus not just in a pedagogical imperative, but also in an ethical one, to which Deleuze allowed himself to return in several seminars, mostly clearly in the brief, two-session question-answer seminar titled 'Anti-Oedipus and Other Reflections', the final classes at the Vincennes campus in 1980. Returning to some crucial insights from *The Logic of Sense* to discuss the possibility of the event's realisation, Deleuze points precisely to the event's dual situation: on the one hand existing only 'in persons and states of things', but also 'however small it is, however insignificant, there is something that exceeds its realization, something not realizable', as if there were 'a "moreness" (*un "en plus"*), an excess', what Deleuze called 'the most *profound* sphere of the event' (TDS AO & Other 2–030680). The ethical message intersects here with the pedagogical one in Joë Bousquet's important dictum, '"Become the man of your misfortunes; learn to embody their perfection and brilliance"' (Deleuze 1990/2015: 149/154), restated in the 1980 session:

> we can better understand Bousquet's phrase: 'The problem is to become worthy . . .'. And here we have his whole moral, 'to be worthy of what happens to us' – whatever that is, whether good or bad – . . . To accept the event . . . doesn't at all mean to resign ourselves or to say: 'Oh God, it serves me right' . . . [but] means identifying in the event that is realized in me or that I am realizing, to identify that part which cannot be realized (*l'ineffectuable*). (TDS AO & Other 2–030680, translation modified)

A student's question interrupted Deleuze at that point, but he reflected fully on this once more, seven years later, providing additional aspects of the event:

> In a certain manner, one might say: every event awaits me! And it's already that. What interests me is an ethics (*une morale*) of the event because I believe that there is no other ethics than that of the nature of people in relation to what occurs to them. Morality is never: what must one do? [Rather] it's: how can you endure what happens to you, whether this be good or bad? (TDS Leibniz & Baroque 18–190587)

Reintroducing Bousquet's dictum, Deleuze added, 'You indeed sense that there is a certain way to live the event as being worthy (*en étant digne*) of what happens to us in the good and the bad. I would say that it's this aspect through which every event is addressed to my soul.'

While Deleuze addressed these points fully and explicitly only in these two seminars, I maintain that he did so implicitly in his ongoing *recherche* in every seminar and session. For this process of encounter with the event along a very fine edge 'is a question of attaining this will that the event creates in us; of becoming the quasi-cause of what is produced within us, the Operator' (Deleuze 1990/2015: 149/153). He describes this process as 'reach[ing] a point at which . . . we are faced with a volitional intuition and a transmutation . . . a change of will, a sort of leaping in place (*saut sur place*) of the whole body which exchanges its organic will for a spiritual will' (149/153–4). And I believe we can see Deleuze's own *recherche* emerging when he says: 'My misfortune is present in all events, but also a splendor and a brightness which dry up misfortune and which bring about that the event, once willed, is actualized on its most contracted point, on the cutting edge of an operation' (149/154).

This 'cutting edge' is the fine line that Deleuze pursued within each seminar. Bousquet's dictum corresponds to his *recherche*: '"Become the man of your misfortunes; learn to embody their perfection and brilliance"', to which Deleuze adds the forceful statement:

> Nothing more can be said, and no more has ever been said: to become worthy of what happens to us, and thus to will and release the event, to become the offspring (*le fils*) of one's own events, and thereby to be reborn, to have one more birth, and to break with one's carnal birth – to become the offspring of one's events and not of one's actions (*oeuvres*), for the action (*l'oeuvre*) is itself produced by the offspring of the event. (Deleuze 1990/2015: 149–50/154)

Each seminar and each session encompassed these dual facets, Deleuze seeking on the one hand the 'counter-actualisation', however fleeting, within 'Deleuze-time', which necessarily included the potential 'actualisations' of ongoing exchanges with participants, and on the other hand, to realise the event beyond one's misfortune, beyond one's battles, beyond one's wounds, and thereby to be worthy of what happens.

We can link this *recherche* in the seminars to Deleuze's ongoing inquiry into the 'supreme subject' of 'what is philosophy?', a focus with which Deleuze introduced the Leibniz and the Baroque seminar with great hesitation: 'So, why this [seminar's] subject [Leibniz]? I wanted to do "What is philosophy?", and then I couldn't. It's such a sacred subject . . . that I didn't dare to take it on. But this [seminar] is nearly an introduction to "What is philosophy?"' (TDS Leibniz & Baroque 1–281087). In fact, Deleuze had already begun this seminar topic explicitly during Cinema seminar IV when he indicated that he would undertake it 'on the level of an encounter of cinema and philosophy' (TDS Cinema IV 1–301084). Then, in that seminar's final session, while speculating on possible topics for 1985–86, he again suggested that while the 'dream course' would be on 'what is philosophy?', another topic would be to link this to consideration of both Blanchot and Foucault (TDS Cinema IV 26–180685). Indeed, Deleuze would spend half a session on this subject (TDS Leibniz & Baroque 15–280487), urging students to connect to philosophy by grasping hold of what suited them personally.

Hence, his ardour: 'So, this is why it matters to me so much to create this lineage in which, across all its innovation, there is always Nietzsche's expression: imagine a thinker as someone who shoots an arrow and doesn't know where it goes. And then, another thinker has to go find it.'[35] Deleuze urged the students to consider the year studying Leibniz and Whitehead as establishing an initial feeling, that is, 'this kind of jolt from the arrow when you have already understood something because you connect with it, . . . as a function of the way in which you yourself live' (TDS Leibniz & Baroque 15–280487). I believe that this insight reflects Deleuze's mission as a professor, his relationship with students as a means 'to teach them the benefit of their solitude; it's to reconcile them with their solitude' ('P as in Professor').

This mission also connects to the question 'what is philosophy?' because in continuing 'to think and live in terms of events', however solitary and strange that might seem, Deleuze reflected, 'it goes without saying that an event's individuation is not the [same] kind of individuation as for a person. Are you sure of being individuated as persons?' (TDS Leibniz & Baroque 15–280487). For Deleuze is trying in this session to urge students away from a mode of exchange based on 'discussion' (understood in the argumentative, objecting sense) and toward being open to philosophy in an entirely different manner, one based on affinity, on feeling. He asks:

> Where do these affinities come from that each of us feels for one direction or another, one vector or another that results in one author communicating something to us and another author, no less brilliant, communicating nothing, that is, remaining abstract and dead writing? It's here, if what is philosophy has a sense . . . These violent affinities that shoot through him/her, really, are like flashes of fire. (TDS Leibniz & Baroque 15–280487)

In many ways, this statement hearkens back to 'the sage' who, like the archer, 'is closer to Zen':

> The sage waits for the event, that is to say, *understands the pure event* in its eternal truth . . . as something eternally yet-to-come and always already passed according to the line of the Aion. But, at the same time, the sage also *wills the embodiment* and the actualization of the pure incorporeal event in a state of affairs and in his or her own body and flesh . . . and this applies to the wound and to archery just as much as it applies to the stroll. (Deleuze 1990/2015: 146–7/150–1)

I would also add 'just as much as it applies to the seminar'. Deleuze's lessons constitute fluctuations connecting the teacher's present to the students', and these temporal fluctuations palpitate constantly between moments of clarity through feeling and moments of corporeal variations and intensity leading away from such clarity, often translated by students as a need for some immediate form of understanding. While this tension within the seminar's 'matter in movement' acceded, in the proper circumstances and with patience, toward the 'pure event', Deleuze's emphasis in his teaching was on reaching those moments, however fleeting, in which he was able to aim this flow of 'matter' toward the in-between of pedagogy and creation.

Notes

1. TDS Leibniz & Baroque 14–070487. See the seminar sessions at The Deleuze Seminars database (deleuze.cla.purdue.edu) founded by Daniel W. Smith (with research support from Purdue and the National Endowment for the Humanities), with whom I serve as co-director as well as a principal transcriber and translator. References to The Deleuze Seminars sessions follow this convention: TDS + seminar title (often abbreviated) + session number and date (day-month-year).
2. See 'P as in Professor', in Deleuze and Parnet 1997. Cited hereafter in the text as 'P as in Professor'.
3. Deleuze often returned to this reference from 'Hamlet'. See 'On Four Poetic Formulas That Might Summarize the Kantian Philosophy', in Deleuze 1997: 27–35. See the phrase's development also in the Kant seminar (March–April 1978) and in TDS Cinema III 5–131283 and Cinema III 12–280284.
4. See the digital archive of Deleuze's seminars located at the Université de Paris 8, established in 1999 at the Bibliothèque Nationale de France (BNF), based on recordings faithfully made by a Japanese student, Hidenobu Suzuki. The archive of 273 cassettes of 180 separate lectures comprises 413 hours of recordings, accessible online from the BNF through the Gallica search engine (https://gallica.bnf.fr). A detailed yet partial summary of the BNF holdings has been published by Frederic Astier (2006).
5. See the two RAI 3-produced videos from the 1986–87 Leibniz seminar (TDS Leibniz & Baroque 3–181186 and 20–030687) and also the YouTube clip from the mid-1970s, clearly revealing Deleuze's compressed spatial circumstances, the professor barely able to pass through the crowd, pointing out that an inherent danger existed for everyone present both for breathing and should a fire break out (TDS ATP I 10–240276, an approximate date). In an earlier session (see TDS ATP I 7–130176), a full-scale revolt broke out concerning the lack of space. This clip's translated title is 'Molar and Molecular Multiplicities'; see deleuze.cla.purdue.edu/node/230 for the YouTube video link, under the title *Deleuze su molteplicità molare e molteplicità molecolare*.
6. In the late 1970s, the conservative government of Valéry Giscard d'Estaing decided to destroy the Vincennes campus (deemed a hotbed of radical activity and drug trafficking) and to move the campus operation to St Denis, in northeast Paris, starting in the autumn 1980 academic year. Hence, Hidenobu Suzuki's recordings correspond to the final year at Vincennes, then continue for the entire seven years that Deleuze spent at Vincennes/St Denis. For discussion of specific political issues on the Vincennes campus preceding this move, see TDS ATP V 10–040380. On the political atmosphere at Vincennes during Deleuze's years there, see Dosse 2010: 347–57.

7. On these distinctions, see 'Plateau 14. 1440, The Smooth and the Striated', in Deleuze and Guattari 1987.
8. Following the November–December 1986 demonstrations that created a four-week hiatus in the Leibniz and the Baroque seminar, Deleuze vigorously encourages the students to prepare a petition to have these bars removed (TDS Leibniz & Baroque 4–161286).
9. For a remarkable overview of Deleuze's vocalisations within his different 'oratorial avatars' (*personnages oratoires*) in the seminars, see Jaeglé 2005.
10. References to *The Logic of Sense* include pagination for both translation editions.
11. Private correspondence with author. For an example of these notes, see the images in the French transcription of TDS Cinema III 18–150585.
12. Translation modified; as the translator Martin Joughin notes, '*discuter* [as well as *discussion*] has in French a polemical resonance absent from "discuss"' (Deleuze 1995: 200). For Deleuze's extended explanation of why *discuter* and *discussions* have no place in philosophy, see TDS Leibniz & Baroque 15–280487.
13. 'Spinoza: immortalité et éternité' (Immortality and Eternity) (Paris: Gallimard, 2001), 'Leibniz: âme et damnation' (Soul and Damnation) (Paris: Gallimard 2003) and 'Gilles Deleuze Cinéma' (Paris: Gallimard, 2006). I focus on the two complete sessions (Spinoza and Leibniz) rather than the excerpts collected from five different sessions (Cinéma). Both Parnet and Pinhas were long-standing participants in Deleuze's seminars. Parnet co-edited with Deleuze their exchanges in *Dialogues* (Deleuze and Parnet 1987) and interviewed him in *L'Abécédaire de Gilles Deleuze* (Deleuze and Parnet 1997). Pinhas is a musician who created, with the Deleuze family's permission, a still active website, WebDeleuze (web deleuze.com) with transcriptions and translations of many seminar sessions and including a range of resources and links for scholars interested in Deleuze's work. Claude Jaeglé's (2005) overview of the seminars is based primarily on the Spinoza and Leibniz CDs as well as *L'Abécédaire*.
14. As a result, the Spinoza seminar continued through the following session (on 24 March 1981) and only culminated after 54 minutes of additional questions and answers on 31 March, following which the Painting seminar began.
15. Each session is temporally distinctive in being considerably edited for the CDs in contrast to the BNF recordings. The Spinoza CD omits approximately 20 minutes of the recorded session, the Leibniz CD omits approximately an hour; many of these omissions in each correspond precisely to interactions with participants, apparently deemed ancillary by the producers.
16. Objections arose to Deleuze's tendentious proposal to reduce the class size to a smaller group limited to the space in which everyone could be comfortably seated, in order to 'return, review and perfect with me what we've already done'. Unfortunately, after extensive discussion but without offering practical details on how this reduction would work, Deleuze never attempted any of these extreme measures, having vented frustration at the seemingly insoluble situation.
17. Notably, during the final semester at Vincennes in 1980, with campus politics upsetting the usual schedule, Deleuze devoted an entire session to assisting the participants in developing concrete actions for non-violent direct protest (TDS ATP V 10–040380); at the next session, continued unrest forced them to stop after only 40 minutes (TDS ATP V 11–110380). See Dosse 2010, chapter 19, for a contextual explanation of the Vincennes situation.
18. Besides student departures and arrivals, noise from sources in and outside the building, including external students interrupting the class, the session I call 'the

day of the squeaky door' reveals Deleuze first irritated by a repetitive screech, then shifting toward dark humour ('I'm going to bring a revolver next time'), before finally linking the hallucinatory squeak to specific points in the lecture (TDS Cinema I 19–180582).

19. See the videos linked to TDS ATP I-Deleuze at Paris 8, seminars to which Guattari regularly contributed, and also TDS Foucault 23–130586. As for Parnet, she is present (seated near Deleuze) in the RAI 3 video of TDS Leibniz & Baroque 3–181186.

20. See, for example, Alliez's contribution (on economic doctrine and mercantilism) in TDS ATP V 7–290180, and also six years later (TDS Foucault 24–200586, nearly entirely inaudible). Pinhas intervened occasionally on digital technology and music, the end of one such intervention located at the start of TDS Leibniz & Baroque 10–240287. I discuss Comtesse's numerous interventions below.

21. For example, musicologist Pascale Criton (TDS Cinema IV 10–220185); director and writer Raymonde Carasco (TDS Cinema IV 12–050285); film and video artist Pascal Auger (TDS Cinema IV 20–300485); filmmaker Dominique Vaillant (TDS Cinema IV 22–140585); a mathematician and colleague at Vincennes/St. Denis (designated only as Marek, TDS Leibniz & Baroque 8–270187); musicologists Pascale Criton and Vincent Walls in the final session (TDS Leibniz & Baroque 20–020687).

22. Notably, Dominique Vaillant's interview/intervention in May 1985 on different aspects of sound and soundtracks in films inspired Richard Pinhas's lengthy (and unanticipated) intervention, followed by another invited intervener, Pascale Criton, who objected to Pinhas's perspectives. Facing precisely the kind of exchange he detested, Deleuze shifted between alternate postures, on one hand defending Pinhas, but on the other hand seeking common ground, finally responding to another student's objections with a peculiar rationale: 'She [Vaillant] wasn't speaking in her own name; she had accepted to answer some questions that I asked her, fine. I wanted to have my technical session' (TDS Cinema IV 22–140585). Moreover, this exchange seems to confirm Parnet's views on the limits of the question–answer/interview procedure (Deleuze and Parnet 1987: 20).

23. One remarkable exchange of this kind occurred during the Spinoza seminar. Having introduced the theme of good and evil through Spinoza's correspondence with Willem van Blyenbergh (a harsh critic of Spinoza's view), Deleuze faced a forceful critique from one participant, whom Deleuze at one point described as 'my Blyenbergh', and yet he succeeded in responding to the student while generally remaining within the focal development (TDS Spinoza 6–130181).

24. However, after the student departed, Deleuze first apologised quite sincerely, expressing his concern for this young woman's 'little burst of delirium', admitting that she had shown up at his home several days earlier, 'in a state of crisis', and that he worried that she might do something extreme. At the start of the following session, Deleuze allowed her to make a presentation which was not preserved on any recordings (TDS Cinema IV 19–230485). On 'les fous' (the crazies) as a phenomenon in the Vincennes seminars, see 'D as in Desire' in Deleuze and Parnet 1997, and in terms of the politics of so-called *marginaux* (marginals), see Deleuze and Parnet 1987: 138–40.

25. Comtesse completed a dissertation in 1974 with Deleuze. The principal Comtesse interventions to which Deleuze responded affirmatively, including extended presentations (noted here with *), are: TDS Leibniz 4–060580*; TDS Spinoza 4–161280; TDS Spinoza 5–060181; TDS Spinoza 6–130181; in the Spinoza seminar, sessions 7 through 11, and 13; TDS Painting 8–050681; in Cinema I, sessions 4, 5, 18, 19, 20*; in Cinema II, sessions 5, 9, 10, 13*, 17,

19*; in Cinema IV, sessions 2, 3, 10, 12; in the Foucault seminar, sessions 10*, 17*, 26*; TDS Leibniz & Baroque 15–280487 and 18–190587. On Comtesse's seminar contributions, see also Dosse 2010: 356.

26. See above for Comtesse's Foucault presentations; Guattari participated in TDS Foucault 23–130586, Alliez in TDS Foucault 24–200586, the musicologist (speaking on Boulez's composition *Pli selon pli*) in TDS Foucault 25–270586.

27. See the last 5 minutes of the 4-hour, 20-minute-long video titled 'Il Senso in Meno II' at TDS ATP I-Deleuze at Paris VIII (deleuze.cla.purdue.edu/node/230) and on YouTube (under this title).

28. The interventions to which Deleuze objected most strongly occur in TDS Spinoza 12–100381; TDS Painting 5–120581; TDS Cinema IV 7–181284; TDS Cinema IV 16–190385; TDS Leibniz & Baroque 13–170387.

29. As regards the matter of textual evidence, a remarkable exchange occurs in the Cinema II seminar (TDS Cinema II 19–030583) in which Deleuze challenges Comtesse on a citation from Proust, based on one word that Comtesse attributed to Proust that seemed suspicious to Deleuze. Upon verification, I have determined that Comtesse misquoted Proust's novel, *Jean Santeuil*, and certainly was unable to provide the reference to Deleuze. Moreover, Deleuze's ire in the cited exchange arose no doubt from his having rebuked Comtesse several weeks before, albeit more gently, on the same lack of sources in a discussion on Élie Faure (TDS IV 3–131184).

30. Of course, Comtesse was not the only student able to upset Deleuze. An exemplary session in this regard occurs in seminar Cinema II. Despite being extremely upset by a dual confrontation with Comtesse and one other student, Deleuze was still able eventually to return to a focused development, quite pertinent for this discussion, in which he encompassed two figures of time, one that is understood as an aggregate of time and another that is time as the instant, the interval, concluding the session with 'next time, yes, we'll see', following which a pause occurred, and, as if picked up by a hot microphone, Deleuze said to someone nearby, 'They were so nasty today . . .' (TDS Cinema II 14–150383).

31. For example, see the discussion on the present, the instant and the interval in TDS Cinema II 17–190483.

32. 'Cette coprésence de tous les degrés de puissance appartient à l'éternité, c'est-à-dire à l'Aiôn', the copresence that Deleuze continues to explore in Cinema III 15. See also TDS Cinema III 14–200384 and Cinema III 16–170484, in which Deleuze juxtaposes Aion to the instant and to the Greek term *nûn*, or *maintenant* (now).

33. Deleuze continued: 'The best students were those who asked questions the following week . . . they would pass me a little note from one week to the next – a practice I appreciated.'

34. Among the most striking locutions in Deleuze's sessions are the phrase 'il faut que vous sentiez . . .' (you must sense/feel that . . .) this or that point or concept under consideration, and the imperative 'Sentez que . . .' (Sense that . . .); also, the complimentary, supportive phrase 'Vous sentez que . . .' (You get/sense/feel that . . .), from which students could infer Deleuze's confidence in their grasping hold.

35. This example from Nietzsche occurs often in Deleuze; see especially Deleuze 1983: 106 and 201, n.31.

References

Astier, F. (2006), *Les cours enregistrés de Gilles Deleuze, 1979–1987*, Mons: Éditions Sils Maria.

Deleuze, G. (1983), *Nietzsche and Philosophy*, trans. Hugh Tomlinson, New York: Columbia University Press.

Deleuze, G. (1990), *Pourparlers*, Paris: Minuit.

Deleuze, G. (1990/2015), *The Logic of Sense*, ed. Constantin V. Boundas, trans. Mark Lester with Charles J. Stivale, New York: Columbia University Press/ London: Bloomsbury.

Deleuze, G. (1995), *Negotiations*, trans. Martin Joughin, New York: Columbia University Press.

Deleuze, G. (1997), *Essays Critical and Clinical*, trans. Daniel W. Smith and Michael A. Greco, Minneapolis: University of Minnesota Press.

Deleuze, G. and C. Parnet (1987) *Dialogues*, New York: Columbia University Press.

Deleuze, G. and C. Parnet (1997), *L'Abécédaire de Gilles Deleuze*, dir. Pierre-André Boutang, Paris: Éditions Montparnasse (DVD: *Gilles Deleuze, From A to Z*, trans. Charles J. Stivale, Cambridge, MA: MIT Press, 2012).

Deleuze, G. and F. Guattari (1987), *A Thousand Plateaus*, trans. Brian Massumi, Minneapolis: University of Minnesota Press.

Dosse, F. (2010), *Gilles Deleuze & Félix Guattari. Intersecting Lives*, trans. Deborah Glassman, New York: Columbia University Press.

Jaeglé, C. (2005), *Portrait oratoire de Gilles Deleuze aux yeux jaunes*, Paris: PUF.

Williams, J. (2011), *Gilles Deleuze's Philosophy of Time: A Critical Introduction and Guide*, Edinburgh: Edinburgh University Press.

Notes on Contributors

Vernon W. Cisney is Chair and Associate Professor of Interdisciplinary Studies at Gettysburg College in Pennsylvania. He is the author of *Deleuze and Derrida: Difference and the Power of the Negative* (Edinburgh, 2018) as well as *Derrida's* Voice and Phenomenon: *An Edinburgh Philosophical Guide* (Edinburgh, 2014). In addition, he is the co-editor of *Between Foucault and Derrida* (Edinburgh, 2016), *Biopower: Foucault and Beyond* (Chicago, 2015), Pierre Klossowski's *Living Currency* and *Sade and Fourier* (Bloomsbury, 2016) and *The Way of Nature and the Way of Grace: Philosophical Footholds on Terrence Malick's* The Tree of Life (Northwestern, 2016). Most recently, he has written articles and chapters included in *Deleuze and Guattari Studies* and *Batman and Theology*.

Charlene Elsby, PhD, specialises in Aristotle and realist phenomenology. She is Vice President of the North American Society for Early Phenomenology, President of the North American Roman Ingarden Society and the General Editor of *Phenomenological Investigations*. She edited the volume *Essays on Aesthetic Genesis*, and her recent essays include, 'The Origin of Theoretical Knowledge in the Organization of Nature', 'Roman Ingarden on Fictional Times', 'Time and its Indeterminacy in Roman Ingarden's Concept of the Literary Work of Art', and 'Gregor Samsa's Spots of Indeterminacy: Kafka as Phenomenologist'. Her fictional works include *Hexis, Affect, Psychros* and *Musos*.

Robert W. Luzecky, received his PhD from Purdue University (2021). He is an Adjunct Professor of Philosophy at George Mason University. His published articles include 'Oppression, Speech, and Mitsein in Margaret Atwood's *The Handmaid's Tale*', in *Clio: A Journal* *of Literature, History, and the Philosophy of History* 46 (3), 2017; 'The Revolutionary Axiology and Non-generalizable Ontology of Kierkegaard's Concept of Repetition', in *Clio: A Journal of Literature, History, and the Philosophy of History* 47 (3), 2020; and 'Deleuze's Elaboration of Eternity: Ontogenesis and Multiplicity', in *Deleuze and Guattari Studies* 16 (1), 2022. His other publications include *Amy Schumer and Philosophy*, co-edited with Charlene Elsby (Carus, 2018); and 'Mitscherling's Reading of Ingarden', in *Essays on Aesthetic Genesis* (University Press of America, 2016).

James A. Mollison is an Associate Teaching Professor at Purdue University in West Lafayette, Indiana. His research focuses on nineteenth-century German philosophy, twentieth-century French philosophy, and value theory. His recent work has appeared in journals such as *Deleuze and Guattari Studies, History of Philosophy Quarterly* and *Inquiry: An Interdisciplinary Journal of Philosophy*.

Thomas Nail is Professor of Philosophy at the University of Denver and author of numerous books, including *The Figure of the Migrant, Theory of the Border, Marx in Motion, Theory of the Image, Theory of the Object, Theory of the Earth, Lucretius I, II and III, Returning to Revolution* and *Being and Motion*. His research focuses on the philosophy of movement.

Dorothea Olkowski is Professor and former Chair of Philosophy at the University of Colorado, Colorado Springs, current Director of Humanities and Director of the Cognitive Studies Program and founding Director of Women's Studies. She is author of more than 100 articles and fourteen books, including her most recent publication, *Deleuze, Bergson, and Merleau-Ponty: The Logic and Pragmatics of Affect, Perception, and Creation* (Indiana University Press, 2021). Her other recent publications include: *Deleuze at the End of the World: An Argentinian Perspective on the Sources of his Thought*, co-edited with Julián Ferreyra (Rowman and Littlefield, 2020); *Deleuze and Guattari's Philosophy of Freedom: Freedom's Refrains*, co-edited with Eftechios Pirovolakis (Routledge, 2019); 'Continental Feminist Approaches to Philosophy of Science', in *The Oxford Handbook of Feminist Philosophy*, ed. Kim Q. Hall (Oxford University Press, 2021); 'Deleuze's Oedipus', in *All About Father: Psychoanalysis, the Oedipus Complex, and the Modern Family*, ed. Lilliane Weissberg (Palgrave McMillian, 2022). She is writing on Tango and Philosophy and is completing an article on 'Postmodernism' for the *Stanford University Internet Encyclopedia of Philosophy*.

Strand Sheldahl-Thomason teaches philosophy at Purdue University Fort Wayne. He received his PhD from Purdue University in 2018. He writes about philosophy and literature, Michel Foucault and practices of the self, and environmental ethics. His recent article 'Foucault and the Use of Exposure: Discipline, Ethics, and Self-Writing' can be found in *Review of Communication*. He is currently completing a book called *Michel Foucault's Ethics of Writing*.

Daniel W. Smith is Professor of Philosophy at Purdue University. He is the author of *Essays on Deleuze* (2012) and co-editor of the *Cambridge Companion to Deleuze* (2012, with Henry Somers-Hall), *Deleuze and Ethics* (2011, with Nathan Jun), and *Gilles Deleuze: Image and Text* (2009, with Eugene W. Holland and Charles J. Stivale). He is also the translator, from the French, of books by Gilles Deleuze, Pierre Klossowski, Isabelle Stengers and Michel Serres.

Henry Somers-Hall is Reader in Philosophy at Royal Holloway, University of London. He is the author of *Hegel, Deleuze, and the Critique of Representation* (2012), *Deleuze's* Difference and Repetition (2013) and *Judgement and Sense in Modern French Philosophy* (2022), and co-editor of *The Cambridge Companion to Deleuze* (2012, with Daniel W. Smith) and A Thousand Plateaus *and Philosophy* (2018, with Jeffrey A. Bell and James Williams).

Charles J. Stivale is Distinguished Professor Emeritus of French at Wayne State University, Detroit. He is the author of books, edited volumes and articles on French language, literature and culture, as well as on Gilles Deleuze and Félix Guattari. He has also translated Deleuze's *The Logic of Sense* (with Mark Lester and Constantin V. Boundas), Franco Berardi (Bifo)'s *Félix Guattari: Thought, Friendship, and Visionary Cartography* (with Giuseppina Mecchia), and the eight-hour DVD interview of Deleuze by Claire Parnet, *Gilles Deleuze, From A to Z*. He is currently co-director (with Daniel W. Smith) of the Purdue University-based Deleuze Seminars archive.

Peter Trnka is Associate Professor of Philosophy at Memorial University of Newfoundland. Born in Prague, he received his PhD and other degrees at the University of Toronto, where he also learned about the time of the strike during his work as president and chief negotiator for the Canadian Union of Educational Workers Local 2. He has published articles on Hume, Canguilhem, Derrida, Deleuze and others, as well a cookbook and poetry. He is currently serving as editor-in-chief of *Janus Unbound: Journal of Critical Studies*, launched in November 2021, and of *Codgito: Student Journal of Philosophy and Theory*, launched in spring 2022.

Index